LOCATING DEVIANCE

Gerald Mars is an analyst in the classical traditions of social anthropology and urban ethnography. He is concerned to first understand and then describe, using classification schemes solidly based in the "how" of crime and deviance rather than by jumping mindlessly into the knee-jerk political reflexes of the "why do bad things happen?" and "how shall society punish what it cannot cope with?" questions. This book is essential reading for those including most operational managers who want to take a mental step back and ask fundamental questions about "what kind of society are we, that these unplanned outcomes occur?" and "how is it that we are all implicated in organizations that co-create deviance?".

David Weir, Professor of Management, University Campus Suffolk, UK, and ESC Rennes, France

This volume displays and also integrates Mars' major contributions over several decades to general social theory, anthropology and criminology. Combining subtle and meticulous ethnography with historically-informed innovation in theory, these studies provide master classes in using empirical work for the most ambitious theoretical arguments. In showing how deviance is central to social organization, he elegantly turns Durkheim's aphorism about the normality of crime into a strategy of general social inquiry into institutional dynamics.

Perri 6, Professor of Public Management, Queen Mary College, University of London, UK

Gerald Mars again demonstrates how, using anthropology's concepts and sensitive participant observation he illumines areas other disciplines find difficult to reach. Via detailed case studies he uncovers the keys to organizational criminality that should appeal to criminologists, anthropologists and managers alike. Easy to read, essentially practical, its final chapter – charting the cultural bases of deviance in the financial service industries – is a tour de force.

Tom Selwyn, Professor of Anthropology, SOAS, University of London, UK

Gerald Mars has been a lifelong student of human behavior as it is shaped and channeled by the cultures and structures of society. But he is at his anthropological best when he delves into the subcultural nuances and situational complexities of ordinary workers. There are few anthropologists of crime and deviance among ordinary folk. Gerald Mars is a master of research on workplace deviance. He digs deep and provides rich layered explanations that illuminate what we take for granted, yet his analysis is central to how we construct meaningful lives. In this latest work Mars integrates his lifetime observations grounded in empirical ethnographies, but reveals a theoretical progression and a deepening sophisticated analysis. This book not only integrates Mars' studies over a lifetime but provides insight into his own academic journey and that alone is a veritable delight.'

Stuart Henry, Professor of Criminology, San Diego State University, USA

Advances in Criminology

Series Editor: David Nelken

Recent titles in the series

The full list of series titles can be found at the back of the book.

Locating Deviance
Crime, Change and Organizations

GERALD MARS
University College, London, UK

ASHGATE

Published by
Ashgate Publishing Limited
Wey Court East
Union Road
Farnham
Surrey, GU9 7PT
England

Ashgate Publishing Company
110 Cherry Street
Suite 3-1
Burlington, VT 05401-3818
USA

www.ashgate.com

British Library Cataloguing in Publication Data
Mars, Gerald.
Locating deviance: crime, change and organizations. – (Advances in criminology)
1. Employee crimes. 2. Applied ethics. 3. Business ethics.
I. Title II. Series
364.1'68-dc23

The Library of Congress has cataloged the printed edition as follows:
Mars, Gerald.
Locating deviance : crime, change, and organizations/by Gerald Mars.
    pages cm. — (Advances in criminology)
Includes bibliographical references and index.
ISBN 978-1-4094-2789-6 (hardback: alk. paper) — ISBN 978-1-4094-7148-6
— ISBN 978-1-4094-2790-2 (ebook) 1. Criminal psychology. 2. Criminal behavior. 3. Organized crime. I. Title.
  HV6080.M363 2013
  364.3—dc23

2012049947

ISBN 9781409427896 (hbk)
ISBN 9781409427902 (ebk-PDF)
ISBN 9781409471486 (ebk-ePUB)

MIX
Paper from
responsible sources
FSC
www.fsc.org FSC® C013985

Printed in the United Kingdom by Henry Ling Limited,
at the Dorset Press, Dorchester, DT1 1HD

Contents

List of Figures and Tables

Figures

Tables

Foreword

It is a special pleasure for me to write an introduction to a collection of essays by my friend and mentor Gerry Mars. I first met Gerry when he gave an inspiring visiting lecture on the Masters course in Criminology at the Cambridge Institute of Criminology in 1972. There was, of course, the intrinsic excitement of listening to a speaker share his first-hand experience of 'fiddling' in a large variety of different kinds of job. Such ethnographic reports contrasted sharply with the often dry findings about populations of incarcerated offenders. But the more important message that emerged was that crime was an essential part of everyday life and did not have to be limited to the often voyeuristic 'studying down' of lower-class offenders (typically those who have been least successful). It strengthened my determination to specialize in the study of occupational crime. (In fact, my doctoral studies set out initially to compare dentists and landlords, a project that I, fortunately, abandoned. But that is another story.)

Gerry Mars typically conducts his research using observation and participant observation, and this book ends with some practical advice for those who wish to practise such methods. But his guiding ideas come from the framework of 'Cultural Theory' developed by the anthropologist Mary Douglas. This (perhaps unfortunately named) approach does not treat culture as a description of an interdependent social context but rather as a classificatory scheme that distinguishes social groups in terms of the relationship between hierarchists, individualists, egalitarians and fatalists. These categories (called 'solidarities' by Cultural Theorists) reflect how much people are integrated into a group – as well as how far they are subject to a high level of imposed rules. (It is important to note that this is a sociological theory, not an effort to understand individual behaviour.)

The essays included here illustrate how Mars applies Cultural Theory imaginatively to a wide range of cases. He shows that it can provide a key to explaining behaviours as different as dockyard and warehouse pilferage, terrorism, and banking fraud. As important, he also uses it to reveal the pathologies of those appointed to control and gatekeep deviance such as managers or management consultants. Surprises are guaranteed. His jointly authored paper (with Mary Douglas) on terrorism, for example, takes us far from the usual type of work on these groups. Here they are examined for what they have in common with other 'enclave groups' (many of whom are animated by egalitarian ideas) and the focus is on their need to restrict the inward flow of information, which then also has consequences for them.

Mars does not think of himself primarily as a criminologist but rather as an 'applied anthropologist' (for which he was awarded the prestigious Lucy Mair prize of the Royal Anthropological Institute). In trying to make sense of different settings, his aim is the empirical explanation of variation using whatever disciplinary tools (such as those found in writings by anthropologists, historians, psychologists, economists or organizational theorists) may be helpful. Although his studies have been influential in the area of occupational crime, this book also suggests some wider implications of his work. Most importantly, it reminds us of the omnipresence of social control as an essential part of the making and unmaking of group life, a factor certainly more significant in its effects than official criminal justice, even as it supplements or circumvents it. Thus, for the subjects of Mars's research, deviance is often a resource for righting perceived grievances and achieving small-scale redistribution of goods (which could be seen as resistance to power and/or a way of diffusing more serious political resistance). Mars shows us the extent to which crime and deviance need to be seen as an aspect of making organizations work, or exploiting them or getting back at them – something that continues to be neglected in much criminological writing, not to mention practical enforcement.

His analyses can also contribute to developing the ever-popular (over-popular?) interest in processes of constructing and deconstructing of crime labels. Attention to such processes in studying matters such as 'pilfering' or 'tax avoidance' is, of course, particularly crucial in the areas of occupational and business crime. His essays show us who is doing (or trying to do) the labelling and the way this works out over time (an important element explaining why there are cycles in the commission of offences and the reactions to them). This book reminds us (as did Mary Douglas's seminal contributions) that responses to social problems and deviance are linked to differential perceptions of risk. Going beyond the somewhat obvious claim that the powerful label the powerless, Cultural Theory argues that different groups (even among the powerful) contest definitions of risks. Hierarchists, fatalists, individualists and egalitarians find different risks (un) acceptable and think differently about risk itself. When, as Mars demonstrates, this approach is brought to bear on the recent economic meltdown, it shows us how deviance was first normalized and then how 'conformity' was redefined, re-empowering the cultural worldviews of both hierarchists and egalitarians.

Mars's work is less concerned with the political or policy choices involved in the legal definition of crime. But arguably, too much concern with this level can obscure as much as it reveals about the relationship between crime and social reaction. This may be seen in the current debate over the growth of punishment, the rise of the alleged 'culture of control' and comparative incarceration rates. It is true that changes in crime rates are not a good explanation of recent rises in punitiveness. Countries with more crime do not necessarily have more people in prison, and, over time, an increased rise in crime rates can be associated with a decreasing use of prison, while a period of reducing crime rates (as recently) can be accompanied by a rise in prison rates. But, in the everyday making of social order, it is misleading to break the connection between conflict, crime and response (indeed, for Durkheim, crime is actually defined by the reaction to it). Mars mobilizes Cultural Theory so as to explain both crime and its control and we learn how difficult it is to separate deviance from the styles of control that shape it.

This has significant implications for the many parts of the world where politicians and police are also in collusion with different kinds of criminals.

The practical (and political) assumptions of Cultural Theory may, at first blush, seem to be relativist ones – all depends on the perspective of which of the four solidarities one adopts. But Mars also uses the approaches of each solidarity to offer critique of excesses of the others (suggesting that there may be some ideal balance). He makes no secret of his views that the current economic crisis can be attributed to an over-emphasis on individualism, even if he has also regularly pointed to the way hierarchical bureaucracies can be a drag on innovation. He has also noted the tendency of egalitarian groups, which reject high grid levels of regulation, to create over-rigid boundaries and to split into smaller groups. When it comes to the problem of enforcement, his analysis suggests that there may be inbuilt (collectively mandated) limits to deviance (as in the way dock workers engaged in pilferage spoke of 'working the value of the boat'). He also warns us that over-reacting to what are considered 'perks' may lead to retaliation by workers. In discussing the reactions to economic excesses in the world of banking and investment, on the other hand, he notes that over-reaction can make the problem worse by discouraging risk taking at a time when bankers' reluctance to take risks may dry up funds for investment and hence make a recession last longer.

With imagination and with sensitive fieldwork, this book well demonstrates (with Lewin) that 'There is nothing so practical as a good theory.'

David Nelken
Series Editor

Preface
A Personal Journey,
a Guide to the Book, Chapter Outlines

My Introduction to Crime and Deviance[1]

I began to be interested in occupational crime in the ten years of work between leaving school and university. Work in over thirty 'ordinary' jobs revealed established fiddling[2] in all of them except one.[3] I found that in some jobs the fiddled medium was cash, in others goods, in yet others, time – and sometimes all three. And I learned that fiddling was not anarchic but operated according to understood rules and was invariably subject to firm moral imperatives. Experience was gained as a tram conductor and in a variety of shops, hotels, pubs, fairgrounds, cafes, offices, a factory, and during two years as a storeman in the RAF.

Most of my jobs in this early period were in Blackpool, then a flourishing seaside resort in the north of England.[4] At that time, Blackpool was Britain's most popular holiday resort, with over seven million staying visitors per year. It could well have been considered 'The Fiddle Capital of the Northern Hemisphere'. Both holiday resorts and ports communities, I later found, were particularly prone to this kind of crime, being, as criminologists term it, 'criminogenic', a topic explored in Chapter 6.

These years of practical training 'on the shop floor' taught me the mechanics: the 'how', 'when' and 'where' of fiddling. I learned the varying routines by which to cheat customers, clients, employers and the tax authorities as well as different ways of manipulating time. This was followed by academic training in economics and social anthropology, then by two years' anthropological fieldwork among longshoremen in Canada (called 'dockers' in the UK). Fortunately for my interests, the pilferage

---

1   Crime is behaviour that is against the law; deviance is behaviour that breaks social norms but is not necessarily against the law. I am aware that different groups define crime and assess norms differently and this is centrally addressed in Chapter 9. But for simplicity here I use the words 'crime' and 'deviance' interchangeably.

2   Minor cheating commonly related to work, is colloquially known as 'fiddling' in the UK and 'scamming' in the US.

3   And that was in a factory where time was strictly controlled and there was nothing that could usefully be pilfered.

4   A product and victim of mass transport, Blackpool flourished over a period of a hundred plus years that began with the development of cheap railway transport in the mid-nineteenth century and lasted until the mid-1960s when cheap package flights to the Spanish Costa Brava led to the town's quick and calamitous decline.

rate in St John's was six times higher than the average of other Canadian ports and, like ports everywhere, was just beginning to face the buffeting of global competition and technical change. Two years' intensive participant observation revealed the techniques, internal controls, managerial collusion and morality that underpinned dock theft, and these are outlined in Chapter 5.

After Newfoundland, through my own employments, industrial consultancy and interviewing, I was able to gain data at different levels of organization in the UK and abroad and to confirm that fiddling was often carried on with the collusion of supervisors and sometimes of management. Where this was so, it involved organizations accepting and adapting to fiddles and incorporating them within their structures. In short, fiddling was not only extensive: it operated at many levels, served a number of useful functions, and was often institutionalized.

An extremely experienced workmate at the start of one of my first jobs told me, 'Every job has a fiddle, Gerry. Our job is to find it.' But if this was so, and it seemed it was, could their different forms justify treating them as a single entity when their variances seemed quite wide?

The Need to Classify

What was needed was a system of classification that would allow effective comparison and understanding. Without it, I merely had a collection of disparate accounts and was unable to compare, say, the group-based fiddles of collectively organized longshoremen with those of individually competitive journalists, the fiddles of waiters with those of garage mechanics, or the deviance of autonomous entrepreneurs with those of accountants – and without classification and comparisons there can be no science.

No existing system of classifying occupations[5] or their fiddles satisfied these requirements. The academic literature revealed a dearth of any generalized and *comparative* accounts of workplace crime.[6]

---

5   For example, white- and blue-collar occupations and class-based categorizations – lower-, middle- and upper-class occupations.

6   The majority of studies in this field have taken, and still take, a 'managerial/ consultancy' and often a moralist approach, to workplace crime, neither of which permits the suspension of morality necessary to dispassionate analysis. Rare exceptions are the pioneering study of managerial deviance, Melville Dalton's early classic *Men who Manage* (1959), Ditton's excellent study of bread roundsmen (1977), and Stuart Henry's *The Hidden Economy* (1978). Ditton's work, being an ethnography, is largely limited to the concerns of a single occupation. Henry's contribution is to link workplace crime to the wider 'Hidden Economy' of which it is a part, but it too does not draw comparisons between occupations. Since their contributions, however, there has emerged a body of useful work on organizational crime, especially Ackroyd and Thompson's *Organizational Misbehaviour* (1999) and Maurice Punch's *Dirty Business* (1996).

This synthesis was later to be provided by Cultural Theory (CT),[7] which originates with the work of Mary Douglas in anthropology. Its effectiveness when applied to classifying occupations and understanding work-based 'amateur' fiddles then became clear[8] – as did its wider application to organizations and to providing a different, non-orthodox, way of understanding professional crime and criminals as discussed in Chapter 2. The revelations that emerged during the widespread economic crash of 2007–2009 extended interest further – taking analysis from the micro-concerns of the workplace to the macro-deviance emanating from boardrooms, a topic explored in Chapter 9.

A Guide to the Book and Chapter Outlines

This book locates the social contexts in which crime occurs – from the local to the global. After an account of the theoretical framework by which the book's material is organized, it considers the social contexts of crime more generally. It then focuses on case studies of behaviour in the workplace, then on cases that reveal the intrusion of influence from the communities in which they are set. Finally it assesses the influence of long-wave economic cycles (Kondratieff waves) on organizational crime and deviance, with particular reference to deviance during the last upturn and the subsequent current crash. An appendix offers a 'how to' guide to doing fieldwork in workplaces.

Chapter 1 discusses the derivation of CT and its four archetypal categories (variously called cultures, 'ways of life' or 'solidarities'): Hierarchy, Individualism, Egalitarianism and Fatalism. These form the book's analytic core.

These archetypal cultures derive from the way people's lives are organized. They are based on two universally validated dimensions – the rules that cultures impose on their people (Grid), and the degree they are integrated into groups (Group). Arranged as continua and presented as a 2×2 matrix, they provide the four archetypes. Each of the four links to a distinct and cohesive 'cluster' of values, attitudes and behaviours. Hierarchy demonstrates respect for tradition, order and precedence; Individualism for unfettered competition; Egalitarianism for the virtues of the bounded group, the Enclave as against the exploitative 'outside'; and Fatalism by a passive acceptance of the status quo. These are compared across cultures to demonstrate their universal relevance across time and place. They are applied here to show how not only organizational deviance but crime more generally similarly reflects the way people's lives are organized and offers the basis of their classification.

---

7   See Mary Douglas's originating article, 'Cultural Bias' (1982). For a fuller account of developments in CT, see Thompson et al. 1990. For an update with examples of articles using the theory, see Perri 6 and Mars 2008.

8   The resultant book was published in 1982 as *Cheats at Work: An Anthropology of Workplace Crime*.

Chapter 2 then applies CT to the wider ranges of crime and criminality and pinpoints the strengths and vulnerabilities of each of the four criminal cultures. The chapter then uses the same model to examine the social organization of the police and military intelligence and to identify their strengths and vulnerabilities when dealing with criminal adversaries.

Chapter 3 applies the four cultures to focus on the 'fiddling' of ordinary people in 'ordinary jobs'. It deals with difficulties of classifying and comparing workplace crimes, demonstrates the collusion of supervisors and often of managements, and assesses their justifying ethics.. The chapter identifies eight 'fiddle-prone' factors that facilitate workplace crime and the sway of three macro-influences: globalization, new technologies, and the growth of Individualism. It shows how occupational crime causes organizations to adapt their structures, distort their functions, and sometimes determine whether they operate at all. These features emerge with different emphases throughout the book. The final part of this chapter considers the changing nature of workplace sabotage, including computer sabotage.

Each of chapters 4, 5 and 6 takes a different CT culture and, by case studies, illustrates the specifics of each distinctive form of deviance.

Chapter 4 concentrates on the politics of the Enclave, on egalitarianism, to examine the political structures of organized dissent. It focuses on terrorist crime to chart the constraints facing enclavic organizations – though, of course, it is not claimed that dissenting organizations are necessarily terrorist or criminal. But enclaves of all persuasions similarly attempt to manipulate and control the information available to their members. This determines the choices they can make and has implications for the organization's structure and the behaviour of its members. It refutes more common explanations for behaviours associated with collective dissent commonly attributed to the personalities of their members and leaders.

Chapter 5, a case study of Hierarchy in action, examines dock theft in Newfoundland, Canada to show the parallel organization of legitimate and illegitimate work. It took two years of participant observation to unpick the complex system by which cargo was obtained and distributed, to appreciate the discipline and controls necessary to regulate it, the system of morality by which it was justified, the community norms that supported it, and the inherent collusion of managers who tolerated it.

Chapter 6 again examines the role of Hierarchy to examine a warehouse with an extremely high level of pilferage. It focuses on the links between community and workplace values and behaviour. Set in a dockland community, though not linked to the docks, it reveals the pervasive influence of community culture in the warehouse and the opposed cultures of distant management and locally recruited labour. This chapter concludes by presenting the concept of 'community criminogenesis' – the proneness of a community to occupational crime. Two types are identified, one dependent on a dominant industry's dealings with goods handled by teams, the other with services offered by individuals.

In Chapter 7, two cases of aberrant Individualism are offered, again derived from participant observation, to develop the idea of 'organizational capture' leading to 'Organizational Tyranny' and the perversion of normative ends. In the first, an enclavic organization of professional recruitment consultants is 'captured' by its individualist elite, its normative moral values being then negated and its resources exploited. The second explores how a university business school was similarly captured to reveal how a new individualist management manipulated resources and controlled information to transform it into 'more of a business than a school'. The concept of 'organizational tyranny' is then refined, showing how the inherent checks of hierarchic organizational power can be eroded by competitive Individualism to pervert its functions – that is, to assert the dominance of instrumental at the expense of normative ends.

Chapter 8, also a study in Individualism, details a further case of 'organizational capture'. It again shows how the resources of an organization can be manipulated to depart from its original purpose. The case details a biscuit factory in Soviet Georgia beset by targets laid down by distant planners. It was 'captured' by its local management, who transformed it into a private free-market enterprise. It circumvented its targets to produce 30 per cent *more* biscuits than the plan specified. This it then supplied to an illicit and enthusiastic private market. Here distant and essentially attenuated control offers strong parallels with the distant, globalized controls and targets set for subsidiary organizations by transnational companies, and it has parallels with government-controlled public utilities.

Much of this book, like much of criminology, takes little account of macro economic factors that appear to influence behaviour at micro levels. And yet the climate created by disparate economic conditions is pervasive and has profound influences, not just on behaviour in general but on criminal behaviours in particular.

It is suggested that a useful approach which links economic conditions to criminal behaviours can benefit from the work of Nicolai Kondratieff, a Soviet economist killed by Stalin in the 1930's.

Chapter 9 accordingly links CT's behavioural approach to Kondratieff's theory of economic long waves to demonstrate how different phases of economic cycles rise to dominance and fall as cycles proceed. Four case studies of economic cycles are offered, each exposing the deviance appropriate to each. Upturns reveal the dominance of individualist values: short-term optimism, boldness in decision making, the legitimating of rewards to risk takers, free market competition, freedom from controls and, on occasion, rule bending. An upturn is always marked by 'deviant exuberance' that ends in a crash, the beginning of a downturn, and then the emergence of Hierarchy. Hierarchy is characterized by opposed values: pessimism, risk aversion, and the denigration and stigmatizing of entrepreneurs, calls for their regulation and control and a respect for rules and precedent. Particular attention is given here to contemporary deviance in the financial services sector.

Finally the Appendix offers a 'do-it-yourself' guide to carrying out an organizational ethnography by calculating grid and group strengths. This offers a 'quick and dirty' means to assign organizations and the occupations within them to their appropriate cultures. So armed, the allocation of values, attitudes, appropriate behaviours and justifying ethics should naturally follow as these are detailed in Chapter 1.

The Ethics of Participant Observation

This is a notably grey area[9] and each case requires separate assessment. But discussion of ethics appears more complicated than I believe is merited. My standpoint is simple – possibly too simple. It is that the interests of informants should be sovereign, which means never publishing material or passing information to a third party that might identify or disadvantage them. As an example, I assured the longshoremen discussed in Chapter 5 that my findings on pilferage in the docks would remain confidential if publication would, *in their view*, damage their interests. This meant that, for ten years, data on dock theft could not be published. After ten years, however, the technology of shipping had shifted to the use of end- and side-loading vessels and the transport of cargo in containers. This obviated the need for gangs and with it their system of pilferage. It was when this new technology was well established and gangs were no longer employed that I asked my key informants and the Union's executive (the executive of the LSPU, The Longshoremen's Protective Union of St John's) to authorize publication, which they did (Mars 1974; see Chapter 5 of this volume).

However, information gained from one context can also damage the interests of informants in another. When working in the warehouse discussed in Chapter 6, I became well aware of the methods by which goods were pilfered and spirited from the warehouse – they replicated many of the methods I had experienced in RAF stores and by the longshoremen discussed in Chapter 5. But I felt bound not to reveal this in my discussions with employers because it would damage the interest of my warehouse informants.

Two Apologies

In a collection such as this, which derives from ongoing theoretical developments in the behavioural sciences, it seems inevitable that different terms should emerge for the same concepts, jostle for dominance and appear in print, only to become redundant and be replaced. While this might be thought indicative of the creative dynamism of its practitioners (or not!), it can cause considerable confusion to readers of a collection when the cores of component chapters, as here, have been published at different times and use different terms for the same concepts. 'Cultural Theory' started as 'Grid/Group', then became 'Grid/Group Theory' before being abbreviated here as 'CT'. The collective term for the fourfold categories

---

9   A fuller discussion of the ethics of participant observer fieldwork is by Jun Li, 'Ethical Challenges in Participant Observation' (2008).

started off as 'cultures', became 'ways of life', and now seems to be settled on 'solidarities'. Perhaps most confusing, however, have been the names describing the 'strong group / weak grid' configuration, which has shifted from 'enclaves' and 'enclavism' to Egalitarianism, with sometimes both terms being linked. Use of the 'weak group / strong grid' term has similarly shifted from 'isolate' to 'fatalist', while 'Individualism' in Chapter 4 is referred to as 'opportunism'.

A second apology concerns repetition. Several chapters have been published at different times and often in a 'stand-alone' format. This inevitably has sometimes meant the need here to repeat the basis of CT, while some case details are similarly repeated.

References

Punch, M., (1996), *Dirty Business,* London: Sage

Ackroyd, S`and Thompson, P ., (1999) *Organizational Misbehaviour,* London: Sage.

Dalton M., (1964) *Men Who Manage,* New York: Wiley

Ditton, J., (1977) *Part Time Crime : An Ethnography of Fiddling and Pilferage,* London: Macmillan

Douglas, M. (1982), 'Cultural Bias', in *In The Active Voice*, London: Routledge and Kegan Paul, 183–254.

Henry, S., (1978) , The Hidden Economy: The Context and Control of Borderline Crime, (Oxford: Martin Robertson.

Li, J. (2008), 'Ethical Challenges in Participant Observation', *The Qualitative Report*, 13(1), 100–115.

Mars, G. (1974), 'Dock Pilferage: A Case Study in Occupational Theft', in P. Rock and M. McIntosh (eds), *Deviance and Social Control*, London: Tavistock, 209–28.

Mars, G. (1982), *Cheats at Work: An Anthropology of Workplace Crime*, London: Allen and Unwin.

Perri 6 and G. Mars (2008), *The Institutional Dynamics of Culture*, Farnham: Ashgate.

Thompson, M., et al. (1990), *Cultural Theory*, Boulder, CO: Westview Press.

Acknowledgements

Some of the material in this book has appeared in the following publications:

Chapter 2: *The Social Psychology of Crime*, edited by D. Canter and L. Alison (Aldershot: Ashgate, 2000), pp. 29–50.
Chapter 4: *Human Relations*, 56/7 (2003), pp. 763–85.
Chapter 5: *Deviance and Social Control*, edited by P. Rock and M. McIntosh (London: Tavistock Publications, 1974), pp. 209–28.
Chapter 6: *Culture and Organisation*, 14/4 (2008), pp. 365–79.
Chapter 7: *Culture and Organisation*, 15/3–4 (2009), pp. 237–56.
Chapter 8: *European Journal of International Management*, 2(1) (2008), pp. 56–70.
Appendix: *A Handbook of Organisational Anthropology*, edited by D. Caulkins and A. Jackson (Oxford: Blackwell, forthcoming, 2013).

I am grateful to my friends and colleagues, Professors Perri 6, Charles Goodhart, Steve Frosdick, Stuart Henry and David Nelken for insightful discussions and inputs on aspects of this work and – a constant debt – to my wife Valerie for her creative support as well as critical and insightful commentaries on much of the material.

Chapter 1
The Basics of Cultural Theory

There is nothing so practical as a good theory.
Kurt Lewin

Finding a Theory

There have been numerous definitions and approaches to 'culture', with one commentator recording over 300 variations. This is because the 'Holy Grail' for social scientists and philosophers has long been to find a key by which they might define, classify and compare typical behaviours and values that would be applicable to all mankind. Numerous proposals as to how this might be achieved have been offered, some seemingly more successful than others, but none has proved fully practical – that is, applicable to the whole range of world cultures and able to offer sustainable comparisons. They failed because they didn't meet the two vital conditions for effective classification: their categories proved to be neither exclusive nor exhaustive. This meant they were always liable to be torpedoed: someone could always say, 'Your categories and comparisons don't apply to the people *I* studied' – a response that has been called 'spiteful ethnography' (Geertz 1967). These earlier attempts at classification may have fitted – but, to adapt Christian Dior's metaphor, 'They fitted like a poorly made frock fits – they fitted where they touched'

It was while searching for a way of classifying occupations and their deviance that I became involved in this larger anthropological problem. Each attempt to classify workplace deviance by applying the usual occupational taxonomies – blue collar/white collar; lower-, middle- and upper class – had proved inadequate. Anthropologists, in facing their similar problem, had accumulated considerable data on a wide variety of cultures – just as I had extensive data on how fiddles were organized in many different occupations. But in neither case could differences be accommodated in a viable system of classification.

At this time, Mary Douglas was promulgating her system for classifying cultures. She produced a taxonomy that not only applied to so-called 'primitive' societies but was, she insisted, relevant to all societies and at all times. She called her taxonomy Grid/Group Theory; it later came to be known as Cultural Theory and is referred to here as CT. Now it was possible to effectively compare Hottentots with, say, Bushmen, Australian Aborigines with Western society professionals, and medieval bankers with their current counterparts. And it was to prove similarly effective as a basis of classification when I applied it in other social contexts and, as here, to occupations, organizations, and their different types of deviance.

The core of Douglas's method was to choose not a single basis of comparison but a duality. Scouring the literature on (so-called) primitive societies,[1] she examined how they were structured according to two criteria[2] and developed further in 1978 to demonstrate how they could be universally applied.[3] The first asks how far is a society able to impose rules and constraints on its individuals, thus limiting their choices. She called this 'Grid'. Therefore a society with many rules and constraints – such as the caste societies of India – would be rated 'strong' on Grid. At the other extreme, societies that allow members many choices – as with, say, Californian swingers – would be rated 'weak' on Grid.

The second dimension measures the strength of incorporation within groups. This she called 'Group'. A Chinese lineage offering full life support to its members would measure 'strong' on the Group scale – so too would an army platoon or the staff of an oil rig where residence, leisure, common interests and identity similarly overlap. In contrast, New Guinea Highlanders, the British Columbian Kwakiutl and, especially in the West, independent entrepreneurs, for all of whom no one group is all encompassing, would measure 'weak' on the Group scale.

By considering these two dimensions as continua – as ranging from 'strong' to 'weak' – and then by placing them on a 2×2 matrix, Douglas illustrated four archetypal ways of organizing – four ways that relationships are manifest 'on the ground': 'weak grid and weak group', 'strong grid and weak group', 'strong grid and strong group', and finally, 'weak grid and strong group'.

The relative strength of Grid can be assessed by the use of space, time, objects, resources, labour and information. Taken together, they determine the strength of autonomy, insulation, reciprocity and competition. An individual's autonomy in a specific milieu – how far they are allowed to carry out tasks in ways defined by them – is a good indication of Grid. Low autonomy is found where constraining rules are strong; high autonomy, where they are weak.

---

1   See Douglas 1961. This was the first unveiling of CT but was not considered at the time to be applicable to Western cultures.

2   The origins of CT (which are more fully discussed in Perri 6 and Mars 2008a, pp. xv–xxix), derive from Durkheim's classic study, *Suicide* (1951) [1897]. There he demonstrated that he could classify social organization in each of the countries for which he collected data by identifying two dimensions. The first, social integration, is the degree to which social life is bounded and bonded within groups to which individuals are accountable. The second is the degree of regulation by which individuals are constrained by rules and defined roles. But it took another 73 years before Douglas (1970) was to cross-tabulate the two dimensions (which she termed 'Grid' and 'Group') to construct a 2×2 matrix that revealed the four cultural types.

3   This had to wait until 'Cultural Bias', Occasional Paper 35 of The Royal Anthropological Society, was published in 1978 – reprinted in Douglas 1982.

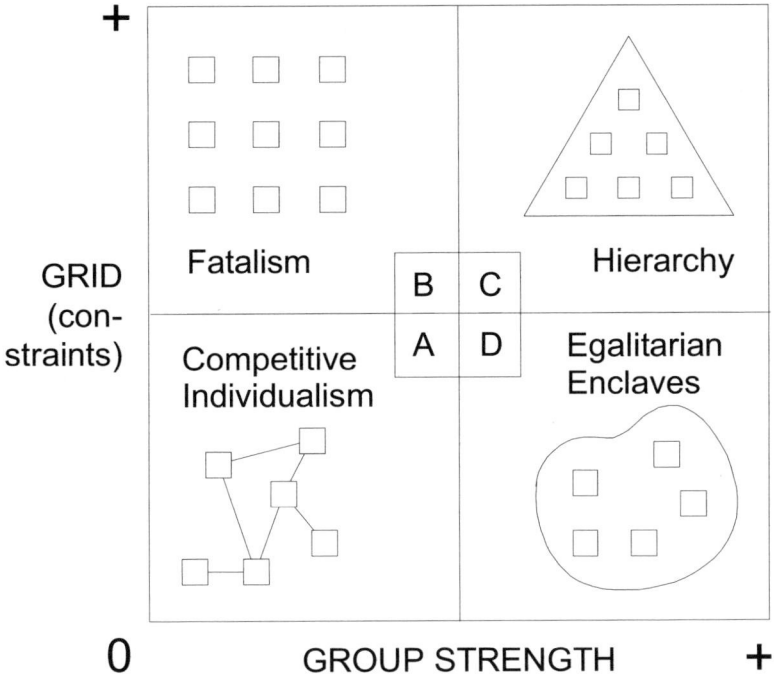

A. Individual networking
B. Isolated and atomized
C. Bounded and ranked
D. Bounded and egalitarian

Figure 1.1   **The four characteristic ways relationships are manifest 'on the ground'**

Source: Frosdick and Mars 1997, p. 110.

The insulation of people from others is also a feature of Grid. A ranking system, for instance, insulates people: it separates them from others and therefore contributes to strong grid. The absence of insulation, on the other hand, readily permits links between people and contributes to low grid. Reciprocity, the third indication of Grid, has to do with how much a job allows its incumbents to offer others and how much they can accept in return. Strongly gridded petty criminals can offer very little to anyone, whereas weakly gridded gang leaders can offer a lot. Competition is the final indicator of Grid. A job with few constraints indicates weak grid that facilitates strong competition – social positions are 'up for grabs', whereas high constraints inhibit competition.

Aspects of Group are assessed by the frequency and mutuality of contact, the scope of activities under the aegis of the group, and the strength of its boundary.

Repeated face-to-face contacts with the same people indicate that both frequency and mutuality are strong. Group strength increases further as the scope of group activities extends. Sharing a common residence, working and taking recreation together, as, for instance, with terrorist cells, or army platoons, all increase group strength.

The strength of a group's boundary is indicated by its members' perception of the distinctiveness of its internal behaviours compared to those considered appropriate to outsiders. Another indicator of the strength of boundary is the ease or difficulty of entry. The more difficult to enter, the stronger the group. Elaborate recruitment procedures thus indicate strong Group. These components of Grid and Group have been codified under the acronym 'LISTOR/SPARCK' and are arranged as a 'do-it-yourself' guide to categorizing relationships in organizations – see the Appendix.

Douglas's next step was to return to the anthropological literature and re-examine these four archetypal ways of organizing from the standpoint of their social values and attitudes – which incorporates their ethical systems. These she found also fell into four distinct clusters, each correlating with one of the archetypes – that is, she found the way people were organized according to their grid and group ratings was congruent with their values, attitudes and appropriate ethical systems – and these justified their characteristically different behaviours. Cultural Theorists refer to these as 'the four solidarities' or 'the four ways of life' terming them as follows: Individualism (weak grid and weak group); Fatalism (strong grid and weak group); Hierarchy (strong grid and strong group); and Egalitarianism (weak grid and strong group). These are marked A, B, C and D respectively in Figure 1.1.

All societies comprise features of all the solidarities since they are the basic institutional forms to be found in any period, in any part of the globe, at the smallest and the largest of scales, and with different degrees of strength.[4] It is worth emphasizing that though all solidarities in a society are evident in different degrees, an overall 'cultural bias' will emerge that emphasizes the competitive dominance of one or sometimes two (and occasionally three) solidarities at any one time.

When I applied this approach to occupations and their everyday deviance in 'everyday jobs' (see Chapter 3) I found the same basic correlates – that the way a job was organized in grid/group terms was also directly associated with their incumbents' values, attitudes and behaviours, and that these invariably involved deviant practices and the ethical justifications sustaining them. Such behaviours had little to do with the psychological make-up of individual participants, being instead based on their social situation – this makes CT a sociological, not a psychological, theory.

---

4   This is one reason why applications of CT are increasing it would seem, exponentially. See the myriad examples in Perri 6 and Mars 2008b.

Now to look in greater detail at the general characteristics of the four archetypal solidarities, each of which. as will be apparent, presents a distinct, strongly cohesive, and coherent worldview.

Hierarchy

Hierarchy is characterized by strong grid constraints and strong encompassing groups. It is one of the dominant forms of social organization found in societies with simple technologies. In the West, Hierarchy is one of the two most influential cultures (the other being Individualism). Applied to organizations, these are termed 'bureaucracies'.

A classic example of Hierarchy is the Hindu caste system. Being strong on grid constraints involving ranking and conformity to rules and strong too on the group dimension emphasizing incorporation, most Hindus have relatively little choice (certainly when compared with most Westerners) over where they live, what they can eat, the jobs they can do, or who they may marry. Their strong groupings are able to maintain and sustain these constraints.

Hierarchies are structured as pyramids marked by divisions of labour, ranking, and differential rewards. In the West, whether a bureaucracy is criminal or legitimate, it similarly subjects its members to rules, reveals ranking with differential rewards, and is able to offers its members a sense of common identity.

Members of Hierarchies, deferring to rank and office, respect authority to those assigned it and give priority to rituals and ceremonials that sustain and justify the group. Their members operate with long time-spans – since groups last longer than individuals – and they consistently use the past to justify behaviours in the present. They tend to defend relatively harsh punishments[5] and are prepared to sacrifice individuals for infractions of the group's moral code since these are seen as threatening the effectiveness and sustainability of the group. In Hierarchies, the interests of individuals are essentially subordinate to the interests of the group.

Hierarchies are marked by a concern with regulation and order that is represented and maintained by those concerned to sustain their structures and processes, particularly their elites, and by those who function to enforce its rules. In the West, these values dominate during economic downturns when arguments for regulation are listened to and effect policies (see Chapter 9) that modify the excesses of anarchic Individualism manifest in the previous upturn.

In less technologically complex societies, divisions of labour may largely be limited to gender differences and leadership roles. Within Western society, organizations with more intense divisions of labour, rank, leadership and authority derive from office and the knowledge of validated experts who rely on orthodox precedents and traditions as their charters for action.

---

5   Or, what in the predominantly individualist West, would be considered harsh punishments.

Boundaries – whether spatial (Mars 2008), social or conceptual – are strongly affirmed in Hierarchies. These not only mark distinctions of rank but define insiders and outsiders and offer barriers to entry at different levels. This applies also to information that is validated only when it flows via accepted conduits. In situations of change, this can sometimes prove unadaptive and dysfunctional.[6]

Because their elites centrally control resources, Hierarchies can 'tax' and reallocate them to celebrate rituals and ceremonials – such as anniversaries – that repetitively glorify and bond the group and allow them to further buttress their own institutionalized positions. In Western bureaucracies, they may use them to carry out research for the same ends.

Hierarchic strength derives from its emphasis on tried and established procedures and the security and rewards this offers members. In return, they are offered support and a 'closure of ranks' if this is necessary in adverse involvements with the outside. As might be expected, if criminality is involved, these characteristics are at their most pronounced. But since Hierarchy is dependent on its lowerarchy's resolute sense of group identity, this can be maintained only as long as an elite can justify to the lowerarchy why it should enjoy an unequal allocation of resources.

Managers will readily recognize the high-grid/high-group structure as appropriate to many organizations and as particularly typical of old established and single-product companies, especially where their functions or products remain relatively consistent – as, for instance, in established banks and insurance companies, especially those run by family dynasties,[7] and government departments, both of which typically make obeisance to their pasts by displaying portraits of past chief executives in their boardrooms. Hierarchic occupations are well represented in accounting departments of head offices, in certain medical specialties, and in the military. It is similarly the defining feature of organized crime groupings, as discussed in Chapter 2. But these defining features may be overturned when an organization is subject to 'organizational capture' by aberrant individualists, as discussed in Chapter 7.

A common feature of organizations is the built-in conflict (or at least tension) that exists between departments with a hierarchic bias (eg. accounts) and those with an individualist one (eg. sales). The Hierarchy, respecting caution, precedent and risk aversion, will invariably be opposed to the short-termist, more risk-prone innovations and practices carried out or proposed by their individualist actors. And this often surfaces when risk-prone individualists engage in rule bending, as they are prone to do.

---

6   The Soviet Union refused to accept intelligence that the Germans were about to invade Russia in 1940. The Americans similarly negated intelligence that the Japanese were planning to bomb Pearl Harbor. In both cases, intelligence came from low-level unorthodox information sources.

7   That is, unless they have been 'captured by individualists', as discussed in chapters 7, 8 and 9.

Individualism

Individualism, defined by weak grid constraints and weak group involvement, is not readily subject to rules, constraints or ranking, and its principle social mode is the network. Individualism, the essence of competitive entrepreneurism, is, with Hierarchy, one of the two dominant cultures in Western industrial society and is becoming increasingly so in the developing world.[8] This is because, with the refinements of technology and its global spread, the division of labour is becoming more pronounced and because people are increasingly shaking off the constraints of involvements in groups, such as those of kinship and neighbourhood.

Innovation, fad, fashion, optimism, opportunism and competitive rivalry are the defining features of Individualism everywhere, attributes that power much of the dynamic in societies. Here social position is more frequently achieved through competition, rather than, as in Hierarchy, often being ascribed by birth and family.

In cultures with a strong individualist bias, such as our own, we therefore find the same emphasis on fad, fashion, competitive consumption and display. And the similarly structured weak-grid/weak-group Kwakiutl and Haida of British Columbia follow similar behaviours. Their leaders and aspirant leaders organize Potlatches – competitive feasts – at which they destroy large quantities of blankets collected by members of networks in order to humiliate rivals who would then attempt to exceed their displays. Individualism is currently well represented in the US, especially in its more entrepreneurial states – New York and California – where conspicuous consumption is readily observable.

Central to individualist concerns are strong drives to autonomy, competition, risk taking, rule bending, short termism, and the fostering of relationships within ever-shifting networks. Individualism is noted for open boundaries and network contacts, chosen from among those thought likely to be useful and offer competitive advantage but who are as liable to be dropped when no longer considered so.

Believing that individual differences should permit disproportionate returns, individualists relentlessly seek support and information of possible competitive advantage, which is why networking is so valued and boundaries are kept open. In weak-grid/weak-group Papua New Guinea, where Individualism is marked and fads and fashionable display are well developed, there is a constant jockeying for competitive achievement measured by success in attracting followers but whose shifting loyalty is inconsistent. Ostentatious feasting in Papua New Guinea or,

---

8   Individualism is not, however, restricted to developed countries. It is sometimes well pronounced in so-called 'simple' societies, as among the fashion-conscious Highlanders of Papua New Guinea, who eagerly embrace novelty (Popisil 1963) and the Kwakiutl, the North American 'totem pole' Indians of British Columbia who, to humiliate their rivals, engage in competitive feasting and conspicuous destruction (Codere 1950).

as among the Kwakiutl Indians in British Columbia, and in the industrial West, is a way not only of maintaining and expanding networks through display but also of economizing on time, a scarce, highly valued resource to individualists.

The individualist perception of time is essentially short termist, in marked contrast to that of Hierarchy, where long-time perceptions dominate. This has widespread and deep implications for policy formation at all levels – for instance, in finance, in the diminishing time that shares are now held compared to even twenty years ago, and in architecture, as evidenced in the reduction of amortization periods for new buildings that now amount to just over twenty years, well within the lifespan of an individual. Hierarchy, in comparison, found no problem in often taking as long as three hundred years to complete a cathedral, as was not uncommon in medieval Europe where the future was perceived as essentially similar to the present.

In Western occupations, Individualism is well represented among industrial consultants, salesmen, designers, freelance journalists and entrepreneurs, who spend considerable time and resources in maintaining and expanding their networks.

Individualism holds little brief for ritual or ceremonial (the hallmarks of Hierarchy) unless these can be exploited for personal benefit. Since competition is pronounced, authority that restricts it is seen as intrusive and is resented. And unlike hierarchists, individualists give no especial value to information derived via approved knowledge conduits: they seek information from whatever source would seem useful for competitive benefit, hence their propensity for networking and their pursuit of the unorthodox and radically new.

Both before and especially since the Victorian era, Western societies have demonstrated a steady shift diagonally down-grid, from the constraints of Hierarchy to the personal autonomy of Individualism.[9] This shift, as stated, follows the increasing attribution of personal power, autonomy and credit deriving from the growth of knowledge and the increasing role of technology and specialization, core features of industrialism. It is a shift becoming more evident worldwide as globalization proceeds.

CT offers two further cultures – Egalitarianism/Enclavism and Fatalism – that, in their alliances and conflicts, are a consistent presence both in macro social terms and at the level of organizations.

Egalitarianism/Enclavism

Egalitarianism (sometimes referred to as Enclaves and Enclavism),[10] the third culture, has strong group identity, so, as with Hierarchy, there are marked

---

9   This is shown as a diagonal shift from 'A' to 'C' on the grid/group chart.

10   For more detailed sources on the nature of Enclaves, see Douglas 1982; the various essays in Flanagan and Rayner 1988; Thompson et al. 1990; and Douglas and Mars 2003 (Chapter 4 this volume, together with its added bibliography).

divisions between inside and outside. But unlike Hierarchy, grid here is weak, so their members eschew ranking, are reluctant to grant authority to leaders,[11] and therefore do not readily validate arbitrators.

Examples of Egalitarianism from 'traditional' societies are the leaderless Nuer cattle herders of East Africa (see Evans-Pritchard 1940, pp. 163–4), who, lacking arbiters, need their disputes to be sorted by outsiders. In the industrial West, degrees of organizational Egalitarianism are found in communes, health food undertakings, and in reforming bodies such as Greenpeace, vegetarian groupings, religious cults, radical political organizations such as the Animal Liberation Front, and the active units of terrorist organizations (see Chapter 4).

Egalitarian occupations are found where groups of workers are not stratified by rank or occupational divisions, as is found among basic-level waiters and waitresses in low-level restaurants,[12] and which was strongly evident in the early days of kibbutzim where all leadership roles were rotated and all significant policies decided at group meetings (see Mars 1988).

Where Egalitarianism is dominant, the absence of legitimated leaders and the lack of accepted arbiters mean that disputes and dissatisfaction tend to be driven underground – often being hidden behind a collective idealism. Conflicts in Enclaves accordingly remain largely unresolved and tend to fester. In industry, their relationships have been characterized as 'erratic' with frequently shifting alliances (Sayles 1958, pp. 39–71) and often marked by sudden bursts of militancy, as in 'wild-cat strikes'. Inter-group discord is common.

Unexpected and often disruptive schisms are mostly resolved by a dissident group's splitting from the main body. Repetitive fission is thus a defining feature of Enclaves, as the histories of many cults and reformist political groupings demonstrate. Vegetarianism, for instance, begat Veganism and then distinctions arose between those who would eat only surface as against root vegetables and Fruitarians, who reject vegetables altogether. In terrorist groups, as we shall see in Chapter 4, the tendency to schism is an inherent weakness for similar reasons.

Lacking structured ranking, the egalitarian enclaves cohere by uniting behind 'a wall of virtue' (inside good, outside evil) and in extreme cases by adopting what appears to observers as a unifying, collective paranoia. In the West, Enclave members see themselves as society's conscience-bearers striving against the greedy excesses of Individualism, whose activities they see as precariously risk prone, and against the policies of Hierarchy, which they view as insensitive and partial. In furthering their causes, they argue on behalf of and recruit from members of the next culture – the Isolated Fatalists.

---

11   However, this role is often granted to charismatic founders, though not as readily accorded to their successors, and accordingly Enclaves are prone to succession crises and schism.

12   In high-class restaurants all jobs are, of course, highly stratified as Hierarchies.

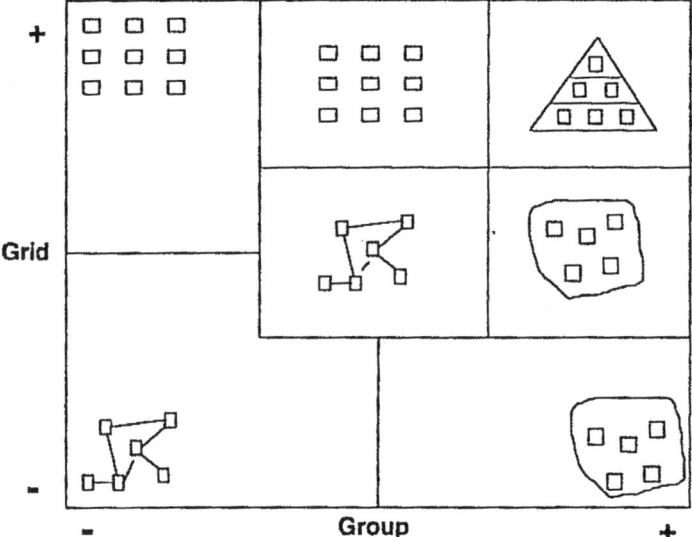

Figure 1.2   Cultural Theory applied to organizations and occupations

Fatalism

Isolated Fatalism is the fourth solidarity. Its high grid position indicates a
subjection to constraints set by others and its low group rating precludes the
identity and support that group membership provides. Fatalists are usually
considered society's casualties due to their position at the low prestige end
of their systems and because they have the least autonomy. 'Rubbish men' in
Papua New Guinea, who live isolated lives on the outside of villages, are an
example: essentially reactive rather than proactive, they are prone to view the
world passively, as Fatalists, seeing the impact of events and risks as something
over which they have little control and the world's happenings as capricious,
with causality due to fate or luck.

The members of Western Fatalist occupations show the same characteristics.
They include dial watchers, call centre workers and assemblers – especially when
controlled by computer monitoring. Fatalists characteristically work alone[13]
and are liable to constraints of space (often having a fixed workplace) and of
time (they frequently have to adhere to pre-set schedules). When controls are
considered too onerous and without group support, they might well respond –
not with collective action but with personal sabotage, as we shall see in Chapter
3.

Cultural Theory, when applied to organizations, assesses them as having a
bias to Hierarchy. This is because all organizations must possess some degree of

13   'Working alone', as used here, includes being socially alone, i.e. as a worker on a
noisy conveyor belt is effectively alone in not being able to relate to co-workers.

both high grid and high group – high grid as the basis of the rules that in different degrees sustain them, and high group that demarcates their varying levels and different functions (Fig 1.2 refers). The staffs of accounts departments, for example, are high group because they relate to and reside together. And because they essentially impose and adhere to rules, they are subject to high grid. In a contrasting example, their more entrepreneurial colleagues in, say, sales, would be of lower grid, especially so if the latter are paid on commission and particularly if they spend most of their time outside the physical constraints of their organization's premises, in 'their territories'. They would also be rated as low group since they lack the constraints (and support) of group membership.

CT can be applied not only to analyze the inherent tensions between competitive solidarities within an organization but also to examine intra-organizational relationships within an industry and to function as an aid to understanding sources of intrusion from their environment. When applied to the study of occupations, the analyses are necessarily simpler since the social organization of an occupation tends to homogeneity – as demonstrated in Chapter 3.

Since CT's four cultural solidarities demonstrate that it is the form of their social organization, their social context, that primarily determines their incumbent's values, attitudes and behaviours, it follows that people can shift between different contexts and behave differently in each. As an example, I once worked with a highly efficient consultant in a multinational company. In her forties, she was always smartly dressed in a dark two-piece business suit and discreet pearls. She knew the name and functions of every executive we dealt with and was extremely competent. And at the end of every working day, she would close her briefcase – and go home to her bohemian squat.

Many texts by CT theorists, including this one, may appear to discuss 'hierarchists' and 'individualists' as if they were psychologically derived – as referring to types of people. Though meant as a colourful way of describing behaviour – it is cumbersome to write 'people living under and cultivated within hierarchical (or individualist) institutions' – it has unfortunately often proved misleading: what is merely a stylistic device has led some to falsely interpret the theory as offering a description of psychological types.

CT does not deny that some personalities might be 'more at home' in some social contexts than in others. An effete, introverted ballet lover with a poetic muse is, for example, unlikely to feel fully 'at home' in the marines. People who face an unamenable environment have five alternatives: they can avoid it (the most common response), adapt to it, leave it, attempt to alter it, or they can psychologically 'crack'.

The four 'solidarities' have been set out in ideal terms, but the majority of real-life situations are less extreme: they reflect a more central positioning on the grid/group chart than would occupancy of its extreme corners. The solidarities should be considered not as 'boxes' or bounded entities but rather as fields.

CT Develops – and Becomes Dynamic

This fourfold schema, while innovative in explaining the link between structures and their clusters of values and behaviours, was criticized because it was considered static – that is, unable to explain how change occurs.[14] The counter to this argument, and the next major breakthrough in the development of CT, was to await the idea of 'regimes' or hybrids (Thompson et al. 1990, p. 4) that show how all four cultures are present in different degrees in *all* contexts.

After this, the next step was to appreciate that it is the mechanics of their interaction that provide the basis of change.[15] This is because Individualism, Hierarchy and the Egalitarian Enclaves – the three active cultures – aim competitively for the promulgation of policies that support their own values at the expense of the others. It is their alliances, competition and interactions that provide the dynamic for social change. They are indeed political – they compete for resources and vie for acceptance. The incumbents of Fatalism – the passive solidarity – lacking the ability for independent initiatives and action, are unable to transact and are accordingly subject to the competitive endeavours of the other three. Nonetheless, though in conflict, all the solidarities are necessarily interdependent because each is essentially in need of the others. There is what Thompson et al. (1990) have termed 'a requisite variety', a theme further developed by B. Schwarz:

> Individualism would mean chaos without hierarchical authority … To get work done and settle disputes the egalitarian [enclavists] need hierarchy too. Hierarchies, in turn, would be stagnant without the creative energy of Individualism, [they would be] uncohesive without the binding force of equality [and] unstable without the passivity and acquiescence of Fatalism. (Schwarz, quoted in Verweij and Thompson 2006)

As Douglas (1999) notes,

> Starting from the initial assumption that each cultural type is built upon a distinctive world view, he [Thompson] sharpened and refined the idea of opposition between world views by introducing the terms 'contradictory certainties' and 'plural rationalities'. A culture builds legitimacy on its own foundation of 'certainties' which contradict the 'certainties' of other cultures. Thus cultures are self-defined as adversarial. This second idea, that they need the adversary in order to know who they are and what they stand for, introduces

---

14   The arguments of these critics are outlined, discussed and I believe, effectively countered, in Perri 6 and Mars 2008a, pp. xxiii–xxiv.

15   A detailed discussion of the dynamizing of CT is to be found in Perri 6 and Mars 2008a, in the section 'From Typology to Dynamic Theory', pp. xvii–xix.

dynamism into the model. The theory now assumes that in any community all four kinds of culture are actualized and in continual conflict.

Members of each culture, therefore, tend to bigotry vis-à-vis the others: they find difficulty in appreciating the 'contradictory certainties' and worldviews of cultures other than their own, or in grasping that societies necessarily accommodate a plurality of rationalities. This makes for perpetual tension and misunderstandings. Thus, like all cultures, the CT solidarities produce their own versions of ethnocentricity. This typically makes collaboration between them a constant source of tension.

Once CT had been reinforced with ideas of 'regimes', 'plural rationalities' and 'contradictory certainties', it emerged well able to refute the most frequent criticisms levelled against it – particularly that it could not explain change.[16] A theory's validity, however, ultimately depends on how well it explains its field better than the alternatives and, as Lewin suggests, on how effective it is in practice – it is on these bases that CT should be judged. This can be done not only by assessing the cases in this volume but by referring to the wide variety of applications exhibited in Perri and Mars 2008: together, they demonstrate an impressive body of material supporting the view that CT is indeed effective in terms of explanation *and* that it is practical in action.

References

Codere, H. (1950), *Fighting with Property*, New York: Augustin.

Douglas, M. (1961), *Natural Symbols: Explorations in Cosmology*, [n] edition, London: Barrie and Rockcliffe.

Douglas, M. (1970), *Natural Symbols: Explorations in Cosmology*, [n] edition, London: Routledge.

Douglas, M. (1982), 'Cultural Bias', *In The Active Voice*, London: Routledge and Kegan Paul, 183–254.

Douglas, M. and Mars, G. (2003), 'The Egalitarian Enclave: Terrorism – A Positive Feedback Game', *Human Relations*, 56 (7), 763–85.

Evans-Pritchard, E.E. (1940), *The Nuer*, Oxford: Oxford University Press.

Flanagan, J.G. and Rayner, S. (eds) (1988), *Rules, Decisions and Inequality in Egalitarian Societies*, Aldershot: Avebury.

Frosdick, S. and Mars, G. (1997), 'Understanding Cultural Complexity', in S. Frosdick and L. Walley (eds), *Sport and Safety Management*, Oxford: Butterworth Heinemann.

---

16   There have been other criticisms, but discussion here is necessarily limited to a single introductory chapter. The reader is, therefore, referred to an earlier work, Perri 6 and Mars 2008b, which, I believe, effectively refutes them.

Geertz, C. (1967), 'Politics Past, Politics Preset: Some Notes on the Contribution of Anthropology to the Study of the New States', *European Journal of Sociology*, 8(1), 1–14.

Mars, G. (1988), 'Hidden Hierarchies in Israeli Kibbutzim', in J.G. Flanagan and S. Rayner (eds), *Rules, Decisions and Inequality in Egalitarian Societies*, Aldershot: Avebury, 98–112.

Mars, G. (2008), 'Corporate Cultures and the User of Space', *Innovation: The European Journal of Social Science Research*, 21(3), 185–204

Perri 6 and Mars, G. (2008), 'Introduction', *The Institutional Dynamics of Culture*, Farnham: Ashgate.

Popisil, L. (1963), *The Kapauku Papuans of West New Guinea*, New York: Holt, Rinehart and Winston.

Sayles, L.R. (1958), *Behaviour of Industrial Work Groups*, New York: Wiley.

Thompson, M. et al. (1990), *Cultural Theory*, Boulder, CO: Westview Press.

Verweij, M. and Thompson, M. (eds) (2006), *Clumsy Solutions for a Complex World: Governance, Politics, and Plural Perceptions*, Basingstoke: Palgrave Macmillan.

Appendix to Chapter 1 by Sarah Mars

My daughter, amused both by my fixation with CT and by my repeated attempts to grow figs against the annual depredations of squirrels, has constructed 'A Grid–Group Analysis of Fig Acquisition Scenarios'. It shows that applying theories can be entertaining – as well as useful.

For Anti-Squirrel Defence Purposes:
A Grid–Group Analysis of Fig Acquisition Scenarios

+

GRID

HIERARCHY
Acting on the authority of the Fig Procurance Subcommittee, a team of management trainee squirrels from Fig Acquisitions is dispatched to report back on prospects for a fig retrieval project. Their preliminary findings detailing potential for immediate harvest are dispatched to the Fig Intelligence Board which forms a working group to produce a report and recommendations. To comply with the consultation schedule, fig harvesting is rescheduled for winter 2007.

FATALISM
Fed up with her production-line existence grading acorns for export to the oakless lands of Tottenham, Squished the Squirrel hides a mouldy turnip in a case of 'Far From the Tree' acorns causing a panic on the nut and seed exchange and a rush into fig futures.

B **C**

A **D**

INDIVIDUALISM
The ruthless squirrel known to some as 'Nutcracker' forms a brief alliance with local birds to secure air cover during a fig raid. He has diverted competition from his less well informed local competitors by spreading rumours of a glut of tinned peaches about to fall from a tree in Gospel Oak.

ENCLAVES (EGALITARIANISM)
Eschewing the cultivated fig as the handiwork of a corrupt mankind, the Squirreline Purificationists fight to keep their diet fig-free. However, their leader, Unsoiled, is found one night feasting upon a freshly-picked fig and driven from the commune. Resentful and angry, he draws on discontented elements among the Purificationists to form a splinter faction, the Army of the Unsoiled, whose diet consists entirely of figs.

0 **GROUP** **+**

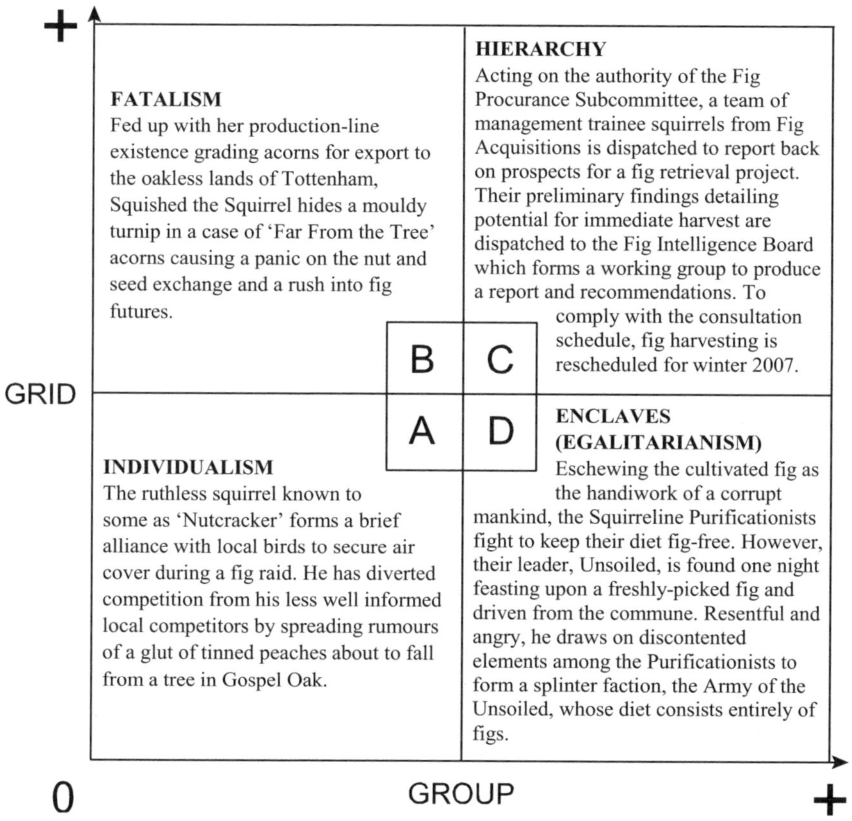

PROVIDED BY THE FIG PROTECTION COUNCIL

Chapter 2

A Cultural Theory Approach to Criminal Behaviours[1] – with a Comment on the Characteristics and Vulnerabilities of Law Enforcers

Introduction

Discussions about crime have long been dominated by legal and lay definitions, many of which are based on intuitive rather than logical inference. In using the four CT categories outlined in Chapter 1, we avoid such definitional traps. The most influential are psychological explanations of criminal behaviour, which undoubtedly supply insights into individual cases of criminality yet prove inadequate when extended beyond this. As an example, terrorist organizations are often defined in terms of the individual psychosis of their members yet are more effectively shown operating as 'regimes' – as mixtures of Enclaves and Hierarchies, operational cells and administrative centres that are symbiotic – with all the opposed and clustering values these encompass. This, too, is why 'eco-warriors', normally 'lumped in' with 'terrorists', are treated more effectively as being biased to Enclavism, an argument developed more fully in Chapter 4.

As so much writing in criminology is divorced from social theorizing, it is difficult to find comparative research that fleshes out the typologies of behaviour, values and attitudes outlined in this volume. There is thus the hope that this attempt to sketch out these characteristics might stimulate efforts to consider criminality in terms of Cultural Theory.

---

1   Much of the material in this chapter has been deductively arrived at through the application of CT and from secondary sources rather than from my preferred research mode – participant observation. This is why I am particularly grateful to a variety of experienced police officers and two ex-military intelligence officers with whom I have discussed its contents. They have confirmed its approach and have made various suggestions, which I have incorporated.

The Four Archetypal Criminal Cultures

Since CT identifies four archetypes, we have Criminal Individualists such as some gang leaders and most fraudsters who are weak on group and weak on grid; the isolated, opportunist Criminal Fatalists, strong on grid and weak on group; Criminal Hierarchists, comprising the 'administrators' of organized criminal gangs such as Mafias who are strong on group and strong on grid; and Criminal Egalitarians, ideologues such as Animal Liberators, Eco-warriors, and the small active cells of terrorist groupings such as Active Service Units of the IRA who are (or were) all strong on group and weak on grid (see Figure 2.1).

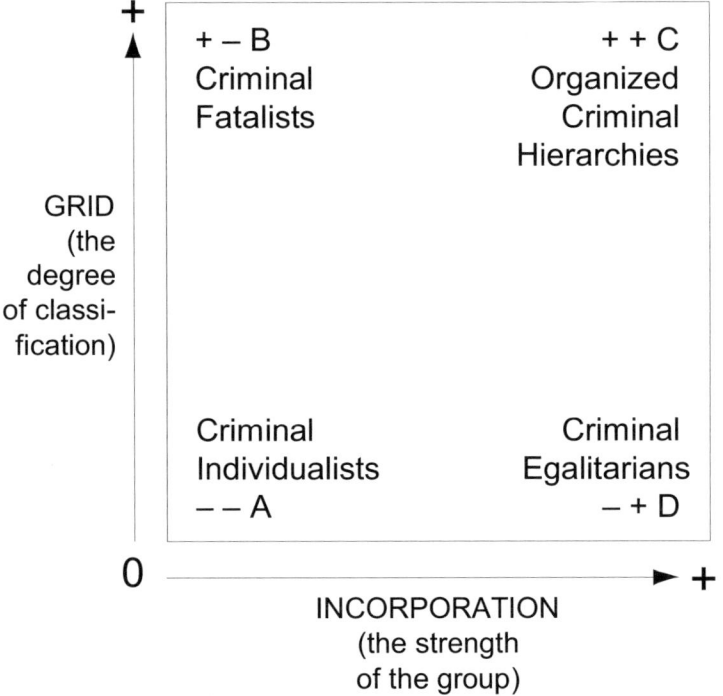

Figure 2.1   The four archetypal criminal cultures

Each criminal culture is first identified by ideal type, then assessed in three ways: their characteristics are defined, their strengths listed, and their vulnerabilities gauged. The treatment then examines them as constituencies of regimes to assess the tensions that arise from competing cultures within organizations. The chapter concludes with a CT assessment of law enforcement agencies (the police and anti-terrorist army agencies). Their characteristics are similarly defined and their vulnerabilities and strengths assessed both internally and in their dealings with different criminal cultures.

Criminal Hierarchies (Strong Grid/Strong Group).

The defining features of Criminal Hierarchies are at first sight much the same as those defining legitimate hierarchies, particularly in their emphasis on an unambiguous system of ranking and the maintenance of a strong boundary differentiating their organization's 'inside' from its 'outside'. This consciousness of boundary, though common to organizations, is, however, more strongly defined in criminal than legitimate organizations, since the costs of permeability are likely to be higher – as will be shown when discussing their vulnerabilities.

Seventeen 'ideal type' characteristics of Criminal Hierarchies

1. Formalized recruitment processes. These are often 'stepped' so that people are first required to 'prove themselves' by performing 'ordeals'.
2. A division of labour and provision of training for specialized roles, with all roles graded in a system of understood ranking.
3. An accepted system of promotion to posts of increasing responsibility and rewards, both material and symbolic. These, too, are likely to be 'stepped'.
4. A respect for authority that is primarily linked to office rather than function.
5. An emphasis on ritual and ceremonial, with close attention paid to significant anniversaries and rites of passage to mark entry, and with formal presentations to mark departures and moves between constituent subgroups.
6. An expectation of loyalty to the group linked to a strongly defined conception of the inside/outside boundary.
7. A 'closing of ranks' to protect individuals from the 'outside' – but only when this does not threaten group integrity. When it does, individuals will be readily sacrificed.
8. The existence of an ambiguous entity of boundary-straddling supporters (Mars 1988) – often retired members, consultants or experts rather than full-time members who mediate between the organization and its outside and who offer support and provide services. Their ambiguous situation, however, can also prove a source of distrust and tension.
9. Respect for the past, with emphasis on tradition and precedents as guides to forming and legitimizing policy and the authority of office.
10. A generally accepted process of arbitration for dealing with disputes.
11. An unambiguous and understood scale of punishments that emphasizes the importance of the group at the expense of the individual.
12. An adherence to long-term time spans (since individuals pass through the group but the group itself has a longer life) that facilitates research, planning, investment and task consolidation at the expense of the 'quick fix' and the quick profit that characterizes the individualist mode.

13. A conservative attitude to risk. This allows new ventures but attempts to have them assessed by traditionally tried-and-tested means and approved by appropriate senior members of the hierarchy.
14. A relative slowness in adapting to change, especially sudden, unprecedented change.
15. A dependency on record keeping that supports the maintenance of procedures and especially those governing the movement of resources both in and out of the organization.
16. An emphasis on vertical communication by which information flows to and from approved sources and through appropriate conduits. This leads to (a) the operation of implicit (though sometimes explicit) 'need to know' criteria, and (b) a tendency to negate information from non-approved sources.
17. A system of insurance and welfare that in well-established Hierarchies can cover payments during sickness and prison terms as well as care of families and provision of pensions.

The four strengths of Criminal Hierarchies

1. Of the four archetypes, Criminal Hierarchies are the most stable and most likely to adapt and survive over time. This is because they can institute administrative procedures and plan and operate internal political checks and balances. They also benefit from the specialization that comes with a developed division of labour, the long-term time spans they employ, and their ability to shift resources to investment in training and research.
2. The mutual support, career structures and welfare facilities that hierarchies can offer members, and their ability to operate sanctions and distribute rewards, all contribute to their effectiveness. And if the strengths of these groups are further enhanced by bonds of ethnicity, they are particularly difficult to penetrate.
3. Because Criminal Hierarchies are essentially bureaucracies (strong grid/ strong group), like their legitimate counterparts, they develop routines and regular activities. They therefore tend to develop high levels of expertise and appear increasingly to be organizing themselves on established commercial lines.
4. Organized criminality has increasingly profited from ongoing globalization. In this it is aided by its relatively unhindered ability to develop and exploit transnational ties with similar organizations (Porter 1985), a process benefiting from the relative lack of cooperation between national law enforcement agencies. In addition, Glenny (2008) points to the over-regulation of immigration controls that encourages the smuggling of sex workers and unskilled labour across national boundaries and the under-regulation and liberalization of global financial and commodity markets

that, with computers, facilitates money laundering. This allows the ready recycling of illicit funds through what can pass as legitimate companies and applies particularly to the movement of earnings from drugs. Deputy Assistant Commissioner Janet Williams of the London Metropolitan Police, has noted:

> Criminals can flit across countries in a split second, hopping from one computer to another, disguising the nature of what they are up to. This makes it difficult for any police service to follow them.[2]

Glenny suggests that, since the fall of the Soviet Empire that 'liberated' many experienced, illicit entrepreneurs, the Tolcachi, as discussed in Chapter 8 of this volume, have effectively extended their networks beyond ex-Soviet boundaries. He estimates that black (or shadow) activities now account for 20 per cent of the world's GNP (though this is difficult to validate) and sees this as set to increase if markets and finance remain unregulated. Lack of control of the illicit market in drugs contributes largely to this figure – and will increasingly do so – as governments continue failing to decriminalize and control the use of drugs.

Just as transnational companies enjoy massive benefits of scale and often have turnovers and bargaining powers greater than many nation states, so some criminal hierarchies enjoy similar benefits. We therefore find symbioses between corrupt or tolerant state entities and criminal organizations (which may not be criminal in their home states).

China provides the emergent pattern in 'people smuggling', with a strong central government remit delegated to locally peripheral administrators. The international trade in drug smuggling similarly benefits from alliances between weak central agencies and organized criminals.

The vulnerabilities of Criminal Hierarchies   The vulnerabilities of Criminal Hierarchy derive from potential 'fault lines' that make them liable to exploitation by rival organizations and opposing law enforcers. Much vulnerability mirrors their hierarchic strengths; some, however, is due to their need to innovate and adapt to change, which makes for dependence on individualists. These and other vulnerabilities are illustrated by considering two examples of the Mafia, one from Italy and the other from the United States.

The first concerns the accidental discovery of an extensive Mafia scam based in South Italy, which came to grief in Milan. Originally reported by David Nelken (Passas and Nelken 1993), it records how one evening police were called to what appeared a noisy drugs party in a Milan apartment. The police noticed two large suitcases. When opened, these revealed a mass of paperwork by which claims were made against Italian government ministries for refunds of payments to be set against spurious exports of EC agricultural products. Though names of legitimate

---

2   Reported in *The Guardian*, 31 May 2011.

firms were used, the notepaper was obviously forged and carelessly completed. The apartment belonged to a freelance accountant, Bruno, who also acted as a management consultant.

It was apparent that Bruno was running a 'paper factory' that was integral to achieve frauds against the EC and that the venture had extensive ramifications covering much of Italy. It was evident, too, that this scam was based on an organization in Sicily run by the Mafia. Under police interrogation Bruno quickly confessed his part as consultant to the scam, and his confession and the false records led to his Sicilian principals. Their backdoor intervention allowed jurisdiction of the prosecution to be shifted to Sicily, which permitted Bruno's prompt release on bail – and, as promptly, his murder.

The second case involves the Mafia in New York. It derives from Maas' classic *The Valachi Papers: the confessions of a 'foot soldier'* (1969). The American Mafia is organized differently from that in Sicily, which is hardly surprising since the social and economic contexts of the two countries differ vastly. In the United States, with its greater bias on Individualism, Mafiosi run their own businesses and operate more autonomously than their compatriots in southern Italy, though they operate collectively for mutual support as members of 'The Mob'.

Valachi, 'the canary who sang', sang because he had a grudge, or rather a number of grudges, and because he was frightened. It appears that the New York Mafia at that time was shifting 'downgrid' from relative Hierarchy to a greater degree of Individualism. Valachi's (crooked) business, he felt, had been intruded upon by senior Mafia members and he believed he was being ousted from control.

As is usual in Hierarchies, there existed a legitimized system of arbitration for settling disputes, but with the organization's shift downgrid, Valachi was not happy with the impartiality of the arbitrator. Also, through political shifts and resultant reorganizations, he had lost his patron, and the replacement, he felt, was unsympathetic to his interests. Further, when threatened by law enforcers, he believed he was not receiving his due protection. Faced with these shifts in organizational values, the possible loss of his business and liberty, and fearing for his life in a new, more cut-throat environment, he decided to 'sing'. And he was able to back his testimony with damning documents. This was the first such case in North America of any significance, one leading directly to the significant findings of the Kefauver Commission (1968) and a serious weakening of the Mafia.

In both cases, internal reactions followed turbulence in the environment. The New York Mafia, set in the milieu of North American Individualism, was more likely to shift downgrid than in the Sicilian case where Hierarchy more readily prevails. It more readily submitted to the pressures of short-term competitive manipulation that negated Valachi's ideal of impartial arbitration. The Sicilian Mafia, on the other hand, more secure in the stability of its own hierarchy, maintained more control, offered fewer alternative opportunities to its members, and suffered less damage.

These comparisons nicely reveal some of the combined vulnerabilities of Criminal Hierarchies: a reliance on records, necessary dependence on alliance with a consultant service provider when out of its 'home' area of competence, and recourse to draconian punishment. This is often counterproductive, however, because it tends to demotivate those who think they might well be next. The accounts also demonstrate the interdependence and built-in conflict that is always at least latent between any two CT solidarities – in this case, the usual example of hierarchic organization on the one hand and individualistic endeavour on the other.

We are now in a better position to itemize the vulnerabilities facing criminal hierarchies.

Eight vulnerabilities of Criminal Hierarchies

1. Like legitimate businesses, Criminal Hierarchies need to be dynamic, which means being competitive – both absolutely and vis-à-vis rivals – if they are to maintain their relative positions and sustain the morale and commitment of their members. This requires continuous expansion and a constant throughput of resources. It means extending operations – not only to milieu where their existing synergies, expertise and experience are readily exploitable but also to where these attributes may not be so developed. Both avenues increase risk and both are likely to involve adaptations of their internal organization that cause discord. Assessments, therefore, have to be made of new forces in possibly alien environments (Porter 1980) that may contain actual or potential competitors, predators and law enforcement agencies. In extending its operations, therefore, a Criminal Hierarchy – like a legitimate one – faces more than just the vulnerabilities normally associated with making strategic alliances: there is also the possibility of making serious miscalculations, as we saw with Bruno and the Sicilian Mafia. This vulnerability is enhanced with the increased cultural and physical distances involved in globalization. Law enforcers might thus find it fruitful to concentrate on areas of *potential* expansion as well as existing activity, a policy already well established by counter-terrorist agencies.

2. Individualist experts, like Bruno, are more likely to 'sing' when threatened than internal experts who are integrated into criminal organizations. They lack the social support that group membership involves and are excluded from insurance and welfare services that are not normally available to consultants and experts. They are also more insecure than regular members. Denied direct access to information by the 'need to know' principle, they typically also lack information about the Hierarchy's collective memory, political structures, and the nuances of power shifts and policy variations. Nor do these collaborators always have an effective 'bank' of reliability based on past services. There is a parallel here with how many legitimate businesses treat their consultants, who also are considered sources of insecurity. It follows that outside experts are likely to be more vulnerable to law enforcement pressures and potentially more valuable as sources of information than regular, full-time gang members.

3. A further vulnerability derives from the necessary dependence of organizations upon effective records, and in the case of Criminal Hierarchies, on incriminating records. And, like other organizations, they are increasingly dependent on computers and are as liable to have their computer systems entered by their opponents' hackers.

4. A fourth vulnerability is the emergence of divergent interests between the Hierarchy and its lowerarchy. As in any business, these can derive from the perceived resentments felt by lowerarchs over promotion, unfair rewards, unjust payments of welfare benefits, and dispute settlements. In Criminal Hierarchies, however, the power of lowerarchies can be decisive in their downfall. Intelligence that focuses on these potential 'fault lines' tends to centre on such sources of information and subversion.

5. Criminal Hierarchies are prone to the instabilities of succession crises unless these are formally prescribed and legitimated. However, it is not easy for them to institutionalize procedures to appoint replacements or arrange for orderly retirements. The same problems apply on appointments and promotions to new and previously untried areas of expansion. Not only can these crises leave vacuums in control by the top, but the resultant insecurity is likely to have unstable repercussions throughout the organization.

6. Due to limits all organizations place on validating information from the outside, there is an enhanced tendency to negate information, especially if it comes via unapproved sources. This makes adapting to change more difficult and slower than is often required. It also means that the planting of misinformation may fail if not preceded by sound intelligence about how and by whom information is normally validated.

7. It has been shown how Criminal Hierarchies, like non-criminal ones, typically need to combine two cultures – Hierarchy to ensure effective administrative procedures and Individualism to ensure quick adaption to new opportunities and flair. This is a common source of strain shared with legitimate organizations, with hierarchs seen as orientated primarily towards policy via precedents, and acceding to established authorities, a concern with internal organization, adherence to rules and risk aversion, while short-termist individualists spend energy, resources and time networking beyond the boundary, looking for new opportunities and being prepared to take risks. In Criminal Hierarchies, information tends to be even more insulated, and boundaries stronger than in legitimate organizations. Here, the tendency of internal individualists to network externally is a marked source of tension, suspicion and potential exploitation by opponents.

8. Finally, all organizations need to recruit. Recruits to Criminal Hierarchies, however, are likely sources of instability, partly because they are unsocialized on entry and partly because even their initial dealings with the organization can give them information of use to opponents. As recruitment, at least to some degree, has to be routinized and involves

organizations dealing outside their boundaries, the 'planting' of informants is more readily effected at the recruitment stage.

Criminal Egalitarian Enclaves (Strong Group/Weak Grid)

These are activist groupings motivated by ideology and idealism, such as the more aggressive animal rightists, eco-warriors, and practising base-level operational terrorists. Their central feature is their identification of a strong boundary, but, unlike hierarchs, they eschew classification, and in so doing embrace an egalitarian approach to their world. This makes for a limit on the acceptance of institutional controls and induces weakness in their operations that can only be overcome by the acceptance of some degree of hierarchic control. In this, their basic dilemma, we find the inherent tensions that exist within these groupings. When they reject controls, this often leads to their disintegration.

Eight general characteristics of Criminal Egalitarian Enclaves

1. A suspicion of the outside, regarded as the source of all evil, with the inside seen as holding a monopoly of virtue.
2. A fear of internal 'contamination', manifest in tendencies to eschew grid differentials such as ranking, records, authority, classification, and indeed any system of controls over the use of space, time, objects, resources, labour or information. Internal contamination is also seen as deriving from insiders having involvements with the outside.
3. There is a tendency to periodic turbulence, factionalism and shifting alliances among memberships because of the focus of these fears on particular people or factions, and especially on leaders or aspirant leaders or those so perceived or suspected. A senior member of the security forces opposing the IRA explained to me that when they had aborted an action or picked up a suspect, they would then exploit this suspicion: 'we'd suggest we had a source by telling them we were "acting on information received" or that "we have reason to believe ...." ' They often thought leaks came from above.'
4. Due to their egalitarian refusal to legitimize authority, it is difficult to apply arbitration to disputants.
5. Thus the only effective ways to resolve disputes are by ejection or withdrawal. There is therefore always the likelihood of schism involving the formation of rival breakaway groups. Coogan (1993) in his book *The IRA* has a chapter entitled 'Splits in the Ranks'.
6. There is a liability to rumour because the rejection of specialized roles means that information has no approved conduits.
7. A belief in total 'whole life' commitment to the group.
8. A belief in the eventual perfectibility of human beings if only the internal view can be extended beyond its boundary.

The Strengths of Criminal Egalitarian Enclaves   The main strength of Criminal Enclaves is the dedicated involvement of their members. However, to effectively mobilize them requires at least a minimal buttressing of hierarchic organization and a limitation on size if they are to achieve their aims and not dissolve into factional in-fighting. Criminal Enclaves, therefore, and particularly the more successful activist terror groups, are invariably found to be small and, at least to some extent, controlled by aspects of Hierarchy. The Criminal Enclavists who made up the IRA's Active Service Units, for instance, could not operate without the backup and control of their Central Command institutions – not only for supplies of arms and resources but also for training facilities, systematized intelligence and the provision of welfare; an extract from the IRA blueprint below, made public in 1977, is revealing.

Reorganization was necessary because the IRA's purely military structure, based on the battalion, was too easily infiltrated. The Central Command therefore moved to a cellular structure based on groups of four, which proved much more effective – the new system thus combined and maximized organizational finesse and commitment, they combined attributes and benefits of both Hierarchy and ideology. However, as they reveal, to operate, they still aimed to maintain central control:

> CELLS: As we have already said, as from now, all new recruits are to be passed into a cell structure.
>
> Existing Battalion and Company Staffs must be dissolved over a period of months with present Brigades then deciding who passes into the (reorganised) cell structure and who goes into the Brigade controlled and departmentalised Civil Administration [explained later].
>
> The cells [each] of four volunteers will be controlled militarily by the Brigade's/Command's Operations Officers, and will be advised by Brigade's/Command's Intelligence Officer.
>
> Cells will be financed through their cell leader, who will be funded through the O.C. co-ordinator. That is, for wages, for running costs, financing of operations (expenses etc., will be dealt with through the O.C.).
>
> Cells must be specialised: sniping cells, executions, bombings, robberies, etc.
>
> The cell will have no control of weapons or explosives, but should be capable of dumping weapons overnight (in the case of a postponed operation).
>
> The weapons and explosives should be under the complete control of the Brigade's/Command's Q.C. and E.C. respectively. (Quoted in Coogan 1993, pp. 578–80)

This extract nicely reveals the tensions between the two levels hierarchs and enclavists, with the hierarchs here determined – no doubt based on past experience – to strengthen the line of command by gaining (or regaining) control of resources, expenses, weapons, recruitment and the allocation of personnel.

Seven vulnerabilities of Criminal Egalitarian Enclavists Note: vulnerabilities can be reduced if there is a sensitive reconciliation of external hierarchical control and lower-level autonomy and if the ideological groups are kept small.

1. Criminal enclaves are relatively easy to penetrate. Rejecting administrative processes, their checking procedures are unlikely to be developed so that opponents with apparently good pedigrees can gain access.
2. Rejecting administrative procedures and having no effective sources of agreed precedents, Criminal Enclavists have to 'reinvent the wheel' each time an administrative decision has to be made.
3. Their resultant lack of administrative continuity is increased because emergent administrators are prone to be deposed. They therefore find difficulty in developing strategic plans.
4. Since legitimacy is not readily granted to leaders, it is difficult for them to negotiate meaningfully with the outside (which here includes their hierarchic controllers). This means agreements may not be ratified, or if ratified may be subsequently reneged by a newly emergent faction.
5. Fault lines are easily apparent, if not from without then certainly from within. Their exploitation can be effected by the planting of rumours.
6. Their externally defined boundary and fear of internal factionalism make members extremely vulnerable to suggestions of a 'sell out' by their colleagues and, particularly, by their own leaders: there is always a potential divorce from the centre.
7. Criminal Enclavists, being essentially egalitarians, are reluctant to judge or discipline their members and in the attempt to keep differences between them to a minimum they therefore eschew overt competition. This does not eradicate competition but diverts it. Just as the members of enclavic religious cults tend to compete with piety, so the more competitive members of Criminal Enclaves compete with maverick risk taking. I was told by a senior member of army intelligence that liability to excessive risk taking had been responsible for the demise of several IRA Active Service Units. (A more detailed analysis of these groups is in Chapter 4.)

Even the most ideologically oriented, spontaneous and egalitarian of enclavic groups, however, needs a minimum administrative structure – that is, a degree of Hierarchy. Grass-root protesters such as the heavily ideological eco-warriors, need to coordinate their activities, obtain and distribute equipment, and arrange minimum budgeting. Similarly, the Animal Liberation Front, and when it operated, the Irish Republican Army, all with strong overall biases towards ideology and Enclavism, also need a hierarchic command structure – in the case of the IRA, an extensive one – with active grid constraints governing space, time, objects, resources, divisions of labour and information.

Criminal Individualists (Weak Grid/Weak Group)

Criminal Individualists are competitive freebooters marked by a reluctance to accept the constraints either of grid or of group. They do not sit happily in organizations, though often find themselves within or on their periphery. Assiduous networking is an activity on which they are likely to spend considerable resources, time and effort. Their cultural collateral (Hobbs 1988) depends on the extent and potency of their network. Like entrepreneurs in the straight world, they operate by linking opportunities to resources, particularly by using their networks to bring together information, specialists and markets. They are concerned to mobilize and plan one-off project crimes, or, like Bruno, as discussed in the section 'Criminal Hierarchies' above, they carry out similar activities as members of or as specialist consultants to criminal and terrorist groups. They are valued as sources of ideas as well as contacts, and they are the recruiters of specialists for specific jobs that are typically dispersed at completion.

Ten general characteristics of Criminal Individualists

1. Since Criminal Individualists chaff at anything that inhibits their autonomy, their loyalty to the organization is suspect to hierarchs. This increases the more their networking takes them outside the organization (Gouldner 1957–58).
2. Individualists, being competitive as well as being networkers, are prone to embrace the latest fashions and fads. Associated with conspicuous display and consumption, they demonstrate status and success to existing members of their networks and serve to impress new and potential contacts.
3. Rejecting the constraints of procedures and due process, individualists emerge as pragmatic short termists, willing to bend rules and more concerned with taking shortcuts than the strategic long view.
4. Accordingly, individualists tend to a robust and optimistic view of their world and, therefore, readily take greater risks than others. This leads to conflict with hierarchs, who treat risk as calculable and subject to the constraints of due procedures and process.
5. Criminal Individualists, being short termist, tend to over-extend their credit – both social and material – to and beyond their limits.
6. Information is hoarded, bartered for personal benefit, and passed along networks that negate or short-circuit an organization's approved conduits.
7. Short time spans mean a lack of regard for tradition and, if employed in an organization, lead individualists to ignorance and disregard of their organization's collective memory.
8. Individualists, being active networkers with adherence to short time spans and enthusiasm for the one-off project, tend to use people as means to ends. They are accordingly subject to accusations of treachery in their personal relationships.

9. Since a Criminal Individualist appears only as successful to his network as the demonstrated success of his projects and since only a minority of projects can come to fruition, an individualist will, of necessity, have to allocate time (and resources) to a variety of projects that might never materialize. Time is accordingly weighed as the scarcest of resources and its expenditure is costed against possible returns. This care over the allocation of time to projects applies also to its allocation to people: the attention they receive is usually related calculatedly to their likely benefit potential.

10. Criminal Individualists deal in information as much as products or services, and they guard and hoard information as a valuable resource. This means arranging both strategic meetings and strategic avoidances. Putting the wrong people together can have disastrous consequences, just as the reverse can be highly profitable. Accordingly, the insulation and tactical merging of different aspects of life is a characteristic of Criminal Individualists.

The strengths of Criminal Individualists Driven by competition and unencumbered by approved procedures or the constraints of group membership, Individualists are the most readily adaptive of the criminal categories. This is enhanced because they are active in using their networks to pursue information and are constantly alert to new possibilities while anticipating the activities of rivals and opponents.

Seven vulnerabilities of Criminal Individualists

1. Their need to network and the conspicuous consumption associated with and necessary to it, mean that individualist patterns of spending and receipts are visible to law enforcement agencies.
2. The constant need to extend their networks makes them vulnerable to the approaches of *agents provocateurs* and to deliberately planted misinformation.
3. As they use members of their network primarily as a resource, they are liable to provoke resentment when they drop them as of no further use. Resentment is often fuelled by envy at their high levels of conspicuous consumption. This, presented as evidence of unjust distributions of criminal returns, is always a possible source of schism to be exploited by rivals and opponents.
4. Never fully integrated into the organizations with which they associate, individualists are liable to be regarded with suspicion by hierarchs, particularly as they operate outside the boundary and are seen as concerned to pursue personal rather than group ends. They are thus more likely than integral members potentially to find themselves, as was Bruno, subject to the harsh sanctions that Criminal Hierarchies are prone to use. This is a source of personal insecurity, readily exploitable by law enforcers.

5. Since individualists are continually tempted by the lure of new opportunities, they frequently have to operate with collaborators and against rivals and opponents with whom they are not familiar. They are, therefore, subject to the increased 'risk premiums' involved.

6. As they are driven by opportunity, individualists are prone to be overburdened by the number of their projects and the often unanticipated demands these involve. Unlike hierarchists, who schedule their activities, they therefore tend to be perpetually short of time and liable to skimp necessary attention to detail.

7. An individualist's lack of group involvement not only reduces the benefits of group membership but also inhibits full awareness of the group's collective memory and the protective precedents these enshrine. This and their relationship to events as 'one-offs' rather than as parts of sequences, involve individualists in short termism and an approach to enterprise that can be termed 'ad hoc' or 'anti-strategic'.

Criminal Fatalists (Strong Grid/Weak Group)

These are the isolated and least-skilled petty criminals, who lack regular association with others and therefore the support of effective group membership. Criminal Fatalists are also strongly gridded. Young (1991), an ex-policeman who turned anthropologist, gives an account of the typical Criminal Isolate in his old patch:

> Ill educated, socially deprived, and often in custody or prison for long periods, especially during his adolescence, he inevitably belongs to the lower socio-economic classes. Poorly educated, physically and mentally undernourished, and often living in squalid and undistinguished surroundings, he has a narrow social existence, living on what is said to be his 'regular diet of brown ale and chips'. Contrary to the moving and freedom of a wild animal, the 'prig' is always oppressed and not infrequently physically constrained. His apparently wild and undisciplined natural life is therefore illusory; indeed, it might more easily be seen to be a dull, sombre world of control and limitation. (Young 1991, p. 158)

The mode of operation of Criminal Fatalists is haphazard, carried out with inadequate competence and a minimum of planning. They have little commitment to specialization, and move from one low-skilled highly gridded criminal activity to another as events present themselves. Just as their criminality is spontaneous, so are other aspects of their lives. 'They spend resources as they get them' (Young 1991).

Hobbs (1988) offers an insightful case study of a typical Criminal Fatalist. Keith drinks in a part of the bar of The City Arms that is restricted to petty criminals. He is 'on no more than nodding terms with the con-men and "businessmen"' who drink in another, more elevated, section of this highly stratified pub, and who hold Keith in demonstrably marked contempt.

Keith ineffectually 'goes through the motions of buying and selling, conspiring to set up various schemes that could never come to fruition' and mixing socially with those who similarly 'shared a lack of cultural capital'. But Keith 'had nothing to trade, he was a punter, and as such could not participate in the core activities of the elite section'.

Keith moves on the edges of this more organized elite world, but is never of it. When his wife dies, however, the elite villains, out of pity, decide to give him a number of chances and he moves over to the elite bar. His lack of ability, expertise and planning, however, and his inability to coordinate the work of others, ensure that he fails at everything he is offered. Eventually he infuriates the elite and is publicly shamed. He ends up back with the rest of the Criminal Fatalists in the low status bar. As Hobbs (1988) remarks, 'Keith had not only proved himself to be incompetent and unreliable but more importantly he had failed to trade successfully'.

Criminal Fatalists: Five characteristics

1. Fatalists are on the outside of organized criminal groups, though they may carry out subordinate actions for them'
2. They are constrained by a lack of both material and social capital.
3. They are reactive rather than proactive.
4. They cannot be identified with any consistent criminal activity.
5. As they lack the ability to plan and are reactive, they embrace a fatalist view of causality and of risk: 'Life is capricious.' 'If you're due for bad luck, there's nothing much you can do about it.'

The strengths and vulnerabilities of Criminal Fatalists   With few choices, little autonomy, and a deficiency of cultural, social and material collateral, Criminal Fatalists are in no position to offer benefits to, or to exert claims on, others. Criminal Fatalists, therefore, have few strengths and are vulnerable to exploitation by other criminal categories and by law enforcers. They are disorganized, with all the liabilities this involves.

As Criminal Fatalists are essentially reactive, lack skills, and possess little capital, they have fewer choices and opportunities than other criminals. They are limited, therefore, to repetitiously but unsystematically commit the same kind of crime in the same contexts. Careful and systematic policing records allow them to be easily identified, and their lack of planning means that they can readily fall into any available net whenever this may be spread for 'the usual suspects'. They suffer the further vulnerability that, being often on the edge of higher-status criminals – the Criminal Individualists and the Criminal Hierarchies – they are a ready target for law enforcers seeking information and are therefore vulnerable to suspicion from such higher-status criminals.

A Concluding Note

Since CT deals in behaviours operating within a total social field, the use of a 2×2 matrix and the resultant four archetypes that emerge are not distinct and insulated behavioural packages. In a messy world, the distinction between upgridded petty Criminal Fatalists and the more powerful bosses of Criminal Hierarchies is, therefore, essentially a question of gradation. Similarly the distinction between competitive criminal entrepreneurial activity dependent on networks and the fully institutionalized controls of hierarchic organization is also graduated.

The Characteristics and Vulnerabilities of Law Enforcement Agencies

Discussions with police in the UK and with Army staff engaged in anti-terrorist actions have shown that CT can reveal useful insights in understanding the workings of these agencies.

An external stereotypical view of police might identify them homogeneously, as hierarchists. When we examine their different elements, however, we identify four different and again archetypal but mutually interdependent and competitive ways of life, four cultures each with a cluster of coherent values and attitudes. In brief, and to simplify, these may be set out as follows:

1. Hierarchy *(Strong Grid/Strong Group)* – primarily represented by the senior uniformed ranks, concerned with procedures, rules, processes, continuity and discipline, and also by the more insulated Public Order Police – the riot squads – who similarly occupy an elite status.
2. Isolated Fatalists *(Strong Grid/Weak Group)* – represented by the disenchanted stereotype of 'PC Plod', who has little autonomy, frequently feels let down by his hierarchy, can see few prospects in his present role, and looks forward to little else but an early retirement.
3. Competitive Individualists *(Weak Grid/Weak Group)* – the detectives, unconfined by the boundary of their organization and its rules, and as much at home socializing and interacting with criminals and outside contacts as with colleagues. These are the most competitive, achievement oriented of the police and have the highest status. It is they who provide the heroes of their organization. Like individualists elsewhere, they are short termist in outlook and actions and prepared to bend rules and procedures to gain a given end. As such, they are a source of worry to their more rule-bound hierarchical superiors.
4. Egalitarian Enclavism *(Weak Grid/Strong Group)* – it might be surprising to some to locate a category of police that satisfies the requirements of Egalitarian Enclavists. These, however, are to be found in the ranks of Crime Prevention Officers who are seen within the police and who see themselves in a sense as social workers rather than enforcers of the law. They tend to

dislike wearing uniforms, and, like the generality of egalitarians, believe in the perfectibility of human nature. They see themselves under siege in the police force and unified in opposition to the insensitivity, and perceived opposition, of the hierarchy. They find it difficult to justify their role to other police constituencies since, like most ideologues, they deal essentially in intangibles – crime prevention is not as calculable as crimes detected. Their status among colleagues is not high. Community Liaison Officers occupy a similar situation.

Standardized police operations are well set up to oppose – that is, to contain rather than to eradicate – organized Criminal Hierarchies and, to a degree, Criminal Individualists. When, through media or political pressures or both, they find it necessary to adapt quickly to changes in operational needs, they have tended to find normal policing structures inadequate. Their response has been to set up Regional Crime Squads. These primarily comprise individualist detectives who tend, through networking and unorthodox extra-organizational means – that is, by rule bending – to bypass normal police procedures. In their early days, their successes are invariably high until they eventually have to be reined in. The problem for the police is that individualist detectives are likely to exceed the constraints required by hierarchists. This leads to a cycle of periodic scandals and the serial dissolution and rise of new crime squads under various names.

The police are prepared to live with and can readily understand and indeed relate to Criminal Hierarchists because their own cultural bias is similar. The police can also deal with Criminal Individualists because they can readily categorize and understand them: they are the over-ambitious who, through greed, go too far. For a similar reason, they have little difficulty in relating to the Isolated Fatalists, who are also readily categorizable, in their case as system failures.

However, an intransigent problem facing the police lies in their dealings with criminal enclaves. As one retired senior policeman explained, 'We're terrified of ideology. Take Liberty [previously the National Council for Civil Liberties]. Police just don't understand that ideology can motivate them to do what they do. It's the same with ALF [the Animal Liberation Front], though they're more easily dealt with.' Not only do the police face difficulty in interpreting motives when these are morally derived, they also fail to understand the ideologists' 'irrational' criteria for allocating resources or their typical lack of interest in maximizing returns.

Interesting distinctions and similarities are apparent in a comparison of the *modus operandi* and cultures of the two law enforcement agencies that operated against the IRA in Northern Ireland – the police, in this case the Royal Ulster Constabulary (RUC), by which name it was known during 'The Troubles', and the Army, the one essentially hierarchic, the other also biased to Hierarchy but with a stronger representation of Individualism.

The Army see themselves as group-based units, as a 'band of brothers' who would perish if need be in 'a glorious last stand'. Their heroic image is essentially collective, as epitomized, for instance, by the Charge of the Light Brigade. They viewed operations against the IRA as a war against another army and, by definition, as leading essentially to a finite conclusion.

The police, on the other hand, saw themselves as dealing with criminals, and their activities as an ongoing fight, spearheaded not by group-based heroes but by their archetypal hero, 'the lone copper'. He tackles his foe bravely but knows this is a conflict that will go on perpetually. Whereas the Army were, until 1984 (when political dictat prevented it), accustomed to identify their opponents by their military ranks, the RUC (and the politicians), however, referred to the IRA in terms of 'gangs', 'terrorists' and 'criminals'. This is indicative perhaps of why there were difficulties in collaboration between the two.

Both the Army and the RUC, however, found a similar problem in understanding and therefore dealing with the enclavists among their opponents. Serving specialists who developed expertise in this area (like the Crime Prevention Officers referred to earlier) felt they had at best an ambiguous status in the Army: they were called 'the Funnies'. And the Army, from its stronger hierarchical standpoint, looked with suspicion on the detective (intelligence) elements in their ranks, seeing them, as my informant put it, 'as almost on the verge of trading with the enemy'.

Conclusion

CT says: 'Let me determine how you are organized and I can deduce your values and attitudes and locate you to your criminal archetype. Not only this, but I also offer a lever to understand your vulnerabilities.' The reverse also applies: 'If I know your typical behaviours, values and attitudes, I am able to deduce the dominant form of your social organization.'

This chapter therefore offers an alternative and a more operational way of classifying crime than is usually applied and is instead based on the ways criminal activity is organized 'on the ground'. It identifies four archetypal ways of organizing but emphasizes that pure forms are rarely found. After identifying the clusters of values and attitudes associated with each type, it demonstrates that it is in their interactions, competition and inevitable conflicts that we gain insight to their strengths – and their vulnerabilities. The same fourfold analysis was then found applicable to law enforcement agencies – the Army and the Royal Ulster Constabulary.

References

Coogan, T.P. (1993), *The IRA*, London: HarperCollins.

Faulkner, D., *International Strategic Alliances: Co-operating to Compete*, Maidenhead: McGraw-Hill.

Glenny, M. (2008), *McMafia: Crime Without Frontiers*, London: Bodley Head.

Gouldner, A. (1957–58), 'Cosmopolitans and Locals', *Administrative Science Quarterly*, 2, 281–306, 444–80.

Hobbs, D. (1988), *Doing the Business: Entrepreneurship, the Working Class, and Detectives in the East End of London*, Oxford: Oxford University Press.

Kefauver, E. (1968), *Crime in America*, New York: Greenwood.

Maas, P. (1969), *The Valachi Papers*, New York: G.P. Putnam's Sons.

Mars, G. (1988), 'Hidden Hierarchies in Israeli Kibbutzim', in J.G. Flanagan and S. Rayiwi (eds), *Rules, Decisions and Inequality in Egalitarian Societies*, Aldershot: Avebury Press, 98–112.

Mars, G. and Mars, V. (1993), 'Two Studies of Dining', in G. Mars and V. Mars (eds), *Food Culture and History*, London: The London Food Seminar, 49–60.

Passas, N. and Nelken, D. (1993), 'The Thin Line between Legitimate and Criminal Enterprises: Subsidy Frauds in the European Community', *Crime, Law & Social Change*, 19(3), 223–43.

Porter, M.E. (1990, 1995), *The Competitive Advantage of Nations*, New York and Harvard, MA: Free Press.

Thompson, M. (1996), Chapter 4 in *Inherent Relationality: An Anti-dualist Approach to Institutions*, Bergen, Norway: Los Centre, 45–74.

Thompson, M., Ellis, R. and Wildavsky, A. (1990), *Cultural Theory*, Boulder, CO: Westview Press.

Young, M. (1991), *An Inside Job: Policing and Police Culture in Britain*, Oxford: Clarendon Press.

Chapter 3
Workplace Crime Including Sabotage – and its Wider Settings

Introduction: Then and Now

This chapter is about fiddles in the workplace – the ordinary crimes of ordinary people in ordinary jobs. Its premise is that one cannot understand how an organization works – with how its relationships function – without understanding its deviance. It is therefore about where to look for fiddles and how to recognize them – about how formally designed work systems are adapted, used, manipulated and bent, and why this is frequently done with the collusion of managements. It is argued that, in these endeavours, it is first necessary to suspend (not deny) one's own morality in order to gain objective assessments of these behaviours.

It is now over three decades since these concerns were first raised in *Cheats at Work: An Anthropology of Workplace Crime* (Mars 1982/1994). In giving accounts of deviance in ordinary jobs, I there showed how its overall practices contributed to 'a hidden economy' and demonstrated the normality by which customers, clients, employers and the tax authorities are exploited and how time is manipulated, frequently with the complicity of management. In revealing the mechanics of fiddling, *Cheats* showed that fiddles were (and are) endemic in a wide variety of organizations. Later experience revealed them operating in different countries at all social levels and to have been markedly influenced by new technologies and the extension of globalisation

Cheats rejected the approach, then common, that classified fiddles according to class and linked them largely to blue- and white-collar crime. This early use of Cultural Theory (CT), in demonstrating that the form and incidence of occupational deviance derived from the way jobs were organized, therefore involved a new way of classifying and indeed of thinking about occupations and the differing forms of deviance associated with them.

Ditton (1976) and Henry and Mars (1978) had earlier shown that understanding occupational deviance involved recognizing that its criminal aspects were of a different order from 'ordinary' crime and that blurring their differences negated understanding. For a start, the motives of pilferers frequently demonstrate a strong social component, with the onward distribution of pilfered items often being of central concern to them. Henry (1987) was later to set occupational crime within the wider context of the informal and formal economies. He demonstrated their essential symbiosis, how they mutually support, complement, adapt to and amend each other. Hollinger and Clark (1983) related these concerns to the US.

Cheats, concentrating on the micro organization of the workplace, argued that occupational deviance, from illicit 'perks' through 'skimming' to outright sabotage, provides the flexibility that makes many organizations work, thus giving theoretical underpinning to what is a commonplace for many workers and – despite their protestations – for many managers. It showed how deviance often permits organizations to adapt to their environments when they might otherwise not readily be able to do so, how it can distort their functions and sometimes even determine whether they can operate at all. However, though these basic tenets still apply, other influences have developed that directly influence the nature of workplace deviance.

Though *Cheats* in 1982 took some account of external influences on the workplace, what it did not do was to specifically assess the growing influences of globalization and continuing changes in technology. To address these external macro influences is one of the concerns of this chapter. Another is to assess whether there is more occupational crime now than three decades ago.

But first, to outline the original approach to the cultural underpinnings of behavior, which, in its essence, remains today as robustly valid as when it was first expounded by Mary Douglas in 1970 and developed by her in 1978. CT, as outlined in Chapter 1, has come a long way in the last thirty years. However, its two dimensions apply equally – then, as now – to understanding the way relationships are organized 'on the ground'. What *has* altered is the influence of external, macro forces on the two dimensions and how, in weakening or strengthening them, new opportunities for deviance emerge in some occupations as they are reduced in others.

When applied to the workplace, the first dimension, Grid, assesses the relative strength of constraints in a job – concerned with whether, for instance, there is emphasis on classifying incumbents by rank, and by the requirement to wear uniforms; with a job's control over its holder's occupancy of space; and with whether it imposes restrictions over their time – by needing them to work within a schedule or timetable, for example. In brief, grid is a measure of autonomy, where 'Strong Grid' means little autonomy and 'Weak Grid' a good deal. A highly gridded job is that of a dial watcher or a call centre worker, whereas a self-employed entrepreneur's job is low grid.

The second dimension, Group, when applied to work, assesses the degree of incorporation in face-to-face workgroups. It would rate an Army platoon as strong on group, since the group is reinforced on the basis not just of its members' work but also of their leisure and residence, and it offers a potent source of group identity and group controls. On the other hand, an independent management consultant's job would rate weakly on the group dimension.

When these two dimensions are placed as continua on a 2×2 matrix, as in Figure 1.1, it identifies the four solidarities as occupational archetypes that, for this chapter, have been given descriptive animal mnemonics.

The Four Solidarities in the Workplace

Hawks

Weak-grid/weak-group, individualist occupations, here called 'hawks', are those relatively free of group membership and group controls. They determine their own *modus operandi* and thus avoid constraints. These are the networking entrepreneurs, fixers and dealers, who competitively swoop to their goals and who value autonomy, competition and the freedom to transact. Jobs that are paid or partly paid by commission usually contain a hawkish element.

Hawks see social positions not as ascribed but as competitively 'up for grabs'. Journalists are commonly hawks, as are many independent professionals. Nick Leeson, who broke Barings Bank, acted as a classic hawk despite – or perhaps due to – operating in a traditional hierarchic context (a long-established, family-owned bank) that encouraged him as long as he was able to produce, or appear to produce, well above average returns for the bank.

Newspaper managements similarly recognize the variable skills of their journalists by permitting 'added-on' expenses for exceptionally good work. Journalists have a motto: 'A good story deserves good expenses.' Such collusively variable rewards are a feature of occupations demanding quick fluid adjustments or/and where talents and flair vary widely.

The characteristic deviance of employed hawks is the fiddling of expenses (as in the European Parliament and by some UK MPs and members of the House of Lords); the manipulation of time (always in short supply for hawks and frequently the basis of fiddles by employed professionals); the evasion of regulations and guidelines; and the switching of resources between different budget headings and the running of an independent 'business within a business' for their own rather than their firm's benefit.

Since hawks value competition, autonomy, innovative corner cutting and new ways of doing things, they are keen to seek out new informants and new information. To achieve their ends, they need to be effective networkers (though their alliances shift with expediency). The new and fashionable are constantly sought and exhibited because hawks continually need to demonstrate success to their ever-potentially extending networks. It is by competing through display and conspicuous consumption that hawks impress and expand their networks. One cannot conceive of an entrepreneurial hawk aiming to seal a deal, influence a prospect or impress a potential network member by suggesting they entertain them for dinner – and then taking them home - to a hovel. Impressive display and awareness of the latest fads and shifts in fashion are necessary to demonstrate success. This often makes criminal hawks vulnerable to law enforcers searching for evidence of crime, as discussed in Chapter 2. It is also a source of data for the Revenue when they assess tax liabilities.

Though innovative flair, adaptability and enterprise are hawk qualities, highly valued in organizations facing competition and change, they can cause mayhem if hawks are not monitored and controlled. A good example is the crew who took over Arthur Andersen, the long-established accountants and consultants who colluded with hyper-entrepreneurial individualists at Enron, leading to the dissolution of both companies, as discussed in Chapter 9.

Despite their value to organizations, hawks face conflict within them since their propensity to rule bending and risk taking are qualities inherently opposed by controlling, risk-averse hierarchists, who are predisposed to the oppositional value of caution and who have an orientation to the longer term. They tend to be rule bound and in decision making operate through precedent. They therefore see hawks as disruptive and their policies as risk prone. This clash of values is most marked when a naive manager or a 'new broom' accountant takes office and fails to recognize or understand the incentive function of the hawks permitted indulgences.

A vulnerability facing normative organizations (those primarily concerned to promulgate ideas, such as universities, museums, professional groups and mutual societies) is the possibility of their 'take-over' by entrepreneurial market-led hawks, as discussed in Chapter 7. This is especially likely during periods of fast change and invariably involves the sacrifice or downgrading of an organization's original social purpose.

Wolf Packs

Strong-grid/strong-group occupations – hierarchies – are here appropriately called 'wolf packs'. They comprise ranked and stratified workgroups with marked divisions of labour. They exhibit a defined sense of boundary and impose strong constraints on their members. They demonstrate assertive self-identity and are controlled, disciplined and strategic in their dealings with bosses.

Dustcart crews (rubbish collectors) are wolf packs. They decide criteria of entry and reject imposed new members who do not match their requirements. They have a well-developed system of ranking, often based on seniority and on their allocation of differential rewards gained from recycling scrap, sharing tips, accepting bribes to clear rubbish they shouldn't, and by selling salvaged items and materials such as unwanted clothes and non-ferrous metals that should be given up to their employers. Wolf packs typically socialize together off the job and act collectively if the interests of any of their members are threatened.

A detailed account of well-developed wolf packs is offered in Chapter 5, showing the structure and values of longshore work gangs. They show how, typical of wolf packs, the gangs adapted their work structure to pilfer cargo as a collective and they jealously controlled entry to their workgroups – usually by making it difficult for a non-approved entrant to work with them. And, also typically, if one of them was threatened by outside interests – their bosses or the law – they resolutely closed ranks in their defence. Wolf packs survive over time by control of entry, control of ranking and, crucially, control of quantities pilfered.

Vultures

Weak-grid/strong-group (enclavic, egalitarian) occupations are here called 'vultures', because – like real-life vultures – they cooperate for some purposes but competitively pursue their own benefits for others, especially 'at the kill'. With few distinctions of function or status, vultures are to be found working from the same depot and are typically responsible to the same boss. Driver/deliverers are vultures. So are bus drivers and same-grade waiters as found in low- and middle-status restaurants (whereas more stratified teams of waiters in top-grade restaurants are more wolf pack).

Vultures have a strong sense of boundary, but because they 'de-emphasize' distinctions of rank they are reluctant to grant authority and arbitrational functions to their members. As a result, dissent tends to be submerged – to arise as sudden spasmodic schisms.

Vultures, being the least consistent or secure of the solidarities, have industrial relationships that tend to be erratic and difficult to manage. A common managerial response is to grant 'fiddle fiefs' to their more valued workers – the 'best' tables to the best waiters, for example. These involve managerially tolerated access to illicit resources, which brings competition into vulture groups and can cause dissent and insecurity.

Unlike wolf packs, vultures lack the stabilizing influences of stratification and the surety of controls generated by the group. And unlike hawks, individual vultures have less independence and personal power. There are fewer professionals among them and more craftsmen and semi-skilled workers.

Donkeys

Strong-grid/weak-group fatalist jobs are those strongly constrained by externally set rules and categories and that lack the support of face-to-face group membership. These are the donkey jobs,[1] characterized by isolation and subordination. They lack autonomy, face controls over time and space, and are therefore socially isolated. Unemployed social security claimants, dial watchers, security guards and call-centre workers controlled d by externally set constraints are in this category.

These workers are powerless if they accept the constraints they normally face, or paradoxically powerful – that is, disruptive – if they reject them. At high points of Grid where constraints are strongest, sabotage is a not infrequent response. Taylor and Walton (1971) offer the case of a worker in Blackpool who, on his last day at work, caused his employer to throw away half a ton of Blackpool rock (candy bars with lettering through their length). Instead of 'Blackpool' running through the rock, his output read 'Fuck Off'. Where constraints are mechanized

---

1   I am NOT here referring to the holders of these jobs as 'Donkeys' but to the *structure* of their jobs that determines behaviours appropriate to them. The same applies to the other mnemonic animal categories used.

– or, computerized – resentment fiddles come into their own. An alienated hotel receptionist working out his week's notice, massively multi-booked the accommodation available, with resultant chaos when angry customers arrived to find their bookings unavailable with the fifty non existent rooms being claimed by several customers

Hopefully it is now apparent that CT's solidarities effectively classify the social aspects of jobs based on how they are structured in the workplace, not on the psychological categories of incumbents based on their personalities. Nor are they derived ad hoc by intuition – as with the common-sense lay categorizations often favoured by journalists.

Variable Moralities and Variable Limits

A primary significance of CT is that it relates each solidarity to a distinct ideology, a coherent 'cluster' of values and justifications that, to its members, makes moral sense of their situation. Applied to the workplace, such value systems incorporate moral codes about who can be a victim, in addition to what can be pilfered and in what amounts. Chapter 5 shows how the Canadian dockworker gangs, referred to earlier as archetypal wolf packs, operated limits on the amount of cargo they permitted their members to take – and they were forbidden to steal passengers' baggage. As one longshoreman put it, nodding towards another,

> He'll take anything [...] He's even taken baggage. He's nothing more than a thief.

Breaches of these rules in wolf packs invariably invoke severe group-based sanctions that can involve ejection from the group. In this they exhibit a well-defined morality, but unlike the morality of their critics this is usually a *quantitative* morality, based on the levels of tolerated amounts taken. Their critics outside the work context tend to see morality only in *qualitative* terms, where an act is perceived as right or wrong irrespective of the amounts taken.

There are occasions when a worker is trapped into fiddling and has little choice whether he fiddles or not. This applies especially where there is group involvement, as in wolf packs and among vultures. A driver/deliverer pie salesman in an archetypal vulture occupation explained:

> There's one woman [...] who runs the canteen at the tech. college. She orders trays of pies. Every day she orders three, every day she sells three, and for years she's always thought there were sixty pies to a tray when there should be seventy-two. This fiddle was passed on to me when I took the job on and the bloke who showed it me had it passed on to him when he started. It must have been going on for years because that woman had been there thirteen years when I took her on and that was two years ago. The fiddle was possible because she'll always sign for three trays with no mention on the voucher of the number of pies.

A refusal to participate in this handed-down fiddle would have alerted the customer that she'd been consistently fiddled out of thirty-six pies every day for at least thirteen years! This driver/deliver's dilemma was compounded since he knew that inevitable repercussions would also affect relationships with his workmates and his boss.

Other vulture occupations, such as waiters, acknowledge similar rules, but, compared with wolf packs, they are less capable of mobilizing group sanctions. When management considers an understood level to have been excessively breached and colluded in but unspoken agreements are aired, then co-worker sanctions are likely to be invoked. I recall a hotel manager's angry protests on discovering that a side of smoked salmon destined for that day's teas had 'walked':

> I know you fiddle and you know I know you fiddle, but – for Christ's sake – leave me a bit.

On this occasion, co-workers' sanctions were limited to strong and unified criticism of the violator since stronger collective sanctions were unable to be mounted.

A supermarket cashier – in a donkey job – recounted the limits and sanctions not affecting quantities but defining categories of customer that should not be fiddled, though in the absence of group involvements, sanctions were limited to gossip and loss of reputation.

> Who isn't fiddled? Well, old people – you'd never do it to an old person [...] this is the girls' ruling [...] and you'd not do it to anyone with young children. You tend to take account of how well dressed people are. 'Oh,' you think, 'they can afford an extra thirty pence', or whatever it is.

We see that rules governing pilferage are widespread and invariably set limits. They run counter to the often-expressed view that, 'Once they start on little fiddles, they'll eventually move to the big ones.'[2] Colluded in management limits and workgroups collective controls invariably apply limits to pilferage. In the days before the widespread use of mobile phones and word processors, it was common to allow clerical staffs and typists to use their office phones to make local calls while managers were permitted long distance calls and the top brass, international calls. This tolerance acknowledged that staff were *expected* to fiddle, but only within the limits defined by their rank.

Clear-cut, morality-based rules voiced by outsiders are invariably too simple to be applied to 'real-life' contexts. We saw that self-imposed worker-based limits on categories and amounts of goods are common, while types of tabooed victim are clearly defined. Added to this is that supervisory (and often managerial) collusion is general. To understand the nature and role of fiddling in the workplace, therefore, it is first necessary to contextualize it – and to do so involves a suspension of

---

2   This view was expressed by the then Chief Constable of Manchester, a Mr Anderton, during a radio program to which I contributed. Neither of us could convince the other!

any externally derived morality. This, of course, need not necessarily involve its denial. The difficulties faced by many managements in adopting this approach and the flawed controlling policies that result are considered in Mars 2001b (part 3).

Fiddle Factors, Fiddle Proneness and External Influences Affecting Fiddle Levels

Under this heading in *Cheats* (pp. 136–59), I moved from the study of occupations to the contexts in which they operate. The aim was to identify factors that facilitate payment of a significant part of an occupation's 'total rewards' in the form of fiddles.[3] Each of these factors depends on an imbalance in underlying structural differences of knowledge, control, power and ability held by some groups over others. Five main areas were identified. Later we shall see how these have been affected by developments in globalization and technology.

The first, 'passing trade', exists where two sides to a transaction typically meet only once, as with tourists in a strange city where any single transaction is unlikely to be repeated. This is different from, say, regular transactions in a village shop where any one transaction is part of a regular flow and where relationships are multi-stranded – that is, a customer can simultaneously be a neighbour, a relative, and a co-member of the village cricket club. Here, a single transaction is likely therefore to also involve relationships of leisure, residence and often kinship, so that damage to one strand would expensively damage others.

In the centre of London, passing trade provides the basis on which staffs in a restaurant I know are paid and is the basis of their 'fiddle fiefs' by which management maintains differentials. Its two most senior staff are reserved the right to serve Japanese customers. There is a stereotype of the Japanese, who are believed not to understand English money since they often do not count their change. Since this restaurant is centrally situated, it is also frequented by drunks, especially at weekends. They are allocated to all waiters on a strict roster but with the greater number going to the most senior.

Burgeoning travel and tourism can be expected to have increased passing trade deviance. John Adams (2000) points to the 'hypermobility' of Western society, which involves steadily increasing distances that its people annually travel. The growing proportions of populations living in urban conurbations also add to passing trade.

The second, fiddle-prone area is 'exploiting expertise', typically found where expertise is involved in a transaction or where this is assumed. As technical complexity is increasing – for instance, with domestic consumer goods – there

---

3   It is the totality of *all* rewards that is important – not only to recipients but to all those concerned with fixing wages and salaries. This *totality* of reward covers the regular though covert arrangements that govern its distribution and the values and attitudes that sustain them.

grows a widening 'knowledge gap' between servicing and maintenance staffs and their customers. Thirty years ago, it was still possible for a reasonably handy amateur mechanic to be able to carry out routine repairs and servicing to an average car. Now, one has only to consider the ever-increasing (and to a degree computerized) complexity of cars to appreciate the imbalance in knowledge and power of present owners as against garage staffs.

As might be expected, women are stereotyped as being more technically ignorant than men and therefore are more prone to be victims. See the repetitive reports in *Motoring Which?* that year after year recount the same findings showing how many garages exploit their more ignorant customers and particularly women customers. The exploitation of expertise can apply either to information or to goods. However, the widespread permeation of computers and the World Wide Web, in serving to spread expertise, has perhaps modified the efficacy of this factor.

'Gatekeepers' are the third fiddle-prone area found where there is an imbalance between supply and demand. This can apply to either goods or information. Whatever the resource, the lack of balance will be most evident at the boundary between supply and demand – and at this point in production or distribution, benefits will accrue to gatekeepers who control what is required. In a command economy, as described in Chapter 8, the factory managers who controlled the supply of a scarce consumer good were classic 'gatekeepers'. In competitive economies where there is usually a surplus of suppliers relative to the demand for them, there is a propensity to bribe buyers in order to gain advantageous terms – a liability found in local authority purchasing, and notoriously in the international arms trade.

'Triadic occupations', the fourth 'fiddle-prone' area, operates where staff in service occupations are involved with customers/clients so that there is the opportunity for two of the trio (employers, workers and customers) to combine against the interests of a third. This occurs when a sales clerk, cashier or waiter gives goods to friends or relatives without charging them, or – as has been described – where management offers differential rewards to staff at the expense of customers, or where management and staff collude to increase the amount charged to customers (not uncommon in supermarkets where ambiguously placed items at the till are repetitively charged for to maintain stock levels, especially prior to stocktaking) (Mars 1982, pp. 66–9).

The level of personal services in Western economies is increasing, which boosts triadic fiddles especially when enhanced by conditions that also increase passing trade or/and exploit expertise involving complex technology. Again, garages offer an archetypal example. In dealing with an obviously ignorant passing customer who needs emergency help, he may well be indented for spare parts that do not require replacing, while inflated charges for labour can be difficult to refute.

The fifth fiddle-prone area, 'rewarding special efforts and special skills', operates where economic return is directly relatable to exceptional individual effort or skill. It flourishes among employed professionals and tradesmen where formal rewards are bureaucratically, often collectively, fixed but where the real market value of such labour is adjusted not through collective means but by individual arrangements (Dalton 1959, pp. 194–217), often through the allowing of over-generous expenses, earlier described as applying in journalism. This factor too is subject to increase with the emergence of new specializations and growing technical complexity.

In addition to these five main fiddle-prone areas, there are four supplementary factors. Whereas the main fiddle categories are concerned with imbalances of power between the fiddler and their victim, supplementary factors derive from the nature of goods and the structures that mediate between them and the people who handle them. They have also been affected by globalization and technological developments

The first supplementary factor is found in contexts where control systems might be effective but are not put in place. This is because of the expense of installation or (and more commonly) because managements decide that the triadic nature of transactions can allow the cost of fiddles to be borne by the customer. Incentive coupons and vouchers issued by stores and petrol stations are not infrequently retained by their staffs, later to be redeemed by them or their friends.

A second supplementary factor is found where ambiguity over the good's quantity, quality or exact category is inherent in its nature. It is not easy to compute the quantity of drink consumed at a wedding, or – in the building trade – the number of bricks delivered to a site, the thickness of concrete on a path, the exact amount of copper used in a building, or the gauge of zinc on a roof.

At busy times – and especially in a seller's market – ambiguity is liable to be deliberately increased, as on hot days when ice cream is sold to eager queues; at New Year sales when customers are surging at points of sale; and when drinks are served at theatre bars during crowded intervals. This is when price lists often go missing and cash register windows become obscured.

Supplying food and drink involves a concentration of fiddle factors that thrive on ambiguity, which is why hotels, restaurants and bars are particularly fiddle prone (see Mars 1973; Mars and Nicod 1984). After a few drinks some customers are unable to distinguish dear drinks from cheaper ones, which encourages over-charging and short-changing. Bar staff, for instance, will sometimes smear gin around the inside of a young woman's glass before filling it with tonic and passing it off as gin and tonic. Tarragona is not infrequently served as port wine, especially at Christmas, while some wine waiters in even the best restaurants, and after careful assessments of their customers, sometimes sell cheap wine as château bottled. Nor is it unknown for them to collect the ends of other customer's bottles to sell in carafes as 'house wine'.

A third supplementary fiddle factor involves the smuggling of goods out of safe storage. When working in the RAF's stores, I found that watches and other high-value/low-volume items were known as V & A, 'valuable and attractive' – that is, they were theft prone and could readily be smuggled from the stores. Items in or awaiting transit that can pass as the property of the pilferer are especially prone to pilferage. Delivery drivers may collude with the loaders of their trucks to load surplus items that can be dropped later or they can collude with the recipient to sign for more items than are received.

A fourth supplementary factor concerns anonymity and scale. The prevailing trend with globalization is to increase economies of scale by increasing the size of plants which encourages deviance, scale having for long being related to a propensity to theft (Smigel 1956). The suggestion has been made that our ethics, having developed from small-scale communities, mean we accordingly fail to appreciate their relevance to large corporations (Cahn 1955).

Sources of Change: Two Related Macro Influences

We now consider in more detail what has occurred since 1982 when *Cheats* was published that might have weakened or strengthened the Grid and Group dimensions of particular jobs, examine their effect on fiddle proneness and assess their influence in new jobs that have arisen in the interim.[4]

In the past three decades, as indicated earlier, there have been changes in two related macro areas that affect jobs and the deviance appropriate to them. These are globalization and technological change.[5]

Globalization

Globalization involves the free and rapid movement of capital, labour and ideas. It is not new but is a long-term accelerating process, aspects of which have been noted at least since the Renaissance. What *is* new is its extent, and the speed of its impact facilitated by computers, and that it has markedly sharpened competition, primarily in finance and increasingly in production and services. (Globalization's influence on the power of organizations and resultant deviance affecting the nation state and its especial influence on international financial services are considered in Chapter 9.)

Transnational companies can swiftly move capital and production around the world and activate financial and human relations directives at a distance. These practices widen divergence between managements and labour and between managements and the more hierarchic, traditional small-scale 'face-to-face' communities in which many labour forces live. This distancing is enhanced by

---

4   This approach, in assessing macro influences beyond the workplace since these affect Grid and Group at the micro level, follows C. Wright Mills's (*c.* 1963) wise injunction: 'Only by moving grandly on the macroscopic level can we satisfy our intellectual and human curiosities. But only by moving minutely on the molecular level can our observations and explanations be adequately connected. So, if we would have our cake and eat it too, we must shuttle between macroscopic and molecular levels in instituting the problem *and* in explaining it' (p. 563).

5   A useful discussion of developments in technology as these have affected fiddling in Australia since Cheats at Work appeared in 1982 is offered by L, Thornthwaite and and McGraw, P (2012).

differences between managers' education, residence, lifestyles, incomes and aspirations when compared to those of their workers.

Much current management education and the manpower policies they attempt to inculcate are based on an implicit stateside ethnocentricity influenced by the competitive individualist philosophy of North American hawks. The texts used in European management schools often derive from the US or are influenced by them. This has resulted in the human relations components of many MBA courses largely being reduced to the bounded concerns of organizations, ignoring the influence of cultural, communal and social values in the workforce.[6] I have often been surprised in discussion with senior managers by how little they know about the communities in which their workers live, by their ignorance of local cultures, and by their over-simple, ethnocentrically derived interpretations of their workers' behaviour, especially in matters of deviance. When they discuss deviance, they predominantly treat it psychologically – as pertaining to the individual. Chapter 6 illustrates such cultural blindness.

This narrowing of management's perceptions can blind them to the sometimes positive functions of deviance. Zeitlin (1971, an article entitled 'A Little Larceny can do a Lot for Employee Morale') records how, unusually, the president of a US company kept an office manager in post though well aware he was fiddling the petty cash of $2,000 per year. He felt he was worth at least another $15,000! But of course, not all functions of deviance are quite so obviously positive.

An airplane assembly plant in the US found difficulty in coordinating the fitting of prefabricated parts that needed to be bolted together but that often could not be aligned (Bensman and Gerver 1963). This problem was overcome by the most skilled workers using tools called 'taps' that cut into the bolts to make them thinner, a solution that was collusively accepted by foremen and lower managers because it permitted the achievement of output targets set by managers. Although strictly prohibited by law as likely to imperil the planes, the distance of managers kept them unaware of these practices. As a result, they were never alerted to the need to redesign the processes of manufacture.

With globalization, then, senior managements are likely to be both physically and socially at a distance from the shop floor and liable to miss the implications of local deviance and what it can teach them. Chapter 8 offers a case study that shows the extreme case of a Soviet factory controlled from afar. Its distant planners could set target levels but couldn't determine working procedures that were necessarily delegated to its local-level management. This allowed them to effectively 'capture' the undertaking and run it as a private fiefdom.

---

6   See D.T.H. Weir (2008), who discusses four different cultural approaches to management.

Globalization and Technology

Globalization and computer technology together, offer an extended arena for hawks. One of the defining features, particularly of employed hawks, is the need to insulate their activities so that parties to one set of their concerns are kept in ignorance of others. Commonly they need to insulate private and alternative activities that take place in the firm's time and often with the firm's resources. Globalization enhances a hawk's ability to insulate and fiddle time on a transnational scale. I know of one highly regarded computer specialist whose London employers believe he works exclusively for them from home, when in reality he lives in the States and works extensively for others. To maintain this deception he has, for the past several years, regularly commuted back to London every Christmas to attend the annual staff party.

An early insight into globalization and technology and their influence on workplace relations comes from a neglected case study by Quataert (1986). He alerts us to their mutual influence and, though he doesn't emphasize it, to the influence of trade cycles. In 1908 they triggered machine breaking and factory destruction at Uşak by Anatolian carpet makers. Massively increased demand in Europe for 'Turkey carpets' during an economic boom led to the introduction of new artificial dyes under the control of German merchants. They dominated the industry, rationalized production, and moved workers from domestic to factory production. Preferring domestic production, the no-longer atomized, fatalist but now collectivized (strong group) workforce, coalesced – they rioted in mobs of over 1,500 to destroy the new factories. The riots occurred during general social unrest and helped foment the successful political revolution spearheaded by the 'Young Turks'.

The events at Uşak point up the social implications not just of globalization and technology but also – a potent cause of unrest in modern society – of shifts in trade due to economic cycles as discussed in Chapter 9. Their effects are more readily transmitted when economies are globally integrated or at least interdependent. These shifts, involving sudden disruptions to social life and frequently having political implications, invariably affect industrial relations. It is the disruption to relationships – the shifts in social organization that amend grid and group ratings and cause shifts in power and control – that are destabilizing, resented, and can lead to the coalescing of previously segmented workforces.

Technology and Sabotage – Old and New

Changes in technology have an evident impact on industrial relations, so that it becomes almost platitudinous to note how computers have radically affected workplace relations and inevitably workplace deviance.

While the extension of IT has undoubtedly reduced workers' control in some jobs, it has increased it in others. Reduced control – an increase in strong grid donkey jobs, as in call centres, for example – encourages deviance, particularly resentment fiddles. However, IT may also increase control: it can reduce grid and give extra power to resentful workers. This can lead to increased opportunities for sabotage (Mars 2001a), as detailed above in the case of the alienated hotel receptionist who added fifty extra rooms to the hotel's database and generated chaos when texpectant guests arrived.

Sabotage that involves computers is not necessarily a new form of sabotage – though some, as will be discussed, undoubtedly is. Hollinger (1997, p. xx) points out that much behaviour involving computers represents merely a 're-tooling' of deviant and criminal activity for the computer age. In many jobs – as in call centres, computers, by charting and monitoring performances and comparatively rating them, increase responsibility as they simultaneously reduce control. This is a sure method, if they are sufficiently out of balance, of raising resentment. However, in essence these conditions are no different from those that existed among workers operating conveyor belts whose responses involved 'throwing a [traditional] spanner in the works', as indeed is any such response to resented Taylorian production methods.

Sabotage as a reaction to upgridding may, as described, be mounted by individuals or by collective action. The form it takes varies and a comparison of responses to coercive technology among Malays and Thai, shows very different responses to similar technical upgridding.[7]

Throughout Malaysia in the 1980s and 1990s there was a rash of collective disruptions in transnational factories assembling electronic components. Staffed mostly by rural young women selected for compliance and dexterity, they were closely monitored by computers that fully controlled their pace and mode of work. Responsibility but not control was inherent, errors were quickly identified, and penalties imposed. They did not, however, go sick, strike or sabotage their controlling computers. Such responses had no place in their 'culture of complaint' that had indigenously involved intervention in disputes by intermediaries. With no intervening trades unions that could take on this role or people so ascribed by kinship, these routes were blocked. Instead, they invoked supernatural intervention: they collectively refused to work because they found their factories to be haunted by malevolent spirits and wouldn't return until elaborate, extensive and time-consuming ceremonies by 'Bomo' (spirit mediums who were specialist shamans) had restored their factories to spiritual purity.

There is no suggestion that the Malaysian response was not one of genuine fear. It bears comparison with forms of spirit possession found among low-status peasants in a variety of cultures analyzed by Ioan Lewis (1971, p. 115) and discussed in Scott (1985, p. 289). Lewis found that among the Indian Nayar such spirits functioned as 'consciences of the rich'. The main difference between the Nayar and Malaysia cases is that the one locates its spirits in individuals, the other in the factory buildings of employers.

In Thailand similar factories to those in Malaysia have the same computerized control systems, but they employed predominantly male workers. There, however,

---

7   Some of the discussion of sabotage here is taken from the Introduction to Mars 2001a.

traditional conflict resolution was not focused through intermediaries but tended to be direct and face to face. Factory disruptions followed, involving direct action against products, machinery and premises.[8]

These cases represent 're-tooled sabotage'. 'Re-tooled sabotage' invariably reveals a unifying and collective grievance, an imbalance of formal power, and the ability and opportunity to communicate and organize. However, the IT revolution has now made possible a qualitatively different, more individualist form of sabotage. It means that a saboteur's grievance does not need to be localized. Nor does it need to be collective – those with an individual grievance can act unilaterally without the need for any support, as did the hotel receptionist who acted on his own. And saboteurs can act across divergent parts of a dispersed organization. Thanks to IT, communication can operate outside of any local milieu. These factors make it difficult to locate and control 'the new saboteurs'. And with the increasing integration of production, often across national boundaries, even a small act of sabotage can prove massively disruptive.

The second distinctive feature of 'the new sabotage', which hardly existed three decades ago, is that, instead of disrupting process and products alongside his fellows, a saboteur's primary and, in most cases, individual concern is now likely to be involved with manipulating information. The most potent and most feared forms of information manipulation derive from devices capable of sending radio signals strong enough to disrupt and permanently damage computer systems. Less dramatic is the planting of viruses that have the potential to steal, erase or modify data and that can travel to all parts of an organization or/and to its customers or suppliers.

Among the most common forms of information manipulation are:

- The deletion, addition, modification, adaptation or distortion of information (which can involve the reprogramming of procedures affecting production outputs and quality).
- The unauthorized promulgation or publication of information, as when two staff members broke into IBM's personnel system and widely disseminated confidential information on staff and managerial salaries that informed and empowered personal negotiation. This same scam recently occurred within the BBC.
- 'Denial of service', by which an 'online service' may be overwhelmed by excesses of unwanted data.
- The above types of information manipulation are most appropriate to resentful donkey job holders. A fourth form, however, appropriate to hawks, is the introduction of 'eavesdropping programmes' that allow periodic or continual access to confidential data that can then be sold on to a firm's rivals.

---

8   More comparative research is needed to examine different cultural responses to similar technologies and to test counter-assumptions of global 'convergence' and technical determinism.

The Growth in Individualism

Individualism's growth derives from increasing specialization and involves a shaking off of both constraints from and the respect previously afforded to hierarchic authorities, employers and regulatory bodies, with a concomitant reduction in group controls. In CT terms, Individualism's growth represents a societal shift diagonally downgrid so that we see increased emphasis on the entrepreneurial aspects of work roles with a tendency to rule bending, short termism, calculated risk taking, and the cultivation of ever-shifting networks favouring the individual. What is occurring is a shift from concerns with the long-term position of organizations to the short-term interests of individuals: wolves are morphing into hawks. The Enron scandal, the sub-prime mortgage debacle, the BP disaster, and others of a similar ilk reflect the increasingly individualist short-term concerns of some top managements who sacrifice long-term corporate interests to maintain short-term share prices and resultant bonuses. These are topics more fully covered in Chapter 9.

The growth of Individualism has been evident in Europe at least since the Renaissance. Hawks, the archetypal individualists, have benefited most from the exponential growth of technology and the resultant specialization involving increases in the overall division of labour. These have ensured that allocations to social positions have had to move relatively quickly from ascription to achievement to accommodate necessary merit. Individualism is most evident in that most technologically complex country, the United States. Insofar as the States exports its technology and its ideals of organization, so it exports its Individualism.

It is not only upper levels of management that are affected by the shift. There is insight to be gained from Shapiro's (1989) explanation of the rise in white-collar crime as due to overall global increases in specialization. Enhanced specialization and the 'flattening' of hierarchies have led to a necessary increase in delegation. These grant more autonomy, discretion, responsibility and control to lower levels. Such delegation involves significant shifts in power, and this entails trust – with all its concomitant opportunities for betrayal.

Increased delegation, if allied to increases in control, adds to a job's autonomy, and together with a loss of group controls, fuels the shift downgrid to increase the deviance opportunities of hawks. But increasing delegation without the trust to grant control is a sure-fire means of increasing the number of donkey jobs with all the problems these involve. Trust is, of course, two way and is consolidated in long-term relationships. However, a gradual reduction in typical lengths of service with a single employer is a further encouragement to occupational deviance.

Lack of long-term commitment to employees by increasingly individualist, hawk-like employers is manifest in reduced pension arrangements for them (but not for senior managements). These, unsurprisingly, generate resentment and lack of loyalty from workers. But there is also a growing disparity between 'shop-floor' pay and the pay of senior managements – particularly since their 'distance' increases with globalization. This is a feature of most Western economies, where pay has been diverging over the past three decades. 'Iniquity theorists' such as Tucker (1989),and Sieh (1993) following Adams (1965), demonstrate that perceived iniquity invariably increases occupational deviance, though Sieh (1987) found this likelihood was minimized where strong unions and workgroups exist. The one institutionalizes the processing of grievances; the other exerts group controls. There has been a noted weakening of both during the last thirty years. Inequality has been shown to have iniquitous social effects extending far wider than industrial relations (Wilkinson and Pickett 2010).

Conclusions: Then and Now

The initial classification of occupations according to grid/group ratings appears to have been sustained, together with its linked clusters of values, attitudes and behaviours, while no alternative classification of occupational deviance has emerged. But since then, further considerations have shown that macro factors now increasingly impinge upon work relationships: the interacting influences of globalization and technology have to be taken into account. Have their growing influences affected levels of occupational deviance?

There are no clear answers to this question. For a start, figures and comparisons in this field are notoriously suspect and often absent – especially so for sabotage. The influence of globalization and technology, when projected onto the 1982 analysis, suggests that developments since then offer a mixed picture. Changes in technology have both created and reduced deviance. More effective technology now records stockholdings, for example, and has made many conveyor belts obsolete, thus obviating the proverbial 'spanner in the works'. But it has created new strongly constrained donkey jobs in industries such as call centres and computer-monitored assembling that are thus liable to sabotage. Computer-derived constraints also appear to be moving up the status hierarchy, thus creating more donkey jobs with their liabilities to sabotage. However, many increases in technical complexity also offer opportunities for its exploitation by hawks against the lesser technologically aware – as in automobile servicing. On the other hand, dock theft has been massively reduced through the use of containers.

Globalization and technology both create conditions that favour hawks and thus facilitate Individualism. They have increased the autonomous elements of many jobs and offer facilities that allow hawks to insulate their different activities within ever-widening arenas. Globalization also facilitates the increasing integration of production and its extension to different geographical locations. The more integrated is production, the more opportunities there are for disruption, which again facilitates sabotage. Deviance can be expected to increase further with the growing expansion of services – and especially of personal services. This is because globalization facilitates the exploitation of passing trade with its ready propensity to utilize triadic relationships.

While two of the four solidarities, therefore – wolf packs and vultures – appear not to have been overly affected by the two macro influences, both hawks and donkeys emerge as having been strongly influenced. The opportunities for hawks have widened through both technology and globalization, while technology alone has tightened constraints on those in donkey jobs, the former restlessly benefiting from increased opportunities for personal gain, the latter succumbing to the constraints of computer-based monitoring with its liability to sabotage.

When we look at the effects of globalization and technology on the five fiddle-prone areas – passing trade, exploiting expertise, triadic occupations, gatekeepers and claims for special efforts and special skills – we see an increased propensity for deviance in all of them except possibly for the role of gatekeeper.

We can say that overall, despite the absence of figures, it appears there will have been an increase in occupational deviance emanating from both globalization and technology. But the all-embracing 'width' and 'depth' of these concepts means that each context will need specific analysis.

Notes on Model of Workplace Crime

Occupational Features	Donkeys	Wolves
Grid - Organizational Controls	Strong - Subordination	Strong
Group - Interpersonal Controls	Weak - Isolated	Strong - tight work groups
Time/Space Controls (Surveillance)	High - "Fenced In", No Discretion	Moderate - Room for Group Maneuver
Co-worker/Colleague Relations	Insulated from Others	Organized, Entry Controls, Status Ranking
Work/Non-work Boundaries	Discrete Division	Social Reinforces Work - Collective Celebration
Socialization	Low - Learn and Fiddle in Isolation	Strong - Moral Career with Rites of Passage
Fiddle Features & Reactions		
Defining Character	Reactive - to Drudgery	Ritualized - Stable and Organized Over Time
Quantity/Quality	Low Stakes - Repetition to Excess	Consistency over Excess, Access Flows From Group Status
Level of Risk	High Given Surveillance	Low Given Group Solidarity
Role Creativity	None in Job - Must Fiddle For It	Low - Stability and Continuity Counts
Organizational Responses	"Crackdowns-Resentment-More Fiddling" Cycle	Implicit Collusion - Look Other Way, Fear Slowdown or Strike
Societal Reactions	Fiddlers are Stupid not Clever	Good Teams Deserve Good Fiddles

Occupational Features	Hawks	Vultures
Grid - Organizational Controls	Weak - Individual Entrepreneuriality	Weak
Group - Interpersonal Controls	Weak - "Statelessness"	Strong - loose work groups
Time/Space Controls (Surveillance)	Low - "Free to Fly", Wide Discretion	Moderate - Room for Low Level Flying
Co-worker/Colleague Relations	Control Subordinates/Competitive Colleagues	Insecure - Competitive/Cooperative Dynamic
Work/Non-work Boundaries	Lines Blurred	Negotiable/Variable
Socialization	Precedent - Professional Credentials	Moderate Moral Acclimization - Share Tricks of Trade
Fiddle Features & Reactions		
Defining Character	Expansive - Create Opportunity	Responsive - to Changing Dynamics
Quantity/Quality	High Stakes - Diversified	Limited & Highly Variable, Flexibility Necessary
Level of Risk	High Given Scope of Stakes	Uncertain, Scapegoating Can Occur
Role Creativity	Central to Job - Essential Element	High - Seize the Moment
Organizational Responses	Hands Off For Fear of Losing, Moonlighting	"Fire Fighting" -- Own = Organization Gain
Societal Reactions	Moral Ambiguity - Fine Line Between Flair and Fraud	Hawk Aspirants - Moderate Creativity But Don't Get Caught

Common Elements	Fiddle Factors	Fiddle Facilitators
Largely Unmeasured	Passing Trade	Control Systems
Pervasive, Endemic	A) Transitory Transactions	Ambiguity
Normative, Not Deviant	B) Multi-Stranding	Converting and Smuggling Goods
Systematic - Follows Rules	C) Social Distance	Anonymity and Scale
Organized - Collusion Occurs	Exploiting Expertise	
Moral/Political Economy Tension	Gatekeepers	
	Triadic Relationships	
	Special Effort & Skills	

Figure 3.1   Notes on a model of workplace crime (derived from Cheats at Work (Mars 1982) as a teaching device by Stuart Henry)

References

Adams, J. (2000), 'The Hypermobility of Western Society', *Prospect Magazine*, 20 March.

Adams, J.S. (1965), 'Iniquity in Social Exchange', in L Berkowitz (ed.), *Advances in Experimental Social Psychology*, New York: Academic Press.

Bensman, J. and Gerver, I. (1963), 'Crime and Punishment in the Factory: The Function of Deviancy in Maintaining the Social System', *American Sociological Review*, 28(4), 588–98.

Cahn, E. (1955), 'Cheating and Taxes', *The Moral Decision*, Bloomington, IN: Indiana University Press.

Dalton, M. (1959), *Men Who Manage*, New York: John Wiley and Sons, Inc.

Ditton, J. (1976), *The Dual Morality in the Control of Fiddles*, mimeo. Outer Circle Policy Unit, London.

Douglas, M. (1970), *Natural Symbols: Explanations in Cosmology*, Harmondsworth: Penguin.

Douglas, M. (1978), *Cultural Bias*, London: Royal Anthropological Institute.

Henry, S. (1987), 'The Political Economy of Informal Economies', *The Annals of the American Academy of Political and Social Science*, 493 (Special Issue: *The Informal Economy*), 137–53.

Henry, S. and Mars, G. (1978), 'Crime at Work: The Social Construction of Amateur Property Theft', *Sociology*, 12, 245–63.

Hollinger, R.D. (1997), *Crime, Deviance and the Computer*, Aldershot: Dartmouth Publishing.

Hollinger, R.D. and Clark, J.P. (1983), *Theft by Employees*, Lexington, MA: Lexington Books.

Lewis, I.M. (1971), *Ecstatic Religions: An Anthropological Study of Spirit Possession and Shamanism*, Harmondsworth: Penguin.

Mars, G. (1973), 'Chance, Punters and the Fiddle: Institutionalized Pilferage in a Hotel Dining Room', in M. Warner (ed.), *The Sociology of the Workplace*, London: Allen and Unwin, 200–210.

Mars, G. (1982, 1994), *Cheats At Work: An Anthropology of Workplace Crime*, London: Allen and Unwin; Aldershot: Dartmouth Publishing.

Mars, G. (ed.) (2001a), *Sabotage*, Aldershot: Ashgate.

Mars, G. (ed.) (2001b), *Occupational Crime*, Aldershot: Ashgate.

Mars, G. and Nicod, M. (1984), The *World of Waiters*, London: Allen and Unwin.

Mills, C. Wright (undated, *c.* 1963), *Power Politics and People: The collected essays of C. Wright Mills*, New York: Ballantine Books.

Perri 6 and Mars, G. (eds) (2008), *The Institutional Dynamics of Culture*, International Library of Anthropology, Farnham: Ashgate Publishing.

Quataert, D. (1986), 'Machine Breaking and the Changing Carpet Industry of Western Anatolia, 1860–1908', *Journal of Social History*, 19, 473–89.

Scott, J.C. (1985), *Weapons of the Weak: Everyday Forms of Peasant Resistance*, New Haven, CT: Yale University Press.

Shapiro, S. (1989), 'Collaring the Crime, not the Criminal: Reconsidering White Collar Crime', *American Sociological Review*, 55, 346–65.

Sieh, E.W. (1987), 'Garment Workers: Perceptions of Inequity and Employee Theft', *British Journal of Criminology*, 27, 174–90.

Sieh, E.W. (1993) , Employee Theft: An Examination of Gerald Mars and an Explanation Based on Equity Theory, in New Directions in Criminological Theory, Vol. 4, eds F. Adler and Laufer W.S., Transaction Publishers, New Brunswick (USA) and London (UK) pp. 95–112.

Smigel, E.O. (1956), 'Public Attitudes toward Stealing as related to the Size of the Victim Organization', *American Sociological Review*, 21(3).

Taylor, L. and Walton, P. (1971), 'Industrial Sabotage, Motives and Meanings', in S. Cohen (ed.), *Images of Deviance*, Harmondsworth: Penguin, 219–45.

Thornthwaite, L and McGraw, P. ,"Still Staying Loose in a Tightening World ?" Revisiting Gerald Mars' Cheats at Work, in: *Rethinking Misbehavior and Resistance in Organizations*, ed by Alison Barnes and Lucy Taksa, Emerald Group Publishing Ltd., Bingley, UK pp. 29–566

Tucker, J. (1989), 'Employee Theft as Social Control', *Deviant Behaviour*, 10, 319–34.

Weir, D.T.H. (2008), 'Management in the Arab World: A Fourth Paradigm', *Transformation/Transformacje*, 39–40, 379–94.

Wilkinson, R. and Pickett, K. (2010), *The Spirit Level*, Harmondsworth: Penguin.

Zeitlin, L.R. (1971), 'A Little Larceny can do a Lot for Employee Morale', *Psychology Today*, 5, 22, 24, 26, 64.

Chapter 4

The Egalitarian Enclave: Terrorism – A Positive Feedback Game[1],[2]

Co-authored with Mary Douglas

Introduction

This chapter, in concentrating on just one Cultural Theory (CT) solidarity, the egalitarian enclave, offers an approach to political systems in closed, dissident minorities.

The chapter seeks to identify different kinds of organized dissent, as well as the constraints they face, most especially those deriving from the manipulation and control of information. The resulting choices have implications both for structure and behaviour, which defy all explanations based exclusively on the personalities of members or leaders.

This approach provides a means of classifying and subdividing enclaves, and proposes, in so doing, a bimodal developmental schema with four forks. The first fork examines demographic security: it focuses on concerns regarding defection and other means of controlling information. The second considers internal organization as well as alternatives to defection. The third fork, on external relations, looks into alternative steps that are available to control factionalism and negotiations with the outside. Finally, the fourth fork explores the availability and control of resources (funds as well as military equipment), and the different effects these have on central versus peripheral autonomy, as well as on the nature of reconciliation. A close examination of how information is shaped by institutions shows that the behaviour and personal attitudes of enclavists are largely defined by the constraints imposed on the options available to them. It is these constraints that ultimately channel their understanding – not their personalities.

---

1 This chapter with some minor variations first appeared in *Human Relations*, 56/7 (2003), pp. 763–86.

2 The argument is primarily a development of the position in M. Douglas, *How Institutions Think* (1987) regarding institutions as systems of information. This chapter benefits from a position paper for an Anthropology Workshop on Enclave Politics, incorporating suggestions by Al Baumgarten, Sean Kingston, Perri 6, Paul Richards, Steve Rayner, Emmanuel Sivan and Michael Thompson. Its development and form here is the responsibility of Mary Douglas and Gerald Mars.

The Cultural Theory of Enclaves as an Alternative Approach

Politics is inherently concerned with hope and trust, and also with belief, ranging from the most tentative to the blindest faith. A political system is founded on cultural values, and an approach from the standpoint of CT is therefore appropriate. Most approaches on the subject tend to be moralistic, philosophical, psychological, politically biased, or all of these and, especially, they tend to focus on the individual political person. By concentrating on other persons around the believer, rather than the single person upholding these assorted beliefs, values, and so on, CT offers a different angle: its own focus is on the different constraints acting on the believer, constraints made, laid and held firm within the framework of interactions with others. These latter who make up the social environment, indicate what is credible, trustworthy, rational and righteous; in other words, individuals have to try to survive in an institutional environment in which they are receiving, and partly controlling, the information on which their own beliefs are grounded.

This chapter therefore demonstrates the use of CT by applying it to a problem of belief within the realm of political theory. This, the problem of the enclave, is the problem posed by the dissident minority that is closed against the outside and whose beliefs are opposed to those of the majority.

In the Western theory of democracy, dissenting minorities are given a crucial role: without their voices of protest and disagreement, there would be no political dialogue. This being so, it is strange that the dissenting group comes under no general theory: when it is studied, the vantage point lies either on the outside or within, yet is never focused on the group's intrinsic and defining relation to its own centre, still less on its relations with other dissenting groups. There is no structured explanation of the ways closed minority groups behave; there exists no unified body of thought or theory for understanding them that would be advanced enough to compare with the theories, for example, of bureaucracy or of markets.

At its most extreme, this means that political science has no systematic way of talking about organized terrorism and, hence, no systematic theory of how to deal with it. A long tradition in social thought has relegated questions of religion to a separate area of expertise – namely, and largely, to that of the religious psychology of individuals. Organized terrorism, however, is a form of group behaviour, and cannot therefore be analyzed in terms of individual psychology alone. As a consequence, and for all the study that has been carried out so far, there is still no way of understanding why some political activists carry out their programmes peacefully, while others, dedicated terrorist organizations, polarize whole communities.

There is a widespread perception that 'fundamentalists' or 'sectarians' are the cause of the world's troubles; a quick look, however, shows that the closed minority groups that might correspond to this description have little in common. Some enclaves have voluntarily withdrawn from a world of which they disapprove, others have been pushed out because they do not conform; some are peaceful and politically inert, others are violently aggressive. Lumping them together can only distort the issue. One of the objectives of this chapter is therefore to suggest how enclaves may be subdivided and classified for further research.

Let us begin with an extreme case – that of a government facing difficulties because it is confronted by a dissident group, which implacably rejects its claims to legitimacy and refuses to negotiate until its demands have been met fully and in advance. The demands are deemed impossible, the situation is inflammable, and the threat of violence arises on either side. Each is convinced of the righteousness of its case, both are certain of their position, and their respective certainties are perforce mutually contradictory. What is the real source of such 'contradictory certainties' (Schwarz and Thompson 1990)? CT seeks to explain how these beliefs have come to be grounded on such conflicting assumptions by examining closely the way information is controlled. In what follows, therefore, the focus is on institutions as information control systems.

Institutions Shape Information

It is well established that institutions hold and convey information. A process of selection precedes all transmissions: an efficient carrier must first choose from the ambient noise what is to be regarded as information; then new, approved information must be graded according to its reliability. What has been recently acquired must be integrated into what has been already defined as knowledge. New knowledge has to be incorporated more or less smoothly into old. To communicate something positive, potential information that has been rejected must be marked as 'trash', so as not to confuse and clutter the channels. All this is not carried out automatically by mysterious robots: it is people who are engaged in sorting out information, channelling it to each other in patterns that best seem to serve their purposes. This is how people create the institutions they live in.

In fact, the metaphor of institution building is not quite right: it is less a question of building, as with bricks and mortar, than of burrowing into a mountain of noise. Living in the mountain requires the making of passages: one must block here and unblock there, create waste dumps, as well as meeting space, and areas for living and storage; systems for retrieval have to be invented and put in place. If successful, the end result will resemble a rabbit warren, whose inmates can comfortably find their way around and anticipate the behaviour of others. They have shaped its passages to suit their collective purposes, but since these are very diverse, there can be many kinds of warren. The representation of society as an information system, which was very fashionable in the 1970s, has run into the ground for lack of a method that would take into account the diversity of human society itself; we shall try to remedy this by considering a number of extreme cases.

The Fatalist Isolate

Let us imagine a society with the minimum level of shared information: it would be a society in which the members hardly relate to each other at all. Either they are so weak in numbers, or else their encounters are so sporadic and unanticipated, that no social conventions develop: to all intents and purposes they are isolates. Another way of putting it would be to say that these people have either no occasion, or no opportunity, to form institutions: they have formulated little or no shared knowledge because they do not have the means to test and control information. Whatever the case may be, they are not trying to persuade or to coerce each other to adhere to permanent arrangements. What each person knows is neither checked nor coordinated with what the others know: social units are small, their communications direct, and their links with each other fragile and haphazard. Correspondingly, their information is less complex, more weakly established and more capricious. They are as different as rabbits and hares: whereas rabbits have a collective life with underground building projects for complex communications, hares are isolates – they shape space by just lying in the heather; they sleep and rear their young on the open ground. It is a different kind of life.

The Opportunist

Let us move on from this, and consider certain other, very different societies, starting with one in which individuals relate to each other freely, unrestricted by historical commitments. Here, its members' choice of action is only limited by the kinds of contractual deals they are able to strike with each other, and by how much flak they will receive if they try to renege on a promise. Information is free, in the sense that anyone has the right to try to generate it, but it only counts as collective information if others accept it.

The structuring process in this individualistic opportunist society depends on hierarchical benefits for individuals, on what Mayer (1960), Mincer (1958) and Rosen (1981) have called 'superstar economics': competition is extensive, anyone can compete to grab the megaphone, no holds are barred. The one who gets it also benefits from a cumulative advantage, namely that what the 'superstar' says, goes. At the same time, what the others are saying gets drowned out. There is no collective censorship here, unless we count as censorship the spontaneous rubbishing of failed attempts to surmount the noise. In this society, authority lies exclusively with the voice of the superstar, yet it is very precarious. Alternative opinions may be expressed, and a few may even listen, in the hope of launching a new fashion and of setting up a new superstar, since time is on their side: in this society, it is hard to hold on to the megaphone for ever, and the currents of fashion move fast.

If this is like a rabbit warren, it is one continually being re-dug and radically redesigned: the shape of the resulting information system will have paths radiating out from a centre, yet at the same time new centres constantly emerge, and old ones decay. It tends to look complex because of its chaotically accelerated processes of change, yet essentially it is only a very simple system, repeated many times over. If it possesses the technology and material means to concentrate coercive power in the hands of a leader, it can be very powerful. In such a case, the leader may reasonably try to turn his or her hegemony over the other voices into something permanent. One way of reconciling incipient opposition would be through a programme of continuous expansion, of continuous recruitment of new followers, as in the empires of antiquity, and likewise of continuous amassing of wealth to attract and reward followers. An alternative might create some sort of hierarchy, which would involve digging out a completely different type of warren. The two can even be combined, with the pattern of information differing at each level.

Information Shaped like an Ant's Nest

A hierarchy rests on a truly complex system of storing and retrieving information, its members observing the habit of using the past as a basis for claims: they like to recognize the validity of past claims that go back over many more generations than would be accepted in the megaphone system. Honouring the past puts strong limits on the competition for the loudest voice. New voices may emerge, although with difficulty. Inevitably, and by the same token, such a practice also projects the past on the future: time, as a result, is structured. At the extreme level, it is like putting the megaphone to the mouth of the oldest person, or that of the senior person of the most senior lineage. This is not so much a warren as an ant's nest, with many finely marked passages leading to chambers at different levels, each serving distinct functions: there are storage chambers, the queen's residence, soldiers' quarters, workers' quarters, nurseries, as well as other passages leading to refuse dumps that are regularly emptied. This particular structure achieves a high level of coordination.

In the ant's-nest type of institution, ambiguity is at a minimum because censorship is strong: exits and entrances are ranked, some allowing for egress from the front, others only through the back, doors are guarded, and passwords required. Alternative information is recognized and blocked, so that it does not flow down the passages. Individuals living within the hierarchy may have it in their hearts to refuse to conform, yet the penalty of nonconformity is to be excluded from information they would surely need, as well as exclusion from the generating processes, and so from influence. The system is organized so as to filter information coming in from the outside, and is further regulated by secrecy rules that stop the free flow of information once it has entered its structure. Members, therefore, only receive such information as 'they need to know' to fulfil the positions allotted to them. Information going out of the hierarchy is also subject to vetting. Hierarchy is the result of a determination to coordinate activities, and hence it makes the shape of information correspond to this very purpose. The interaction is self-sustaining: activities shape information and the shape itself retains the memory. It constitutes its own retrieval system, efficient. Yet hierarchy is also endowed with its well-known downside.

Enclave

This leads us to the enclave, the group that defines itself by its alternative vision of life. It is, by its very nature, a group, and so has an internal and an external aspect. It may opt to organize itself as a small hierarchy, as the Mormons did, for instance, in which case it is ant's nest shaped, and the previous paragraphs apply. However, there are strong pressures on an enclave to avoid all ranking; when these anti-hierarchical pressures have been institutionalized, the enclave's pattern of information is characterized by strong control against outside sources, amounting even to strict censorship. On the other hand, once any information has been accepted, there is competition over its control, as well as over the proclamation of a preferred interpretation, very much as we saw also in the opportunist or megaphone system.

The grid/group 2×2 matrix diagram used as an organizer to produce four archetypal cultural categories can be applied to these four types of information systems, as shown in Figure 4.1.

At the top is the range of enforced rules and derived classifications that are imposed by the social context. The column on the right contains the communitarian systems, the one on the left the individualists – that is to say, individuals whose identity cannot be absorbed by any one group, consisting of the opportunists and the isolates. It is one of the axioms of CT that these four cultural positions are potentially present in any community: they are all there – the fatalists who want no part in the competition for control, the competitive opportunists, the secretive hierarchists, and the dissident enclavists.

It ought to be clear from the foregoing that the enclavists and the fatalists are usually withdrawn from the central struggles for power. Hierarchy and competitive Individualism, on the other hand, are engaged together in organizing and deciding on behalf of their followers and of others. Setting aside the fatalists, who contribute little, the remaining three cultural types together produce a rich political dialogue: the hierarchists, concerned with consistency and continuity, provide the framework and a degree of stability; the opportunists, getting and doing, provide the action; the enclavists, as the conscience of the community, generate interest in moral issues and take it on themselves to speak for the poor, the outcast and downtrodden. As we have seen, information is channelled in each by their distinctive institutions. When the excitement of the dialogue grows heated, each side tries to capture the moral high ground and steal the rhetoric of the others. The interaction of their different voices indicates a thriving community life.

strong grid weak group	strong group strong grid
ISOLATES Individuals insulated Information capricious, not graded or classified	HIERARCHIES Roles prescribed Information censored, partitioned and stabilized Secrecy used for control
weak grid weak group	strong group weak grid
OPPORTUNISTS No censorship Superstar generates information Information subject to fashions Secrecy disapproved Information hoarded to be allocated strategically	ENCLAVES Outside sources censored Information partitioned by factions Maximum ambiguity Secrecy used for control

Figure 4.1   The Cultural Theory organizing chart applied to information systems

Narrowing the Enquiry

Here we must pause, and explain the virtues of this new approach to Enclavism. In one sense, the field has been much researched already: ethnographic and historical case studies of religious sects and of secular communes are numerous. Reports, however, are episodic, and comparative frameworks rare, whereas the researchers themselves have different interests and tend to look at haphazardly selected aspects. There are many gaps and, at the same time, some significant writings (e.g. Coser 1974; Hobsbawm 1959), which have gone beyond this level of enquiry, have not received sustained discussion. Furthermore, research into 'movements', though voluminous, is also not systematic. Usually the interpretation of violent behaviour in movements or enclaves draws heavily on individual psychology ('These people are sick in the head'), or on so-called deprivation theory ('After all those hard times the under-classes can stand it no more'), or on crisis theory ('Political uncertainty increases the perception of injustice') – or simply on feelings of distress, misery or insecurity.

Political scientists themselves pay little attention to dissenting groups that have withdrawn into a secure niche where they can put their principles into practice without interfering with others. Such groups tend to make the cosmic claim that their demands are directly ratified by nature, or by the universe. They do this when they start actively to resist oppression, or for other reasons become confrontational and violent. Peasants' wars turn easily into religious uprisings: God will eventually be brought into the argument, even if the dissent was based originally on a secular demand for constitutional change, as, for example, was the demand of the Irish for Home Rule. The end result is that, as soon as they become important for political studies, dissenting minorities are assigned away to religious studies. This is an impoverishment for political science, not least because one of the biggest contemporary threats to world peace is thought to be posed by so-called fundamentalist movements.

It is a pity that the language of the social sciences tends to be pejorative on this subject: the adjective 'sectarian' implies negative personal characteristics such as narrow-mindedness, anger, fanaticism, bigotry and intransigence. In order to remain open, we are only going to talk about enclaves – that is, groups that have withdrawn from the rest of society and hold themselves apart. This allows both for the existence of non-sectarian enclaves, as well as for the possibility of the outside society adopting sectarian values and employing sectarian rhetoric. It also allows for a hierarchist organization to adopt sectarian attitudes without altogether giving up its hierarchy. Richard Griffiths in *The Reactionary Revolution* (1966) presents the French Catholic church in the interwar years as a beleaguered minority group surrounded by an anti-clerical, rationalist culture. The strongly sectarian attitude he reveals in formal church pronouncements, and even more in Catholic literature and the novels and essays of the time, exemplifies E. Sivan's insight that world religions, even those reputed to be very hierarchical, tend to adopt sectarian attitudes. As the scientific secularism of the West becomes entrenched and they find themselves marginalized, they erect a stronger wall of control against information from the outside (Sivan 1995).

By narrowing the enquiry as to how institutions frame and direct information, we can challenge some common assumptions and convert them into questions. Do sectarian, terrorist organizations spring fully grown out of nowhere? Surely that is not a reasonable supposition. Do their origins (religious or secular) determine something about their future development? Probably not, since we are arguing that there is another, crucially formative experience, namely the threat of mass defection. Does being marginalized account for their behaviour? Hardly: most people are marginalized at some point in their lives. Does the origin of the enclave make a difference as to how it develops once it has joined the margins? Not very likely, following the account we are giving here. Are religious enclaves different from nonreligious ones? Probably not. What should the target of their attack (the outside community or communities) do in order to maintain peace? Why is negotiation difficult? If negotiation is impossible, should the larger community seek to mollify the law breakers, or should it use armed force and apply exemplary punishment?

Enclave Insecurity

First it is necessary to identify the different kinds of organized dissent. We are looking for an organizational basis for comparison that is founded on a theory of information. It will be to our advantage here to set aside religious factors for the time being, and concentrate instead on the problems that all enclaved organizations have to solve. Unless we know how an enclave originates, recruits or casts off members, splits and disperses, we might seem to be talking about different types of organization when we are actually dealing with one single kind at different stages over time.

As long as its boundaries remain fluid or open, a 'movement' may not be counted as a dissenting group: the concern to maintain a boundary between the inside and the outside is definitional for an enclave. An enclave is a community forced out, or voluntarily withdrawn on grounds of principle from the mainstream society, so its first preoccupation must be to hold members to their commitment. To be effective, it must somehow prevent defection. But in the early stages it cannot use force or physical constraints or it will find itself in trouble. Upholding principles with which the rest of society disagrees, the newly founded enclave cannot call on organs of public control to protect its interests: for example, trying to escape from a closed community is not seen as a crime in the wider society, and therefore the runaway cannot be beaten up or imprisoned without the enclave risking public sanctions. Whether it is safe to defect, or whether defectors need to be afraid of being kneecapped or shot, depends on the outside world and its attitudes.

If, however, the concern to prevent defection is a characteristic of one type of enclave, we can also list other types to which this will not apply. For example, the enclave whose founder is still alive and at the full height of his or her leadership, may not have time to develop a concern over possible defection. Also, if recruitment is lively and numbers are up, no one will worry about a few defectors. The intractable problems of organization tend to set in most acutely only after the death of the founder. The Jim Jones church, therefore, and other such sectarian societies that have ended in mass suicide, or other dissenting groups that are only just beginning to form, are not necessarily covered by what will be said here. The typical organizational problems usually become acute only at later stages; yet they might have been anticipated and prevented by the foresight of the founding fathers.

There need not be a succession crisis if institutionalized procedures for installing a successor have already been set up. Of course, the case may still exist where criteria for choosing a replacement after the founder's death are unambiguous (a child, for example, or a best friend may be nominated) or where the outcome again partly depends on the reaction of outsiders.

Some enclaves nonetheless manage to bind their members to them without letting the dread of defection become a dominant preoccupation. This is the first crucial fork along the road. It may be they do not need to worry about keeping their members because of heavy exit costs confronting anyone attempting to defect. For example, the membership of German Pietist groups in nineteenth-century America was stabilized by the fact that the immigrant peasants did not speak English, to say nothing of reading and writing it. Some enclaves are only moderately withdrawn, and not strictly dissident: for example, the Salvation Army might be called a dissenting group in modern industrial society, but they can presumably avoid focusing on the risks of defection because they are carrying out strongly approved philanthropic work. Similarly, it might not have been necessary for the land-rich monasteries in Christian Europe to worry too much about recruitment or defection if the law was on their side. Some enclaves can further secure their membership by legal means: for example, if the would-be entrants must make a legally valid deed assigning all their property to the community and formally accepting to receive no individual pay for their work, they cannot easily escape, since they lack what would be required for a new start. We shall bracket aside all of these as being 'demographically secure' enclaves, with good reason not to worry about defection; they are better equipped to resist the choices that drive some other enclaves to adopt perverse solutions. At this first fork in the road, a bimodal development pattern begins to emerge.

First Fork

Figure 4.2 shows possible development patterns.

The dissident enclave generally tends to lack both the resources to reward followers and the sanctions to punish defaulters, for the simple reason that it cannot call on established authority. Where leadership is weak, there is scope for internal competition; as a result, loyalties become divided between rival contestants. When there are no other available means for strengthening leadership, life in the enclave must be made attractive to its members, the appropriate virtues need to be fostered, and members themselves try to further justify the way they live by comparing it with the evils of life outside.

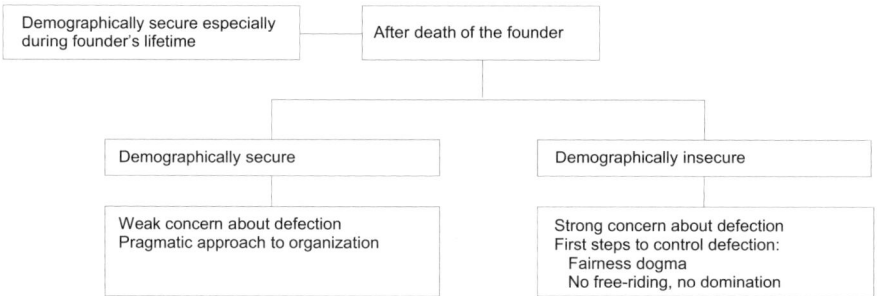

Figure 4.2   Attitude to defection and demographic security post death of founder

One device adopted almost uniformly is to establish fairness principles for all internal dealings: any show of power or attempt to impose control is denounced; attempts to give oneself a 'free ride' by taking advantage of the work of others are checked by the principle of equality. Equality implies no domination, hence attempts to dominate are checked in advance by making unanimity a prerequisite. When adopted as an alternative solution to the problem of defection, perfect fairness can be disastrous if pushed to dogmatic proportions; it is adopted because of weak leadership, and it quickly stultifies any emergent leadership with a veto on decision making.

Among several untoward effects of taking this path is the encouragement to covert factionalism; another is a tendency for ambiguity in internal public discourses. Ambiguity, used initially by the covert leadership to attract consensus, backfires as members learn to exploit it for factional purposes. The longer the enclave has been in existence, the more wholly intertwined will its members be: they will have ingeniously devised institutions intended to entrap each member definitively in the enclave. Yet the weakness of coordination, the price they pay for the fairness dogma, ensures they can never cease to be concerned about possible defection. And the more successful they are in achieving an egalitarian enclave structure, the more prone they become to selecting other solutions that dig them deeper still into sectarianism. Covert factions play out their rivalry by monitoring behaviour closely, especially deviations from the principles of fairness and equality, and suspected attempts to seek power. Close mutual surveillance is exercised for signs of subversion or plans for defection; precise rules, even if unformulated, come to govern apparent behaviour, such as posture, gesture, and use of space; confessions and mini-trials harness factional opposition to central concerns; finally, internal discourse becomes highly structured in the hope of restraining jealousies and resentments. However, there are equally recognized routes by which future leaders aim to attract favourable attention: for instance, by means of conspicuous generosity, exemplary piety, trance, prophecy, or speaking in tongues (Calley 1965).

An enclave that has adjusted to weak leadership by installing rigorous rules of equality must keep its internal structure to a minimum; this means that, in the case of disputes, arbitration has no institutional authority behind it. It follows that disputes remain unsettled and friction, though covert, is rife. Furthermore, objectivity is equivocal and agreement difficult to attain, hence the appeal to oracles, lots, or a holy book; as a result, a random, aleatory element is introduced to all decisions. These organizational problems, which follow from the initial concern about defection, affect the information system.

Information control   To foster commitment to its founding principles, the outside world is denigrated: the fairness principle in itself justifies favourable moral comparison; enclave members are thus given reasons to be proud of the egalitarian way of life they have established (Richards 1996). Black and white dichotomized values, which allow no credit to outsiders, are strategies for exercising a hold on members: they build a wall of virtue between saints and sinners. In this way, relations with outsiders are governed by the concept of an untraversable moral boundary.

However, the enclave's inherent weakness of organization and its factionalism combine to lay the enclave continually open to subversion from within. In these conditions, free-flowing information is a very dangerous commodity, yet there is no founding mandate to check its movement: on the contrary, to be seen trying to control gossip and rumour might be taken as anti-egalitarian pretension. This weakness further increases the difficulty of reaching decisions, since the common basis for interpretation is insecure. The only acceptable control on behaviour becomes the one that can be justified by accusations of disloyalty, disaffection or subversion: the most disparaging attack is to accuse someone of planning to defect.

The following list gives examples of some of the techniques used for controlling information:

- *Graded sources*: Sources are rated according to loyalty. The same piece of information is refracted differentially to the various internal factions. 'No go' areas are created, from which no information can be trusted. Information from the wrong sources is rubbished (Caplow 1947).
- *Accredited sources*: Acceptable sources of information are clearly indicated, and by means of electronic communication, the use of record players and Walkman tapes, accredited information can flood out less trusted sources.
- *Evasion*: When action is agreed, it has to be stated without too much precision, so that public commitments can subsequently be evaded, if necessary.
- *Secret knowledge*: A store of secrets is successively unveiled to adepts who have proved their worth; the special knowledge of the inner initiates is regarded as sacred; possession of the sacred secrets also gives an aura of power to those in command, thus stabilizing the fragile community (Urban 1998). Initiates must never seem discontented or, if they do, they come under heavy suspicion: if they defect they cannot be trusted not to reveal the secrets they know; in some cases, this, the ultimate betrayal, may be rated a capital offence.
- *Distorted time dimension*: Members of an enclave may affect to ignore differences of age for the sake of equality; they also tend to distort the time depth of selected historical events to fit the worldview they are jointly constructing (Rayner 1982).
- *Defective risk perception*: The calculation of probabilities in enclaves is severely biased, partly because of what has already been done to manipulate incoming information. They are thus likely to make little of what would seem to outsiders as high-risk operations.

We are now beginning to reach the heart of the problem of enclaves: that the basis of their contradictory certainties lies not in the personality of their members but in the way their institutions channel knowledge and understanding. At this stage, relations between the enclave and the outside world become too fraught for negotiations to be easy; what we have argued so far suggests how the second forking option might be drawn.

Second Fork

Figure 4.3 shows the patterns that might follow at the second fork.

External relations   One of the dangers for factions arises from weak leadership, which derives in part from the refusal to validate authority positions but also – as this analysis has shown – from the concern to prevent defection. One way of healing

Justice as equality
Internal organization
Steps to control defection

Organization pragmatic Leadership feasible Rational decision capability Majority principle Information partitioned Clarity Negotiation possible Hierarchy possible	Fairness dogmatic Leadership weak Appeal to sacred authority Unanimity principle Information distorted Ambiguity Negotiation impossible Factional strife

Figure 4.3   Organizational steps to control defection

the rupture caused by divisive factionalism is to confront the outside: whether its members engage in controversy, heckle public speakers, hold demonstrations in defence of fair principles, or sally forth to rescue victims of injustice, a warm glow of comradeship and righteousness transcends all incipient rifts. The confrontation can be entirely peaceful and nonviolent yet is very likely to be contested by the guardians of the peace. Here, then, comes a third forking point in the development cycle of enclaves.

At this stage, when new choices present themselves, concern about defection may take a more radical form: the demonstrators could accept the police warnings and go home, or they could provoke more conflict. The choice is between tightening the circle round the group or keeping some gates open: which path is chosen depends on how important it is to prevent splitting the enclave, or on how near its culture is to cracking point. The problems of internal organization lead members to behave uncompromisingly in external relations; their public behaviour has little to do with personal psychology, deprivation or misery, and much to do with adjustment to the institutional constraints described.

Real choices can exist, yet the enclaved leaders may be blind to them. They may well be up against a wall in more ways than can be imagined by outsiders: they cannot get reliable information; they know their colleagues are their rivals; they cannot trust their envoys; and they cannot trust their followers to accept their guidance. Their followers, in turn, do not trust the leader. The weakness in the organization has become acute and exacerbated. If religion were not the original principle of dissent, it is now likely to become the prominent justification of the enclave. This may lead to another forking point: the religious protest enhances the existing sense of separateness, and further justifies intransigence.

Furthermore, the ambiguity that was so carefully nurtured to avoid internal conflict makes representation not merely impossible – it renders it irrelevant. Apart from the moral boundary, there is no common or shared opinion to represent. The envoy who is sent forth to parley cannot yield any point to the enemy; apart from the temporary and not highly esteemed role of negotiator, he or she has no distinct role or status, or even source of internal authority. Often, the selected envoy is a very junior member who can expect to be shot down if he or she returns from the negotiation table without a result that all factions regard as unequivocal victory. Only a very hostile and uncompromising rejection of all proposals made will satisfy them. It is therefore safest to stonewall and effectively refuse to negotiate. Hence the unyielding behaviour of 'delegates' to whom no authority to transact can be delegated: they risk their lives when they accept (usually reluctantly) to be envoys, and they risk their lives when they come back bringing peace proposals.

In a crisis, some factions will succeed in splitting off and making their own new enclave, yet the original founding group is not disbanded. Future developments diverge here, depending on whether relations between the original and the new enclave are friendly, like daughter colonies to the mother institution, or rancorous, fired by mutual accusations of having betrayed the founding principles. One might expect that enclaves that have split off from a common root would support and befriend one another, yet in many cases there is more anger against the enclaves that are nearest to them than there is against society outside.

Third Fork

Figure 4.4 shows how conflict with authorities may follow different paths.

Resources and their control   The choice of openness or closure depends partly on what resources are available and on what decisions are taken regarding the acquisition of wealth. A large donation or other significant source of funds will tend to change the organization: it puts the equality principle at risk because someone (or even a committee) will be endowed with financial control above that of others. On the other hand, some funds provide the leaders with the means of rewarding loyalty. An enclave that develops positive inducements for members to stay with it, changes its organization in radical ways; above all, many of the inherent tensions are relaxed.

Who would ever want to be a leader of an egalitarian enclave? Apart from enduring the hostile suspicions of followers, such a person would be acutely aware of being under surveillance from outside authorities. Leadership itself is gagged and bound; if it can claim charismatic virtues and divine inspiration, it is indeed fortunate. If, however, it never succeeds in acquiring authority, the enclave is condemned to smallness of scale and a fissioning future when internal factions get too powerful to be contained within the original single, fragile frame. A small acquisition of funds, nonetheless, can open up the way to hierarchy: the rank and file may concede authority to an inner council, or to an elected leader. However,

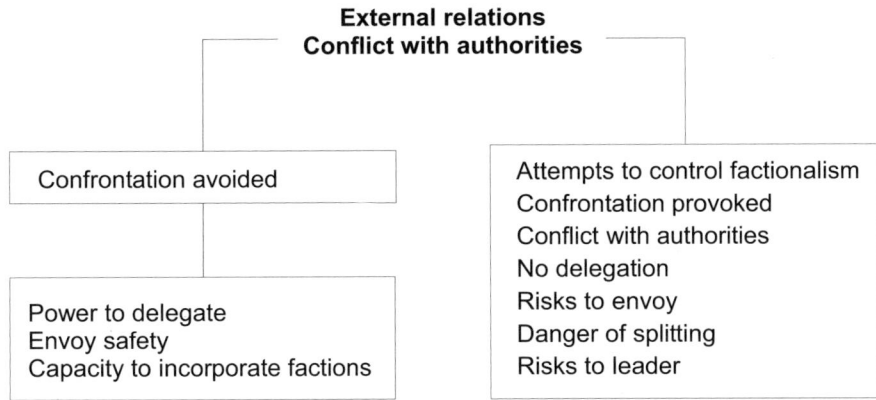

Figure 4.4   Conflict with authorities

even great capital resources will not necessarily improve relations between followers and leaders.

The fear of a treacherous sell-out is always present in the minds of followers. This is partly because unequal access to wealth is a sore subject and partly because leaders are always under suspicion: if a leader should abscond, he or she would be suspected of having taken the community funds, thus jeopardizing the future of the entire group. This very rarely happens, yet it is rumoured and feared.

Better organization in itself would enhance coordination. It may improve the chances of gaining a better livelihood, and thus of attracting recruits – nothing succeeds like success. An interesting negative case is the history of the Quaker movement, which started among the poor in the seventeenth century. Then in the eighteenth century individual families became rich. They were able to offer selective benefits to their allies and their poorer members who took the option of not closing their ranks, and thus were able to keep their vision.

When new funds come to the group as a whole, another choice might lie ahead: the funds could be distributed equally among members. More commonly, however, members shelve the equality principle and proceed instead to make the organization more complex, reserving equality for the common run of members, and creating a covert hierarchy or inner council to look after the wealth. Another method is to set up a charismatic figure who has the constitutional role of making enigmatic utterances from a higher position. In that case, the inner council that manages the allocation of funds to lower-level members does not pretend to have any equality with them: inevitably, it assumes direction. Because of the resulting contradiction with the founding principle, such leaders may find it convenient to be situated far apart from the other levels. The system can then develop into a cluster of enclave cells grouped around a central powerhouse, where the training college, the financial officer, the benefactor and the successor to the original founder, exert remote control over a network of egalitarian enclaves. An example of such a structure in antiquity is that of the New Covenant Community in 200 BCE, which seems to have made the Dead Sea caves at Qumran into a missionary training centre and a powerhouse for the dissemination of their teaching (Talmon 1993). The contemporary IRA in Ireland has a similar organization: it consists of a centre with small cells radiating out from it.

The inner council can probably afford to be openly hierarchical, if the wealth is substantial enough to give it real power, or if the several subordinate enclaves at the outposts can be played off against each other. Other things being equal, the centre tends eventually to be more accommodating to government authority and to outsiders than the outposts. Does this imply that even the worst intransigence can be countered by giving incentives to the enclave to develop a more complex structure? This depends on how it deals with its confrontational members at the outposts, and on what keeps the balance between central council and outposts – though this partly depends on where the resources come from, and the level at which they enter the grouping.

Resources may be provided by foreign agencies in the form of cash, with the intent of fomenting civil war; such contributions may be received as net cash, or in the form of weaponry or training, provided every time with the understanding that they are to be used for violent terrorism. The effect of cash benefits will normally be to strengthen the central administrative core, yet if military resources are given directly to the activist outposts, the balance of power between centre and fringe is reversed: when followers have the guns, leaders cannot call the tune. Then the chance that the acquisition of material resources might minimize hostility is reduced to nil. Naturally, however, the weakness of a leadership that lacks funds makes it readier to embrace a programme of violence, or to delegate fund getting to those on the periphery, by means, for instance, of tolerated extortion, robbery, or other illegal activities.

Fourth Fork

Figure 4.5 shows the possible effects that resources can have on an organization.

In all probability, if the main body of society acts repressively at the first confrontation, the armed enclave will respond in a similarly aggressive manner; how little or how much the members or leaders have to gain by a compromise peace needs to be assessed separately in each case. If the leaders know that they are going to be prosecuted for violation of human rights, it is almost certain that they will not make peace – this is one of the problems of forgiveness that should be on negotiators' agendas. Another forgiveness issue is the major policy problem of how to reincorporate the young members who have been corrupted in the ways of violence as part of their initiation. If they were recruited in desperate circumstances, they may be willing to make a new life; on the opposite side of the conflict, however, it is difficult to bring their former targets – the citizens whose kin the violent aggressors have killed and mutilated – to agree to offer them peace. If, as part of their training and as a test of their commitment, the young recruits

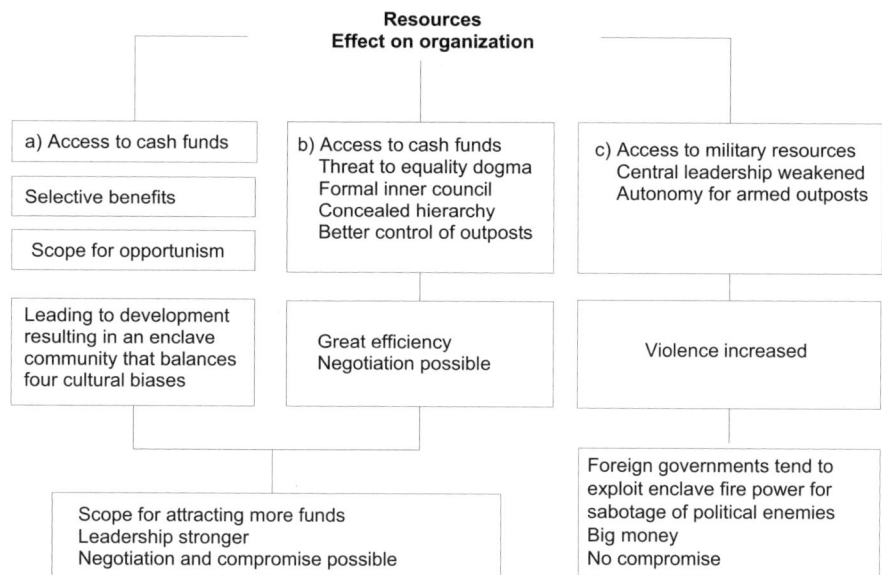

Figure 4.5   The effect of resources on the organization

have been made to commit such horrid atrocities that they may never expect to be accepted in civil society, some special provisions or rituals of reconciliation may be needed, as was the case with the rituals of reintegration of Mau Mau terrorists in East Africa in the 1950s.

Conclusion

Many important aspects of the enclave development cycle have not been mentioned. One example would be the way in which its choice at each juncture is affected by the strength of cultural commitments that lie outside the enclave; another would be the way that it relates to 'daughter' or 'brother' enclaves and other affinity groups. It will be important to note how in some recorded cases the confrontation has been allayed, or what special circumstances have led instead to upward-spiralling hostility. We should investigate the records of subversive movements that led to violence and civil war, asking questions such as the following. Were the reforms that the partisans were demanding feasible? Could they have been achieved without violence? In the outcome, did violence effectively establish acceptable justice? Alternatively, was insurrection simply repressed? If the enclave started out with modest demands, and has come to the point of requiring nothing less than the regeneration of the whole society, can anything be done to satisfy it? Would meeting the demands that caused the initial withdrawal into an enclave, or that provoked the initial confrontation, have any effect once the polarization has got under way?

This focus on how information is shaped by institutions has led to a different understanding of the problems of the enclave. Instead of explaining the behaviour of enclavists on the basis of personality, the reverse is the case: personal attitudes and choices are explained by the constraints that other people, in the form of institutions, impose on the options available. At many points along this process the enclavists seem to have no choice but to continue on a course that will lead to the break-up of their movement or to violent confrontation. Ultimately, the pattern that defines information in the developing cycle of an enclave is neither that of an ant's nest nor of a rabbit warren, but rather that of a conch shell: it is hard, smooth and resisting on the outside, and life inside the shell flows in whirling eddies, through a narrowing funnel – furthest inside are the secrets, and the dead end.

Harsh choices shape the enclaved institution. The outcomes imply the costs of trying to think independently, away from the majority. It may start out with high principles, great confidence, joy and pride in its mission; if it were only half successful in changing the world, everyone might be the better for it. Yet obstacles emerge and unexpected problems lead members to oppress each other, and thence to perverse results. When the enclave inspires enmity in outsiders, it experiences no surprise, but rather a grim satisfaction; yet it is a surprise, and a grief, when harmony remains elusive even within – especially within – and among its own following.

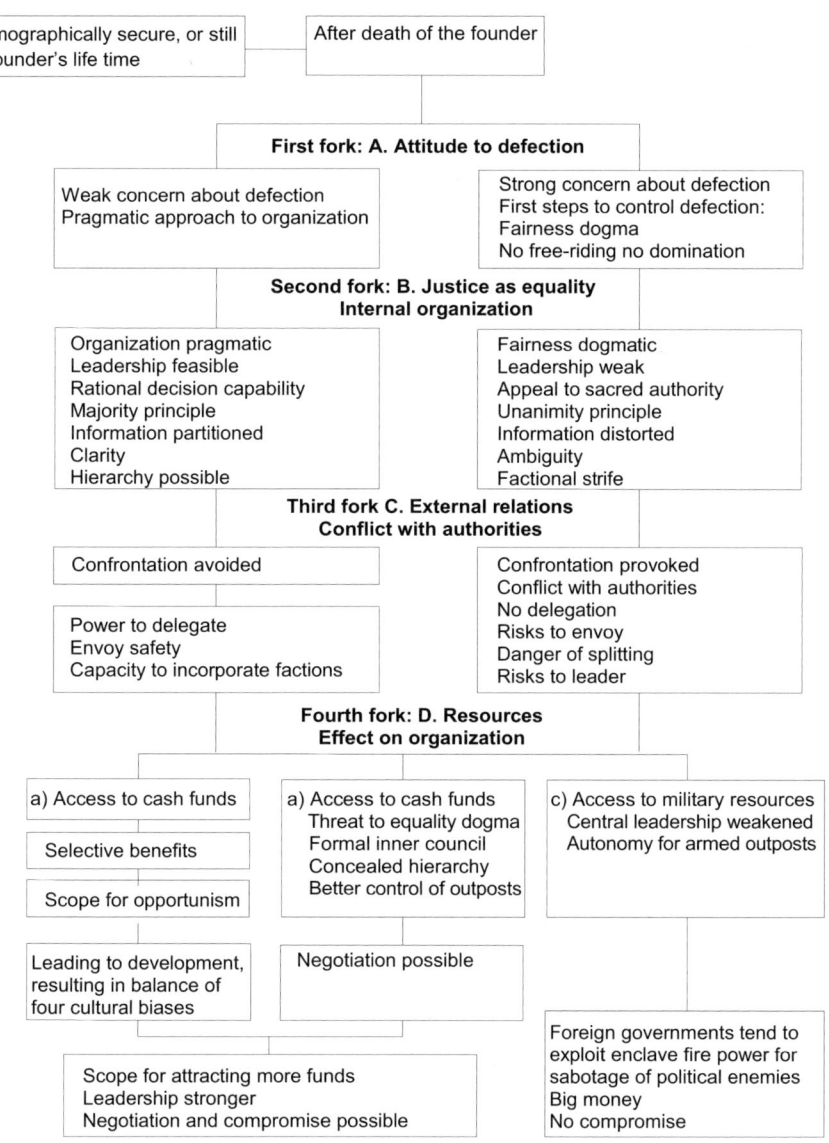

Figure 4.6   The four forks: Provisional developmental cycle derived from the organization of enclaves

References

The sources named here are an idiosyncratic collection not designed to cover the subject; their purpose is rather to introduce material that most cultural theorists know, but which is probably not on the usual reading lists of sociologists or historians dealing with sectarian movements.

Baumgarten, A. (1998), *The Flourishing of Jewish Sects in the Maccabean Era: An Interpretation*, Leiden, The Netherlands: Brill.
Calley, M.J.C. (1965), *God's People: West Indian Pentecostal Sects in England*, Oxford: Oxford University Press.
Caplow, T. (1947), 'Rumors in War', *Social Forces*, 25, 298–302.
Coser, L. (1974), *Greedy Institutions: Patterns of Undivided Commitment*, New York: Free Press.
Douglas, M. (ed.) (1982), *Essays in the Sociology of Perception*, London: Routledge & Kegan Paul.
Douglas, M. (1987), *How Institutions Think*, Syracuse, NY: Syracuse University Press.
Douglas, M. (1992), 'Institutions of the Third Kind: British and Swedish Labour Markets Compared', in *Risk and Blame: Essays in Cultural Theory*, London: Routledge, 167–86.
Douglas, M. (1993), *In the Wilderness: The Doctrine of Defilement in the Book of Numbers*, Sheffield: Sheffield University Press.
Griffiths, R. (1966), *The Reactionary Revolution: The Catholic Revival in French Literature*, London: Constable.
Hobsbawm, E. (1959), *Primitive Rebels: Studies in Archaic Forms of Social Movement in the 19th & 20th Centuries*, New York: W.W. Norton.
Mack, P. (1996), *Visionary Women: Ecstatic Prophecy in Seventeenth-century England*, Berkeley, CA: University of California Press.
MacNeill, W. (1993), 'Epilogue: Fundamentalism and the World of the 1990s', in M. Marty and R. Scott Appleby (eds), *The Fundamentalism Project, Volume 2: Fundamentalisms and Society*, Chicago, IL: University of Chicago Press, 558–74.
Mars, G. (1988), 'Hidden Hierarchies in Israeli Kibbutzim', in J.G. Flanagan and S. Rayiwi (eds), *Rules, Decisions and Inequality in Egalitarian Societies*, Aldershot: Avebury Press.
Mars, G. (2000), 'Criminal Cultures', in D. Canter and L. Alison (eds), *The Social Psychology of Crime: Criminal Teams and Networks*, Aldershot: Ashgate Publishing, 21–50.
Mayer, T. (1960), 'The Distribution of Ability and Earnings', *Review of Economics and Statistics*, 42, 189–95.
Mincer, J. (1958), 'Investment, Human Capital and Personal Income Distribution', *Journal of Political Economy*, 66.

Perri 6 and Mars, G. (eds) (1988), *The Institutional Dynamics of Culture: The New Durkheimians*, 2 vols, Aldershot: Ashgate Publishing.

Rayner, S. (1982), 'The Perception of Time and Space in Egalitarian Sects', in M. Douglas (ed.), *Essays in the Sociology of Perception*, London: Routledge, 247–75.

Rayner, S. (1988), 'The Rules that Keep Us Equal', in J.G. Flanagan and S. Rayner (eds), *Rules, Decisions, and Inequality in Egalitarian Societies*, Aldershot: Avebury, 20–42.

Richards, M. (1998), *A Time of Silence: Civil War and the Culture of Repression in Franco's Spain, 1936–1945*, Studies in the Social and Cultural History of Modern Warfare, Cambridge: Cambridge University Press.

Richards, P. (1996), *Fighting for the Rain Forest: War, Youth & Resources in Sierra Leone*, London: Heinemann.

Rosen, S. (1981), 'The Economics of Superstars', *The American Economic Review*, 71(5), 845–58.

Schwarz, M. and Thompson, M. (1990), *Divided We Stand: Redefining Politics, Technology and Social Choice*, Hemel Hempstead: Harvester Wheatsheaf.

Sivan, E. (1995), 'The Enclave Culture', in M. Marty (ed.), *Fundamentalism Comprehended*, Chicago, IL: Chicago University Press.

Talmon, S. (1993), 'The Community of the Renewed Covenant: Between Judaism and Christianity', in E. Ulrich and J. Vanderkam (eds), *The Notre Dame Symposium on the Dead Sea Scrolls*, Christianity and Judaism in Antiquity Series, vol. 10, Prague: University of Notre Dame Press, 3–23.

Thompson, M. and Wildavsky, A. (1986), 'A Cultural Theory of Information Bias in Organizations', *Journal of Management Studies*, 23(3), 274–86.

Thompson, M., Ellis, R. and Wildavsky, A. (1990), *Cultural Theory*, Boulder, CO: Westview Press.

Urban, H.B. (1988), 'The Torment of Secrecy: Ethical and Epistemological Problems in the Study of Esoteric Traditions', *History of Religions*, 27(3), 209–48.

Chapter 5
Hierarchy: Dock Pilferage –
A Case Study of the Methods
and Morals of Occupational Theft

This chapter focuses on workgroups that are strongly hierarchical and derives from an anthropological study of longshoremen in St John's, Newfoundland[1] carried out by participant observation.[2] Participant observation was necessarily limited. I spent eighteen months in fieldwork, living and spending leisure time with the longshoremen and their families. But since work in the port was limited – Newfoundland has a winter unemployment rate of over 40 per cent and a summer one of over 12 per cent – I was unable to work on the dock. Instead, I spent much time in the Union Hall, wandering round the wharfs and sheds and on and in vessels observing, chatting to men as they worked, and drinking with them in the evenings. My interest in pilferage was originally peripheral to other interests and arose relatively late in fieldwork.

This chapter is primarily concerned to demonstrate how 'normal' work roles are adapted to serve the needs of institutionalized pilferage and how this influenced relationships on the dock, particularly within the longshore work gang. It then shows how the men saw their actions in terms of a prevailing system of ethics that ran counter to the general population of the town.

1　Fieldwork was carried out as Research Fellow of the Newfoundland Institute of Social and Economic Research, whose support I gratefully acknowledge. It was conducted between 1962 and 1964. I briefly returned in 1966, when the situation was much the same. By 1972, when I last returned, containerization had been introduced, which abolished much of the need for gangs. As a result, the wide variety of longshore informants who read the draft of this article, including members of the Longshoremen's Protective Union (the LSPU) and its Executive, had no objections to publication (Mars 1974).

2　These include studies of restaurant and hotel workers (see Mars 1973), in addition to fairground staff, seaside deckchair attendants, health service consultants, ice cream sellers, public corporation executives, driver salesmen, storemen, barmen, and supermarket cashiers. Details of most of these were later published in Mars 1982/1984/1994.

Background to the Port and its Operations

The port of St John's hired its labour on a casual basis by a procedure known as 'the shape-up'.[3] When a ship docks, a hiring foreman stands on deck, the men form a horseshoe 'shape' beneath him, and the foreman then picks the twenty-six men from the gang he will later supervise. The picking of men is carried out in the same way as schoolboys pick their football teams. Men are rehired only for a particular boat, which may give as little as two or as much as twenty hours' work, and they are paid hourly. The hourly rate was $2 and the average annual pay of regularly chosen gang members was only about $2,000. 'Outside men' – those who fill in on vacancies when they occur and who are not normally hired as regular gang members – have even lower earnings than those of regular men and their access to pilferage is much less.

In spite of the apparently casual nature of hiring, close observation reveals that predominantly the same men are rehired at each shape-up by their regular foremen. This is because a bargain exists between members of tightly organized work gangs who need the security of regular selection, and their foremen, who need an output of work satisfactory to their bosses. But a further aspect of the bargain is that the men are, in effect, also granted a tolerated access to pilferage.

Gangs comprise tightly knit, inward-looking groups of friends and neighbours, who spend their leisure time together and among whom there are frequently considerable kinship connections. The gang is, therefore, the unit of work and leisure. It is also a source of security and insurance. One gang supplied fourteen pints of blood for a sick gang member, while another raised funds to re-house a member whose house had burned down – house fires are common in St John's, since houses are mostly of wood. It is this tightness of organization buttressed by kinship, work, residence, leisure and mutual support that facilitates the organization of pilferage and its distribution. Foremen, excluded from social activities, have in recent years largely moved away from longshore areas of residence and take no part in obtaining or distributing pilfered cargo.

The techniques governing pilferage can be explained only in the context of normal work roles and their organization. This is because the organization of both legitimate and illegitimate work is based on the same work-group structure – the gang. It is therefore only by understanding normal working that we can see how work roles are adapted by men to carry out illegitimate tasks under cover of legitimacy.

When a vessel is unloading cargo, men start the process in the bowels of the ship – the hold. Cargo has to be lifted by winch or crane and dropped alongside the vessel to the quay. Here it is loaded onto a fork truck and moved to a shed for sorting, stacking and checking. The total task is performed in much the same way in any port, which means that the dock work gang system is, with variations,

---

3   For an insightful description of shape-up hiring and its social effects see Larrowe (1956).

basically universal.[4] This discussion can therefore be regarded as having a wider application than its single source might suggest.[5]

Figure 5.1 reveals the working situation in St John's and shows the distribution of a twenty-six-man gang among its different sections. The discussion refers to a gang structure designed to unload general cargo, the kind of cargo found in shops, since this is the predominant type of gang structure in the port.

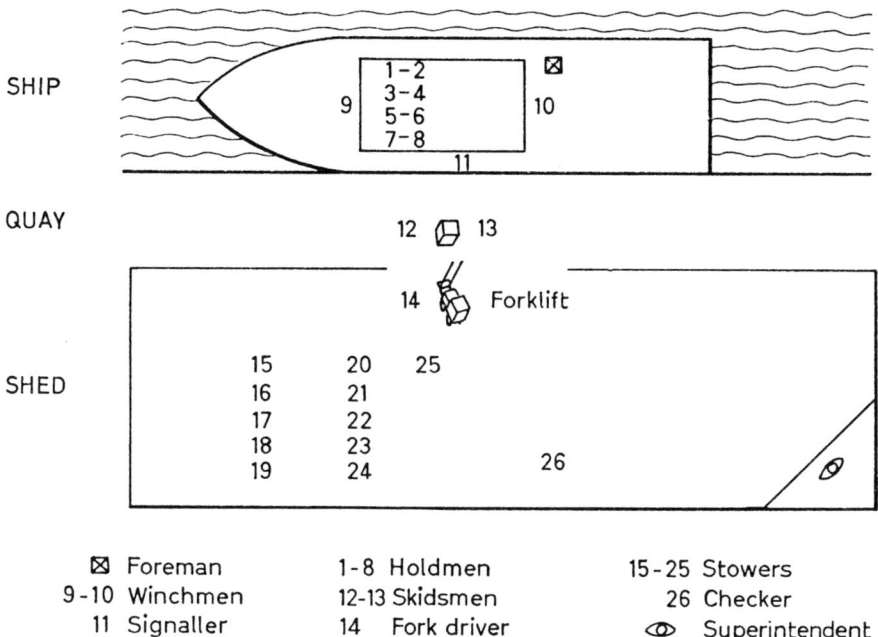

Figure 5.1   The Deployment of a 26 man Gang to Unload General Cargo

The Vessel Crew

The Eight Holdsmen

Men who work in the hold, often collectively called 'the hatchcrew', are organized in four pairs. Where possible, two pairs move cargo to the sling and two pairs load the sling together. Sometimes it is not feasible for all members of a hatchcrew to work together – a cargo's nature or the way it is packed might mean that two pairs of men have to stand idly by until their workmates have cleared a sufficient space.

---

4   Or rather, it was – until the later introduction of containerization became universal.

5   This discussion does not apply to the new wave of cargo-handling technology in docks – containers, lighters aboard ship (LASH), or side- and end-loading vessels.

This enforced idleness contributes to the high incidence of pilferage from ships' holds. Most pilfering of cargo takes place here rather than in the sheds. Another contributory factor is that normal work involves burrowing for cargo below the level of the hatch and therefore legitimately working for much of the time out of sight of passers-by on deck.

There are two slings to each hatch. A sling is a square board, to each corner of which is fixed a hawser; these are linked to a cable and hoisted or lowered by power-operated winch. Each sling is loaded alternately and when it is fully stacked men in the hold pass a signal by hand to a signaller standing on deck, who similarly transmits it to the winch driver. The loaded sling is then raised, swung out over the ship's side, lowered to the quay, and an empty sling lowered into the hold in its place. This in its turn is reloaded and the process continued until the hold is empty.

Winch Drivers and Deckman (or Signaller)

The two winchmen and the deckman work in close partnership both with each other and with men in the hold. Perched in the rigging, one on either side of the hatch, winchmen perform a highly skilled job, as, in response to signals of the deckman below, they raise and lower slings in and out of the hatch beneath them and over the vessel's side to the quay. They are completely dependent on signals from the deckman since they are usually behind the line of vision into the hatch; it says much for the skill of these four men that accidents are relatively few. It seems almost incredible to an outside observer that, acting purely in response to signals, the winchmen can, with practised ease, deposit a swaying, heavily laden sling exactly where it is required on the quay from its loading area in the hold while often unable to see either loading area or quayside. To obtain such polished, almost elegant handling demands a rapport between winchmen and signaller that requires considerable time to perfect. 'You've got to be buddies to do this job,' one winchdriver remarked, 'and you've got to understand his signals – they've all got different signals.' This rapport unites all the vessel crew and though derived from legitimate work organization is, as we shall see, indispensable to the organization of illegitimate pilferage.

The Shore Crew

Skidsmen

Skidsmen work on the quay at the side of a ship. In this situation, they are both physically and socially isolated from the gang's two main sections. Skidsmen work as a pair and handle the sling as the winchman lowers it over the ship's side. If the fork truck is waiting to load, they manoeuvre the contents onto the truck's fork; if the truck is in the shed, they see the sling unloaded directly to the quay.

The job is unskilled and rated low on prestige. Skidsmen have little autonomy since their rate of work is entirely set by the vessel crew. The job has a further disadvantage in that it is visible to anyone walking along the quay. This means that superintendents or managers can at any time detect an absentee or investigate a pile-up of cargo on the quayside. This visibility also of course inhibits skidsmen from pilfering and helps make the job the least desired of any in the longshore work gang.

Fork Truck Drivers

Truck drivers are regarded by longshoremen as relatively skilled. The ability to manoeuvre not very easily controlled trucks in and out of narrow passageways is rated lower in skill than the winchdriver's job but higher than the stower's. The job involves collecting cargo from the quay and taking it to stowers in the shed. The truck drivers can seriously affect the stowers' task: a fast-moving driver, working with a fast-moving vessel crew, can set a pace beyond what stowers consider reasonable. Further, a truck driver not in harmony with his stowers can make their job even more difficult by dropping cargo some distance from their sorting area, forcing them to manhandle it to its destination.

The social position of the fork truck driver is somewhat ambiguous. Sometimes he is regarded as a foreman's man. As one stower remarked, 'He'll work for the foreman, not the gang – he sets the pace for the stowers.' He will, however, sometimes act as a medium of communication between stowers and vessel crew when grumbles come from the shed that the vessel crew are 'hoisting' too much too quickly. This area of ambiguity about his role is thus, in part, a reflection of his physical position in the gang. Working on his own as he does, trundling his truck between shed and quay, he is – like the skidsmen – in little position to integrate with any group. Yet a truck driver does not always 'work for the foreman'. Just as his position in the gang allows him to serve the foreman by setting a pace for shed stowers, so it also allows him to perform certain services for the gang. These services include facilitating pilferage.

The Stowers

The eleven stowers are divided into two groups, of five and six. Working under direction of the hatch checker, they sort cargo in the shed brought from the quay by the truck drivers. The job is regarded as unskilled, not requiring specific abilities, and not very onerous. Among stowing gangs are older men who are 'carried' by the other members; men who have been injured (more often in the hold than elsewhere); men recovering from sickness; and newly inducted outside men. It is among the stowers that most executive members of the Union are found – a result of their opportunity to communicate at work to a degree not available to other gang members. Holdsmen are isolated in groups of eight and work in pairs; winchmen and signallers relate as a group of four; while the skidsmen and truck drivers are relatively isolated. Stowers, on the other hand, in the normal course of work mix with at least four or five, more usually with ten or eleven, co-workers, and also have opportunities to contact stowers in other gangs throughout the shed. Because of this, stowers are able to offer more complicated support to each other in organizing pilferage, and stowers of one gang sometimes give warning of the approach of authority to stowers of adjacent gangs.

Hatch Checkers

A hatch checker's job is twofold: to check cargo against documents and to guide the work of stowers in allocating cargo, in piles, to await individual consignees. A hatch checker is regarded as the foreman's unofficial deputy in the shed. He must be literate and highly skilled at 'knowing the marks'.[6] His position vis-à-vis the foreman is extremely secure, as this knowledge is not widespread and many foremen are illiterate. He is not paid extra for his knowledge,[7] but gains in security and prestige. One experienced member of the Union executive described checkers as 'unpaid policemen'. By this, he hastened to add, he knew of no cases where a hatch checker had reported a man for theft, but rather he felt that some checkers limited the amount men took. I could find no evidence of antagonism between checkers and stowers.

All hatch checkers during my fieldwork seemed well established, and relationships between them and stowers were affable. One event serves to point out the nature of this relationship. During fieldwork, one hatch checker who had a record of sickness was off on holiday. His replacement was a shed checker whose position in the shed was regarded as none too permanent and who, it was suspected by some of the stowers, was 'after Hughie's place'. They combined to missort cargo so the relief checker had no idea where any specific consignee's material would be found. By constantly mixing up different cargo, they made the checker's job intolerable.

There is some ambiguity in the relationship of hatch checker to stowers. The case above demonstrated dependence of the checker upon stowers. In pilferage, however, as we shall see, stowers necessarily depend upon the checker. In this connection, it is noteworthy that most checkers and stowers enjoy a symmetrical joking relationship (Radcliffe-Brown 1952). One checker, for instance, was constantly ribbed at the vast amount he was alleged to have pilfered: 'Clears 'em out Hughie does, don't you, Hughie?' Hughie's reply was always jocular.

---

6   That is, able to recognize contents of a package by code marks on its outside. 'Each parcel, known as a bill of lading from the covering document of title, bears a separate mark; this is shown as a rule, on each case, bag or carton. This identifying mark is known as the main mark; often there are sub-marks that denote the shipper or the quality and size of the contents' (Oram 1965, p. 31). The hatch checker's knowledge is of obvious value in facilitating pilferage.

7   Due to the Union policy of 'not splitting the membership'.

With this account of 'normal working' by a twenty-six-man gang engaged in unloading general cargo, we can see how they perform an interrelated series of tasks. We must now consider how these work roles are adapted and how they interrelate for the performance of covert and illegitimate tasks.

Four Cases of Theft

It must first be made clear that I was not able to observe actual examples of theft taking place in the dock. Details of instances were obtained initially from management or from traders who suffered loss in their consignments. Later in fieldwork, material was obtained from longshoremen themselves but again without direct observation. With such information, however, it was possible to go back to several informants and to cross-check material received.

Case 1: Men's Suits

I first heard from a manager of one wharf that a cargo of men's suits had been broken into and some pilfered. In checking with the trader, I found thirteen out of a consignment of a hundred suits had disappeared between despatch in Montreal and arrival in St John's. With this background of information, I then went to informants who worked on the wharf concerned. The sequence of events was fairly clear, and cross-checking with several informants confirmed what had happened.

The hatch checker had been alerted by details on his bills of lading concerning the contents of the crates; messages had passed from shed to vessel crew to warn them of 'good pickings' to be expected. The crates were then loaded by the hold crew so that two would fall when the winch was jerked. At the appropriate moment, as the sling was poised over the quay, the signaller gave an all-clear sign to the winchman. The winchman adjusted his levers, the winch jerked, and the crates fell. They were only slightly damaged, but this was enough to permit entry. Following normal procedure, the crates were then moved by fork truck to the shed for the attention of the stowers.

The shed is hardly a safe place for pilferage as the wharf superintendent or even the company manager may appear. Superintendents, in particular, frequently walk round the sheds to make sure work is proceeding, and, presumably, also to restrict pilferage. In this shed (as in several others), the situation of the superintendent's office offers a further hazard to stowers. It is commonly set high in the shed roof and typically has large glass windows, so the superintendent, sitting at his desk, has an overview of operations throughout the shed. First, then, it was necessary to block off this view of what was going on in the sorting and unloading area.

In this instance, much other cargo unloaded with the suits was bulky and packed in large cases. The fork truck driver stacked this cargo to block off the superintendent's line of vision so he could not see the sorting area from his office. At the same time, the driver also built up other packing cases to form a hollow square. This enclosure then served as a changing room. Thus equipped, men were able to choose their suits at leisure, trying on different ones for size and being secure from the prying eyes of the superintendent in the roof.

Throughout the day, holdsmen, signaller and winchmen left the vessel and made their way individually to 'the changing room'. Stowers, as they went about their normal job, kept a wary eye open for authority, but the procedure went unobserved. This cargo was removed from the dock in the usual way, secreted in the clothing of men who took the goods home at the end of the day. Longshoremen are extremely skilful in this matter. (I once walked with a man half a mile through busy streets to his home. Once inside, he pulled out bottle after bottle of whisky until there were six bottles on the kitchen table.)

The following day, the hatch checker reported that two crates had arrived damaged. By this time, the missing suits had already been moved and were almost impossible to trace. Neither was it possible to localize the pilferage to St John's: there was no evidence to prove the crates could not have been opened in Montreal, while the vessel was at sea, or at other ports on its route. In this connection, it must be pointed out that cargo often arrives in the port that has been interfered with prior to arrival, and longshoremen in the port are often blamed for pilferage they know has been accomplished elsewhere. In this case, though cooperation of vessel crew, stowers and fork truck driver were all necessary for a successful operation, actual pilferage was effected in the shed. Both management and men, however, are of the view that most pilferage occurs while cargo is still in the hold.

Case 2: Transistor Radios

I heard about this case, involving a cargo of radios from Germany, when discussing the general question of pilferage with one of the superintendents. 'Oh yes – they'll steal anything. They're the worst thieves in the world – only last week a crate of radios en route to Montreal was completely cleared out.' I asked how he was so sure they'd been taken in St John's, but he was hesitant to say. The account obtained from informants was as follows.

With stereotyped Teutonic efficiency, the forwarders had marked on the outside of their crate the name of the radios, a full description (which pointed out that they were portable!), and the quantity. The holdsmen had noticed this crate lying behind other cargo they were unloading. In a situation like this, however, one cannot just break into a crate: a member of the ship's crew will frequently be pacing the deck and occasionally peering into the hold. He is there specifically to restrict pilferage. Usually, this lookout is a ship's officer – the mate or one of his deputies. Sometimes, if cargo is not particularly valuable or not easily pilfered, the job of lookout may be delegated to a more junior officer. In this case, the man keeping an eye on men in the hold was the ship's mate. The threat to security posed by the ship's officer is a serious one, though holdsmen can stay out of his line of vision if they know where he is positioned.

On this occasion, as in other cases where holdsmen were involved, their insecurity was reduced by the signaller. His 'normal' job, discussed above, involves passing signals to the winchman. By quick and deft movements of his hands, he tells the winchman by how much to raise, lower and move the slings. To do this, he must stand on the ship's deck on the vessel's shore side. He is thus in perfect position not only to carry out his normal signalling but also to keep an eye on the ship's officer who, in his turn, is keeping observation on the hold crew. His arm movements, however, are used not only to coordinate the work of winch-, hold- and skidsmen: in his contribution to pilferage, they serve also to warn men in the hold below of the activities of the ship's officer above. So rapid and well understood can these signals be that I was never able to recognize or locate them.

Though the crate was opened by holdsmen, its allocation was divided among all gang sections; nevertheless, I neglected to find out whether this included the normally isolated skidsmen. My main informant, a stower, had two radios, one of which he sold. Not all the gang participated, and there were some disputes since several men were scared to steal such valuable items (the radios retailed at over \$150 each). They were removed from the dock under men's coats.

Except for the high value of items involved, the procedures in this case would appear to be more typical than those in the previous case, in that activity was largely restricted to the vessel crew. The vessel crew's 'leavings' were then made available to stowers and, as this was a cargo in transit, there would presumably have been no need for cooperation from the hatch checker. I neglected to find how packaging had been disposed of in this case, since 'the cargo had been completely cleared out'. The usual methods are for it to be broken up, find its way into the harbour, be carried out of the docks, stuffed into other cargo – cardboard, for instance, being flat, is likely to be slipped into other cargo (mattresses, for example) – or to end up, minus identifying marking, among the normal and considerable rubbish of the shed.[8]

Case 3: Whisky

One British ship's captain recounted what happened on a previous trip while observing the unloading of whisky. As stated previously, overseeing men in the hold is normally the mate's duty. However, in situations where cargo is particularly likely to be pilfered, especially where high-value consumption items such as whisky, for which there is an almost insatiable demand, are involved, a captain or mate might himself take on the task. On this occasion, as the captain was leaning

---

8   As a general rule, men try to take the whole of a case and to dispose of both contents and packaging, since an absent case is less likely to be noticed than one that has been tampered with. Sometimes, though, it is not possible to dispose of a whole case and inconspicuous entry is therefore necessary. In these instances, nails are removed from wooden crates with sharp knives and are later carefully replaced. Razors are used to slice imperceptible U shapes in cardboard containers.

over the hatch, he saw that crates were not placed quite securely on the sling. As they were hoisted, the sling wobbled and one crate fell back in the hold, landing on a corner. This was sufficient to break a couple of bottles, which started to leak their precious liquid. He stated:

> Almost before the damned crate was down, they were there with cups and cans and what-have-you. I was ready for it, you see. I knew what was going to happen. As soon as it fell, I shouted to them to stand back and made them wait till it had run away. They were pretty angry at that and wanted to know why I'd wasted the stuff, so I told them, 'Because I don't want any more cases falling – alright?' They all laughed at that. Yes – you have a hard job with thieving. Mind you, it's not even safe to do this – they can be bloody-minded. Pilferage is found in any port, but it is worse here in my experience than anywhere else in North America. It's petty though – not organized on a large scale.

Such an operation's apparent casualness, as the captain was aware, requires the practised cooperation of winchmen, hold crew and signaller. First, the hold pair must load a crate on the sling with great care so it falls neither too early nor too late. Second, the signaller must be well aware of what has been arranged so he can pass signals to the winchman to treat this sling load rather differently from usual. Finally, the winchman, on whose particular expertise this operation largely depends, must know exactly when to shift his gears so that, with sound science and some elegance, he can cause the crate's demise. The captain told me that a friend of his, also a captain employed by the same company, had some years previously caught a man in the port red-handed and had called the police: 'The men for devilment stole a lot more. "Never again," he swore. "Let the insurance pay up."' The captain said his company 'had largely stopped shipping general cargo to the port' and now mainly confined its operations to coal – 'directly because of this type of pilferage.'

Case 4: Foodstuffs

Having looked at some specific examples, I now turn to consider pilferage of a general category of goods taken regularly in relatively small amounts. These are often foodstuffs, particularly those considered luxuries. Those actually stolen vary, therefore, with the tastes of each individual and of his family. Access to foodstuffs is particularly easy since their packaging is minimal – they usually arrive in single-thickness cardboard containers, and often these become damaged in the normal course of a cargo's discharge.

Quite a lot of the men and their families like sprouts, which are imported from the mainland and, being expensive, are considered something of a delicacy. When a cargo of sprouts arrives, it is usual for several men to fill a pocket or two. Holdsmen might also 'take care' of the interests of winchmen or signaller, and stowers similarly 'take care' of a truck driver. Some men have more esoteric tastes. One had a taste for anchovies, also considered a luxury good, a middle-class treat.

When this man, a stower, handled cargo including anchovies, he pocketed two or four tins. He had a friend with similar tastes, a stower in another gang on the same wharf. When either gang handled anchovies, each stower made sure his friend was also catered for. Men similarly take special foods for their wives. They will make an especial attempt to do so on occasions when liquor is also taken from the dock. Longshore wives are generally 'against' liquor; and anchovies, sprouts, or similar delicacies are used on these occasions to reconcile them to the heavy drinking that is likely to follow 'good liquor pickings'. Stolen liquor offends the more moralistic women on two grounds: that it is liquor and that it is stolen. The implication of wives as receivers serves to undermine wifely opposition.

A System of Pilferage

It is apparent that a system for the operation of pilferage exists, if by system we mean a set of interconnected parts organized together to perform a particular job with the boundary to the system being largely congruent with the work gang. To state that pilferage operates within a system is not at all the same thing, as suggesting that pilferage in the port of St John's is facilitated as an aspect of organized crime in the city. For one thing, pilferage appears to be random – advance planning has little place in its organization; second, it does not usually involve financial profit – personal use and social-based distribution are prime motives; and third, it provides a secondary source of resources restricted to men whose primary source of income is legitimate longshoring.[9]

To understand the social relationships involved in this system of pilferage, we must recognize two complementary facilities that need to be exploited for theft to occur. These (with one exception, to be discussed below) are not found together in the same work role. The key to understanding the system lies in observing not only that these facilities are complementary but also in perceiving how they work in alliance. They may be termed facilities of access and support – see Table 5.1.

Two clear groups emerge that correspond to the technical organization of the work gang. Extreme cases within the system are the skidsmen (– –) and the hatch checker (+ +). Foremen are excluded from the system.

When we examine work roles of men in the longshore gang, we therefore find the technical system imposing a twofold specialization that has crucial effects on the way pilferage is organized. Some men spend their day actually handling cargo: these men who have access to cargo are holdsmen, stowers and checkers. Other men, though involved in the process of moving cargo from ship to shed, do not actually handle goods but instead provide support for men who do in fact handle and have access to cargo. Thus the winchmen, signaller and fork truck drivers perform services with or without machinery such that each may pass long

---

9   A very different situation is found in Bell (1959), reporting on the then situation in New York.

Table 5.1   The division of labour in the system of pilferage as organized in St John's

Work role	Pilferage function	
	Access	Support
Holdsmen	+	− Vessel
Winchdrivers	−	+ crew
Signaller	−	+
Skidsmen	−	− Special case
Fork lift driver	−	+ Shed
Stowers	+	− crew
Hatch checker	+	+ Special case

periods without ever touching a crate. If men with access to cargo had direct and untrammelled opportunities to procure goods, dependencies within the gang would be very different from what it is in fact. Access, as we have seen, however, is limited. Cargoes often arrive in cases that are difficult to open; men in the shed are subject to prying eyes of superiors; men in the hold must beware of ship's officers; documents have to be squared and evidence of packaging disposed of if 'access men' are to be successful pilferers.

All these hazards to effective theft can only be overcome by use of the second facility – support. It was shown that for holdsmen to gain access to the contents of crates involves the support of winchman and signaller. It is a dangerous operation for a winchman simply to drop a crate from a sling, whether this is done onto the deck or back into the hold. There are many people milling around when cargo is being unloaded, and without the sure guide of the signaller serious accidents would almost certainly occur. The signaller, therefore, minimizes this risk and at the same time grants support to the holdsmen by being in a position where he warns them of the presence of ships' officers. Within the shed, the facility of support for access men, the stowers, is provided by the fork truck drivers and the hatch checker. The truck driver's support, as we saw, is necessary to stowers' access because he can move cargo to where it can (a) be more readily interfered with, and (b) provide a screen against outsiders' eyes.

Hatch checkers, as Table 5.1 shows, occupy a distinctive place in this pilferage system: theirs is the only work role to combine both facilities of access and support (+ +). A hatch checker's normal work involves direct physical handling of cargo, which grants him access, while his support is necessary to others on two grounds: first, in squaring documents; second, 'knowing the marks' (i.e. recognizing contents of a box from its markings), and receiving bills of lading, he is in a strong position to point out the most fruitful crates or packages to open.

Two workers are excluded from this system of dependencies: these are the skidsmen who lack access to cargo and who cannot gain support (– –). Their access is extremely limited because they work in the open on the quayside and, therefore, within sight of any passing member of the hierarchy. Further, their handling of any package is only transitory as they unload it from sling to fork truck – it usually needs time to delve into a box or wrench off a lid in order to get at its contents. Not only is their access thus limited, but skidsmen are also in no position to supply support to other gang members.[10] The implications of the skidsmen's lack of function in this total system of dependencies overflows the work situation and affects non-work relationships. Skidsmen usually have no close kinship affiliations with the gang. They tend to have closer connections with the foremen, and are likely also to be excluded from drinking cliques that stem from the work organization.

We see from Table 5.1, therefore, that nearly all gang members are enmeshed in a system of mutual dependencies made necessary by the technical, safety and security limitations that act against open access to cargo. It is because access and support are differentially allocated within the gang, however, that no one individual can exert a monopoly over either facility. This means that no one man is able, in pilferage or in other matters, to maximize his own benefits without incurring effective group sanctions. On one occasion a longshoreman, known to have a car off the dock stacked with cargo, returned to find it broken into, its contents completely cleared. It was well understood this had been accomplished by his workmates. This story was told and retold with some hilarity throughout the waterfront; the general view was that it served the victim right – he was known to be greedy and his behaviour was likely to prove a danger to all longshoremen involved in handling the same cargo.

Convictions for pilferage in St John's are extremely rare: there were no cases during the period of fieldwork or in the immediate past. Managers, in discussion, always insist that the lack of convictions is due to the fact that 'longshoremen always stick together. You can never get one to testify against another.' Managers and superintendents also realize that they are in a poor position to institute proceedings. Even if they caught a man red handed, testimony would involve retaliatory action that would make work relations even more difficult than usual. Men have walked off a boat because management once placed 'watchers' in the

---

10   It was not always the case that skidsmen and truck drivers were not integrated into the gang, or that they had relatively little part to play in pilferage. In the 1940s and 1950s, when work was much more plentiful in St John's than in the 1960s and 1970s, night work was common. At night time, 'good pickings' in one hold were occasionally loaded from the dockside not into the warehouse but into an adjacent hold. This operation required the coordination of skidsmen and truck drivers from both gangs. In return for their help, they would often be allowed on board and into the hold.

hold to supervise the unloading of whisky. Convictions, where they have occurred, have usually been instituted by men largely outside the waterfront system of relationships; they have usually been due to alert ships' officers rather than any measures taken by management.

When longshoremen talk of relationships within their work gangs and indeed within the Union generally, they frequently emphasize the mutual trust that exists between members. Where cooperative illegal activity occurs, necessity for absolute confidence in the dependability of colleagues is of crucial importance. When talking of the induction of new gang members, one informant recounted the case of a Salvationist who moved into his gang before the war. Because he refused to take cargo, men were suspicious and reluctant to confirm him to membership. At this time, police enquiries started into the theft of a valuable cargo of wristwatches, and they 'grilled' the new member over a period of four months. 'All that time he didn't give anything away,' said my informant. 'He was really firm in the gang after that.'

Pilferage, as a cooperatively organized illegal activity, reinforces technical culture and serves therefore to bind members of gangs further into tight exclusive groups. But the institutionalization of pilferage also affects relationships beyond the gang and extends links beyond wharf boundaries. This extension of links derives from management who, when they have exceptionally secured a successful prosecution, also suspend the culprit for six months from all work on the wharf concerned.

One of my informants, a stower, had a conviction for being in possession of stolen groceries taken from the dock. He had been fined in the magistrates' court and the company then suspended him for six months from all hirings on their wharf. This extra-legal penalty could have reduced him to a position worse than that of any outside man, who at least could attend all the shape-ups on each wharf. Instead of this, however, his earnings actually increased. 'In those six months, Gerry, I was never out of a job. The men on Y's wharf saw I was always in. You see, it could happen to anyone. Who knows when one of them might get caught and need a job on X's [his home] wharf?'

'Working the Value of the Boat': The Morality and Regulation of Pilferage

When examination is made of different cargoes and attitudes taken to them, we find most longshoremen make a sharp distinction between cargo it is permissible to steal and that which should remain untouched. Normally all consumer goods are suitable for pilferage, but taking personal baggage is considered despicable. This distinction is seen and expressed in terms of cargo addressed to impersonal firms and covered by insurance, on the one hand, and personal property belonging to individuals, on the other. This distinction is well demonstrated in the following quotations: one longshoreman, justifying his dislike of another, remarked, 'He'd take anything – he's even taken baggage – he's nothing more than a thief.' Another, discussing pilferage of general cargo, commented:

> I can't understand what they make all the fuss about, it's all insured and nobody's heard of an insurance company going broke. In any case, they've made millions out of this port and it's us who do the work.

When the first speaker used the word 'thief', he limited the definition to cover a narrower range of behaviour than is usual. Pilferage of cargo other than baggage is by the implication of this view not regarded as theft. The second quotation makes this explicit: pilferage is here seen as a morally justified addition to wages; indeed, as an entitlement due from exploiting employers.

Longshoremen have a phrase to describe the process of obtaining this entitlement – they call it 'working the value of the boat'. Thus, if a boat is expected to provide ten hours' work at $2 per hour then the boat is 'good for' $20 in wages. 'Working the value of a boat' in this case would mean obtaining cargo up to but not more than an estimated value of $20. The application of this concept can be seen to fulfil a number of functions. First, it tends to institutionalize pilferage, to grant it the status of a recognized and regularly occurring activity and a normal part of life. Second, the concept expresses a level of achievement men should aspire to. To say of a man, 'He always works the value of a boat', is a compliment, a confirmation of his independence and ability to outwit employers.

Not all longshoremen, however, engage in pilferage. Some members of the smaller religious sects are uncompromising in this respect. A few Salvationists and Seventh-day Adventists are known never to steal and are respected for their views. But the respect accorded them does not regard abstinence as an ideal to be emulated: indeed, their behaviour is seen as crankish. In response to my suggestion, 'Aren't these "good people"?', one informant expressed the common view. He replied that he thought they were 'good – but stunned', meaning stupid. The men respect their sacrifice in the same way as many people respect the strength of character of vegetarians, but without feeling they should join them. In neither case does respect imply the regard for ideal behaviour felt by men who are only able to maintain a lower-level norm.

A third function served by 'working the value of a boat' is the provision of a formula that fixes an unequivocal limit beyond which pilferage, no longer thought laudable, is instead perceived as a danger to workmates. If men go above 'the value of a boat', they are likely to attract official intervention. Persistently doing so will involve sanctions applied by co-workers.

Such a formula, though readily applicable to the generality of cargo that normally arrives on regular runs, is not readily applied to exceptional items with high unit value such as the transistor radios discussed in Case 2. When items such as these are taken, a division of involvement and interests occurs between those who participate and those who do not – and this is seen by men as a likely source of disruption to gang relationships. These occasions are, however, justified in terms of being exceptional occurrences, each occasion being regarded as a one-off event that does not disturb the validity of the general rule applicable to 'normal' cargo.

This upper limit also serves to retain pilferage within the sphere of the moral and thus the justified. If a man takes more than the value of the boat, he is taking more than his moral entitlement and this alters the nature of his action. Though to an outsider the difference might well appear only one of degree, to a longshoreman the difference is essentially qualitative. Up to an agreed level, pilfered cargo is seen as a moral entitlement; beyond this, additional pilferage is theft. Thus, when a gang sets levels of aspiration and operates controls to limit pilferage, it is acting not only from a standpoint of economic rationality but also, and this is a paradox not readily appreciated off the waterfront, from one set firmly in the prevailing morality.[11] It is a morality based, unusually, on qualitative criteria as against society's more common qualitative assessments

This fixing of an upper limit can be understood as allowing men to operate within limits of certainty: men know and can forecast not only the reactions of their workmates but also managerial reactions to pilferage – but only when it is kept to known and specific limits. This strongly suggests that managements are also, in a very real sense, conspirators with the men: they in effect collude in accepting a specific level of pilferage as part of an understood indulgence pattern.

More work needs to be done in a variety of industries to determine the extent of such collusion and to assess the factors permitting variable levels of pilferage in different milieux. Where pilferage is the norm, it may well have implications for analysis of industrial unrest. It appears here that pilferage, in the actor's definition of his position, is perceived as a legitimate means of redressing an exploitive contractual relationship. Considered in this light, pilferage can then be appreciated as having possible implications for working-class consciousness. It is behaviour that, in part at least, expresses alienation in an alternative manner to more open industrial and political action. This may well be one reason why managements have been reluctant to take action to eradicate it – preferring instead, despite the cries of moralists, to devise limits to its growth.

At local levels, consideration might be given to the effects of technology and work organization, as these influence control over access and support facilities. In some workplaces, such as the St John's docks, technology, in determining how work is organized, has meant that these are distributed within the work group – a fact that has important effects on culture and the emergence of a group morality. In other situations, technology or managerial direction could mean one or both facilities may well be held by persons outside the work group, or not distributed at all but monopolized by one individual. In some cases, control over access and support may well be used to buttress or detract from formal authority. In others, absence of control can perhaps distort planned hierarchies and relativities, while similar results can follow encapsulation of both facilities within individual roles.

This chapter has concentrated on deviance and its supporting system of morality within a strongly defined hierarchic work group – the traditional longshore work gang ('dockers' in the UK). It shows how close and detailed participant observation

---

11   See Gluckman's classic discussion of 'reasonable' role playing (Gluckman 1955).

can prove a powerful research tool, here revealing how such groups are able to 'bend' legitimate work roles to perform their illegitimate ones; how they control their levels of deviance; and how they can – and do – apply sanctions against those who break their own group norms. In doing so, it demonstrates the existence of a highly specific system of morality that has coherence, consistency and a structure of its own, and how tolerated and agreed levels of deviance are inherent to it. It reveals how such agreed levels were colluded in by bosses as part of the work/ effort bargain informally agreed between them and their labour. Finally, it shows how deviance in the workplace, through its system of distribution, influences behaviours and prestige not just in the workplace but in the wider community. This is a topic developed in the next chapter.

References

Bell, D. (1959), 'The Racket Ridden Longshoremen', *Dissent*, 6, 417–29.

Gluckman, M. (1955), *The Judicial Process among the Barotse of Northern Rhodesia*, Manchester: Manchester University Press.

Larrowe, C.P. (1956), *Shape-up and Hiring Hall*, Berkeley, CA: University of California Press.

Mars, G. (1973), 'Hotel Pilferage: A Case Study in Occupational Theft', in M. Warner (ed.), *Sociology of the Workplace*, London: Allen & Unwin, 200–210.

Mars, G. (1974), 'Dock Pilferage: A Case Study in Occupational Theft', in P. Rock and M. McIntosh (eds), *Deviance and Social Control*, London: Tavistock, 209–28.

Mars, G. (1982/1984/1994), *Cheats at Work: An Anthropology of Workplace Crime*, London: Allen and Unwin; Aldershot: Dartmouth Publishing.

Oram, R.B. (1965), *Cargo Handling and the Modern Port*, Oxford: Pergamon.

Radcliffe-Browne, A.R. (1952), *Structure and Function in Primitive Society*. London: Cohen & West.

Chapter 6
Hierarchy: The East End Warehouse and a Note on Criminogenic Communities

Introduction

The level of deviance in a workplace is not usually related to deviance in its surrounding community. But it was in chatting to an executive of a large car company that connections could be seen between levels of occupational deviance, type of community, and whether dealings were mainly in goods or services.

This executive was complaining that overall pilferage from his company's various spare parts storage premises was maintained at a steady level. But what puzzled him was that thefts from some sites were consistently higher than others. He listed those sites with a disproportionately high rate. Then I realized – they were all situated in towns that were also ports.

The place of crime in ports has a long history. It had long been noted by Colquhoun (among others), a London magistrate in the late eighteenth century. But no connection has since been made between deviance in docks and its possible influence on adjacent workplaces – let alone on the communities in which they are situated. The implications for criminogenesis derived from work cultures dealing in goods, and those supplying services, are discussed in the final part of this chapter.

The East End Warehouse

The following case shows how the cultural elements of London's dockland community were manifest in the working life of a warehouse that stored goods unconnected to the docks and which employed mostly local staff. It is based on fieldwork carried out as one of a small team of consultants[1] called to advise on improving the warehouse's efficiency. The East End warehouse stored and distributed goods – food and drink – on behalf of a number of contractor clients. Its market was expanding and the site well positioned. Nonetheless, contracts went un-renewed and 'stock shrinkage' and resultant losses were massively increasing.

---

1   A fuller account of this consultancy, which is focused on reorganizing the warehouse, is in Mars 2009.

Fieldwork lasted for four weeks.[2] It involved charting workflows, administering an attitude survey, conducting a census, and assessing both the workforce's collective East End culture and that of its management.[3]

The communal culture of London's East End was revealed as pervasive: it governed the way pilferage was organized, who had access to pilfered goods, and who didn't. It determined who was recruited to the workforce and who excluded. And when men were recruited, it controlled who worked with whom, how work was performed – and why it was often neglected.

A shipping company had recently acquired the warehouse as part of a larger takeover package. Its executives were all ex-merchant navy officers and their ideology – exclusively hierarchic and rule bound – set them in opposition to the collective and hierarchic East Enders they employed. Both defined people in terms of insiders and outsiders – and to each, the others were outsiders. Unsurprisingly, their values conflicted.

Early Impressions

First impressions were gained before going to the site through briefings and discussions with the holding company's senior management. They attributed their problems to 'under-utilization of resources', 'worker apathy', 'poor teamwork', and 'the low morale of the workforce'. They were also concerned that the union was 'difficult and 'recalcitrant'. They wanted to be told how these problems might be solved.[4] One explained to us:

> There are far too many warehousemen and most are too old for the job. They're nearly all over fifty, some are over seventy. So when we took over we thought we'd pension some of them off and since they'd all been with the company for years they'd earn a decent pension. Do you know, the Union turned the scheme down flat – out of hand – wouldn't even negotiate.

---

2   Fieldwork in London's East End was carried out in 1975, when there was full employment and 'the wage/effort bargain' (Baldamus 1961) favoured labour. Shortly after this, full employment markedly declined. However, it is not considered that the time between fieldwork and publication detracts from the validity of this case or the generality of its derived conclusions.

3   Charting work flows and designing the attitude survey were carried out by Prof. Ken Eason of Loughborough University, aided by two students Bertrand Nusbaumer and Phillipe Toccanier of the LEAP International Business School, who were all involved part time. I was full time in the warehouse, supervising the students and devising and carrying out the cultural analyses and the census.

4   We suggested we would need to explore wider concerns before proposing how their problems might be approached, underlining our role as facilitators rather than directing experts. We could show the implications of different policies, but we emphasized it was their responsibility as managers to initiate, optimize and involve.

Another was angry at the level of pilferage, which, with damage, had in the last year amounted to over half the company's losses:

> They're thieves. There's no other way to describe it. But it's damn near impossible to catch them. There's no help from the Union, that's for sure.

A third was concerned at having to regularly hire out-of-house trucks to cover shortfalls in the availability of their own when these achieved only half their annual expected mileage of 20,000.

It was soon apparent that senior management, who worked in an office building several miles from the warehouse, made only rare visits – and when they did call in, they talked only to the local managers,[5] not to the men.

Early interviews with local managers suggested they were dispirited and fatalist – especially at what they saw as relentless Union pressure. They assessed most policies of the Union as 'mindless'. One told me:

> We wanted to make one of them up to foreman. They just wouldn't discuss it – and no one wanted the job anyway. Can you begin to understand that?

These initial interviews therefore raised many questions. Visiting the site raised even more.

My first view of the warehouse was depressing. In the yard, a couple of rusting fork trucks awaited repair and the roadways between sheds had pitted, uneven surfaces with holes of brackish water. Congestion caused problems to drivers manoeuvring trucks in and out of crowded roadways. Randomly parked cars offered further hazard.

In the sheds, piles of seemingly unsorted produce littered the alleys between racks, were left on loading bays, were hanging out of the racking, or were stacked on stationary fork trucks. Boxes and sacks of flour, damaged and torn, leaked their contents. A contractor's truck at the ramp had what seemed like a team of five unloading it. I later found they were the foremen acting – as they often needed to – as an ad hoc back-up reserve labour supply. In the main shed, teams of four to

---

5   Such insulation presents problems for tightly knit and bounded elites – there is a block on the upward communication of information necessary to adapt internal manpower policies, a topic more fully explored in Chapter 8. However, Prof. David Weir in a personal communication writes: 'My old friend and mentor John Harvey Jones [an extremely successful chairman of ICI] was prone to argue that the "essential democracy" of shipboard life had framed him as a manager and made him effective at ICI because on ship officers and men have to work as a team.' But perhaps a ship's crew has more of a shared ideology – the same view of hierarchy is acceptable at all levels. And on a ship, hierarchy is mediated by physical closeness – and because an NCO cadre can keep in contact with both levels, above and below them. At EEW this didn't apply: the levels were separated by divergent cultures and the top hierarchy was distant – socially, culturally and physically – as was the NCO cadre represented by local managers. So at EEW, hierarchy went unmediated.

six warehousemen sorted and picked produce, while ten more were drinking tea in a storeroom that doubled as a restroom and sitting on salvaged seats rescued from broken-up trucks. They comprised both the old who, I later found, were being 'carried' by younger men doing their more onerous work, and members of teams that had completed their immediate tasks.

Divisions between staff levels were marked and were evident in their different lunching arrangements. There were eighty staff members: five managers, twelve clerical staff, twenty-two drivers and mates, thirty-five warehousemen (including five foremen), three vehicle maintenance men and three female canteen staff. Yet though the food was identical and cooked in the same kitchen, the groups ate in four separate dining-rooms. The five managers enjoyed waitress service, their table covered with a clean tablecloth. Clerical staff had their own dining room, served themselves from a side table, and ate at a large scrubbed pine table. Warehousemen, drivers and mates collected their food from the kitchen and ate in their rest room, the floor of which was filthy – as were the adjacent lavatories.

When I suggested it might be beneficial if all groups ate together, the opposition was universal – but strongest from the warehousemen, drivers and mates. This was a system of stratification with which they were at ease.

Though early impressions raised lots of questions, they offered few answers. One question was, why did different staff levels appear unable to understand or communicate with each other? Part of the answer seemed due to the senior manager's hierarchic idea of authority: that in any organization there is only one legitimate source of authority.[6] This view grants no legitimacy to trade unions and offers no place for collective representations. Lower-level professionals in the company asserted that the senior managers' hierarchic ideology derived from the company policy of recruiting its senior managers solely from ex-merchant marine officers. The two cultures appeared preset for mutual incomprehension.

Other questions addressed the senior manager's views on worker motivation. One could appreciate how some behaviours might, at least in part, *seem* to be due to 'worker apathy', 'lack of morale' and 'over-staffing' – as senior executives asserted – or 'mindlessness', as local managers insisted. But union activity appeared anything but apathetic and some areas of the depot exhibited a shortage of labour while others – as the tea drinking evidenced – suggested a surplus. And why, if the company's own trucks were underused, did they consistently hire those of outside firms?[7] Why was the site's 'housekeeping' so neglected? Why was no one willing

---

6   This kind of managerial culture is described by Fox (1974) as 'Unitary' and represents much of what Martin later described as 'an integrationist perspective' by which 'organizational leaders believe they can create a unified, internally consistent, consensually endorsed, organizational culture, cast in their own image [and] reflective of their own personal values – a promise of a kind of organizational immortality' (2002).

7   Several informants on the site asserted that the excessive hiring of externally supplied trucks was facilitated by the site manager, who, it was widely believed, took kickbacks from the hiring firms.

to become a foreman? And why had the union rejected a non-contributory pension scheme? Was all of this due to 'mindlessness'? And why, when the depot had only one entrance/exit, was pilferage so difficult to control? Many of the answers had to do with the intensive and intrusive dock-based culture of the East End.

East End Culture

London's long-established East End community is physically and socially located at the core of London's Docklands. Two features are paramount – the social inheritance derived from the traditional organization of dock work and the strength of localism underpinned by relationships of kinship, marriage and residence.

Historically, East End culture has been moulded by insecurity and poverty. Dock work, the main source of male employment, is inherently erratic and traditionally depended on casual labour.[8] Accordingly, much value in this community – even outside the docks – is still placed on the mutual dependencies that came from union membership and from working within kin- and neighbourhood-based work gangs. The main focus of male affiliation and identity was membership in these dockers' gangs[9] of sixteen men. In the warehouse, smaller teams are similarly valued.

London's East End population has intermarried and lived closely together over many generations. Thus kinship affiliation and residential proximity – localism – operate alongside the positive value afforded to teams, to underpin community relationships (Hobbs 1988). Their combined influences are reinforced in the warehouse by the traditional way work has long been allocated in the East End – through personal patronage, by 'speaking for' a relative, neighbour or friend (Willmott and Young 1957).[10] One in four drivers and warehousemen is linked by close kinship ties (brother, father, uncle, cousin or close male relative by marriage). Overall, two thirds owed their jobs to being 'spoken for' by a patron. We realized the strength of localism when our census revealed that 60 per cent of the labour force live within half a mile of at least five workmates and that none of the foremen or local managers lives in the East End.

How East End culture influences 'normal' working   One way to understand social relationships in the warehouse is to consider them as a system of kin- and locality-based obligations and reciprocities that are owed and repaid over extended periods. These permeate the warehouse and reciprocally feed back to the 'outside' community. The converse also applies: an absence of local links militates against

---

8   It was not until after World War II that London's casual dock labour was 'regulated' – that is, 'decasualized'. See Larrowe (1956) for an explanation of the different sociological implications of regulated and casual labour.

9   Such teams pre-dated introduction of the containerization of ships' cargos.

10   Wilmott and Young (1957) note how the system of 'speaking for' relatives in this community was operated by women to influence the municipality in its allocation of housing to ensure the residential propinquity of mothers and daughters, with parallel practices applying to work allocation by men.

social involvement – the further one originates from the East End, the more distant one is socially and the more removed from the locally derived network of obligations and reciprocities. As we shall see, this explains why foremen frequently unload trucks rather than act as supervisors.

In established dockland communities, kinship and neighbourly obligations and the dependencies and trust these involve are invariably stronger than in comparable urban locations. This is because the bonds of dock employment are buttressed by the erratic nature of the work and the necessity of cooperation, dependability and trust when pilfering cargo. The values these engender extend from the dock to the community in which it is set and to the permeation of workplaces beyond the dock.

In the warehouse, these bonds are manifest in the constituency of work teams so that shed staff arrange to work in self-selected teams, mostly of four to six men. These are strongly cohesive, with members having high commitment to co-workers and demonstrating efficient team coordination. They do not readily take to moves that disturb these relationships. But these very strengths mean there is little readiness for teams to cooperate across their boundaries or to help other teams when they complete their own work. Such 'boundary maintenance' makes them unavailable to do 'housekeeping' work in the shed, so cargo remains where it falls, holes in the roads remain unfilled, and nobody feels it appropriate to sweep the restroom floor. In short, it is the narrow cohesion of the teams that militates against a wider sense of 'communal' responsibility.

Pilferage

Pilfering cargo in the Port of London, as in other ports, has a long history. As stated, Colquhoun (1800, 1806) recorded well-established and extensive pilferage in London's Docklands at the end of the eighteenth century. This work-based pilferage can be considered institutionalized, since traditional dock work had long dominated the local economy and since the basic task in a port – the loading and unloading of cargo by gangs of dockers – had largely remained constant through the centuries.[11] So, too, had the gang's structure of interlocking roles.

Though the gangs had been formally designed and structured to load and unload cargo, they were then informally redesigned and restructured by gang members to facilitate pilferage, as we saw in Chapter 5 (also in Mars 1974 and 1982/1994). And since regular pilferage demands regular distribution, the gains were then routinely allocated through kinship- and community-based networks, thus consolidating relationships in the community. This, then, formed the basis of expected behaviours in the community.

Dock theft and warehouse theft have many similarities. The organization of warehouse theft and its distribution is relatively simple[12] and builds upon the same

---

11   That is, until cargo containerization replaced traditional dock working and new kinds of ships revolutionized cargo handling.

12   See Mars 1982/1994, ch. 5.

sets of expectations. Warehousemen will 'overload' more goods than are invoiced onto trucks manned by drivers with whom they are in alliance, many of them in this warehouse being their sons and nephews. The drivers then drop them off at suitable staging points en route to their destinations. A second method is for a driver to 'drop short' on deliveries – and then collude with a consignee's 'bent' employee to 'check in' less than a full invoiced load.[13] The traditional organization of dock and warehouse pilferage and their distribution therefore celebrate both kin-based and coordinated team enterprise, collective support, mutual trust, and the assertion of autonomous independence.

Unlike in docks, where cargo is heterogeneous and its throughput more erratic, in the warehouse the throughput of stores was both homogeneously routine and regular. This meant that pilferage techniques were there continually reaffirmed and refined, which made them extremely difficult to observe – let alone to detect. The result, combined with managerial distance from the workforce and its ignorance of pilferage's *modus operandi*, was marked: in the year prior to fieldwork, total losses in the warehouse amounted to 2.5 times the estimated total annual wages of the nearly sixty men having access to stored goods.[14]

The returns from institutionalized pilferage are often valued as much for bonding communal relationships as for increasing material gain (Henry and Mars 1978). Pilferage ensured the status, prestige and confirmatory identity of the originators of the process, as it did to those who managed the distribution.

In addition to the intrusion of culturally derived values that directly influence pilferage, three further aspects of 'cultural intrusion' are now considered: warehouse careers; work, gender and identity; and foremen as maligned outsiders.
Warehouse careers and the lifecycle: Allocation to jobs and workgroups   The usual career, as stated, begins through recommendation – by being 'spoken for' by an existing staff member, typically a relative, friend or neighbour, which means workers start employment under obligation to a patron. Their first job is usually on 'order picking' (filling orders for disparate items stored in different locations), which is considered boring and is lowly regarded. As vacancies arise, and if workers are young and fit, they move to be driver's mates and then drivers. These jobs are valued most because of the higher pay earned with allowances, the autonomy enjoyed when on the road, and the enhanced opportunities offered to pilfer goods. As men become older and less fit – bad backs are common – they then move back to the shed. Which team a man will work in thereafter depends on the agreement of existing team members. Those unfit to load or unload trucks can expect to be looked after by younger and fitter colleagues.

---

13   The details and implications of such arrangements are more fully discussed in Mars 1982/1994, ch. 5 and Mars 2001.

14   The figure is based on management-supplied figures for both pilferage and stock shrinkage, which includes the cost of damaged items. Annual earnings are equated with the average household income (Institute for Fiscal Studies 1994).

East End cultural values, therefore, not only influence recruitment: they affect the 'flow' of men between jobs, their placement within work teams, and the unspoken, often unrecognized, obligations and reciprocities that operate between workers.

Work, gender and identity   Gender divisions are marked in the East End: work is the domain of men, home the domain of women (though admittedly these divisions are now weakening). Male status derives from work and obtaining and distributing pilfered goods. To be a man, it is necessary to be seen as a provider not just domestically but within the wider community also. The high proportion of relatively old workers in the warehouse, the refusal to accept a retiring age, and the Union's rejection of the pension scheme can thus be explained by reference to East End culture. As it was pertinently put by a 73-year-old warehouseman when discussing the union's wholehearted rejection of the pension scheme,

> Why should I take a pension? I'd be under the feet of the women all day – and get only half pay.

So older men stay at work, spending much of their time drinking tea. This is perfectly acceptable to the younger men, who do the hardest work on their behalf. East Enders see the lifecycle as a long-term cyclical process with its own essential balance. The young look after their fathers and uncles (and by extension, other older workers), and they can expect to benefit similarly when their time comes: this is part of the community's obligations and its reciprocities, understood by everyone at the warehouse – except the managers and clerical staff. Meanwhile, older men enjoyed both an easy life in the rest room and ongoing prestige at home and in the community.[15]

Foremen as maligned outsiders   As previously stated, the recruitment and selection of foremen is also subject to East End cultural values.

Of the five foremen, none lives within two miles of any other member of the workforce – except another foreman. These men are outsiders. This is a job East Enders do not want, considered suitable only for non East Enders – and other than these five men, there are no other eligible outsiders. This cultural exclusion means not only that foremen are outside the normal net of obligations and reciprocities but also that, being outside the pilferage networks, they have no access to this source of extra 'earnings'. Moreover, it limits their formal authority and in doing so exacerbates their well-understood and stressful role as 'men in the middle' – that is, as situated between management and labour and subject to pressures from both (Whyte and Gardner 1945). It is for these reasons that they are 'forced' into 'fire-fighting' – having to load and unload trucks at short notice – because the autonomy of warehouse workgroups precludes their members working outside

---

15   It has been noted that cultures such as that of the East End, with a strong sense of communal identity and which firmly acknowledge the obligations of kinship, tend also to have an extensive consciousness of time depth. It should not be surprising that this is manifest as an extension of obligations from the young to the old.

their narrowly defined roles. It is hardly surprising that warehousemen should be resistant to becoming foremen when acceptance would involve harder work, material loss, and reduced prestige.

The Consultant's Proposals – and Reactions to them

In an attempt to overcome the near-complete absence of contact and understanding in the warehouse – particularly between management and the warehousemen and drivers – our consultant's report suggested establishing a multilevel steering committee. It would meet regularly to discuss possible grievances and new forms of organization – a variety of alternatives and amalgams were proposed that could take account of and accommodate appropriate aspects of East End culture and provide a conduit for channelling change.

We offered proposals of how alternative payment systems might be proposed – perhaps based on the inbuilt collectivity and team orientations already existing. And, building on the existing collective ethic, the management might consider team- or warehouse-wide bonus systems and/or the payment of awards to individuals or syndicates for productivity suggestions or increases in efficiency.

Our report emphasized that much might be learned by listening to and harnessing views at all levels, that changes could initially be incremental, small scale, testable as pilots, and that – initially at least – they would benefit from consultation rather than imposition. The men were in favour of the proposals and after some scepticism and initial rejection had finally come out firmly in support. The Union was enthusiastic about the idea of a consultative assembly with its step-by-step and testable proposals. This perhaps had something to do with the managers' alternative proposals – they had announced that they were contemplating the warehouse's closure.

The senior managers were appalled, however, when I presented the report. I was told I had 'ignited a hornet's nest in the East End' (!) and was asked, 'Are you trying to set up a Chinese commune?' It seemed the incompatibility of opposed cultures[16] would not easily be bridged.[17]

In East End Warehouse, the management were distant from their labour force – socially, physically and ideologically – which made it difficult for them to understand how different behaviours (including their own) are largely a product of the way jobs are organized and of how workplace behaviours may be influenced by outside cultural factors They were therefore unable to understand the values and motivations of their workforce, which made them ineffective in their dealings with them (Likert 2003). In addition, the insulation of their own cultural values precluded

---

16   An incompatibility of cultures might also be considered as applying between those of the management and the consultants. This was emphasized when I refused to explain the system of pilferage or to identify individuals ('Dammit – we're paying you') – see the 'Ethics' section of the Preface.

17   The report and its proposals are more fully discussed in Mars 2009.

them from suspending (not necessarily abandoning) their moral stance on pilferage, which prevented them analyzing it with clarity. And when they later found I had written extensively on workplace crime but had not incorporated details of it into my report, they were furious. (See the section on ethics in the Preface.)

So What Happened?[18]

The company did not retain the Steering Committee or develop the idea of working in teams, nor did it incorporate others of our behavioural suggestions. Despite its threats and the dire straits it was in, the warehouse was neither closed nor sold but was retained to become a viable business. A new manager was installed, new racking, new trucks and better fork lift trucks were purchased, and the holes in the yard were repaired. At the same time, employment prospects in the East End markedly declined, which reduced the Union's bargaining power, and a compulsory pension scheme with resultant redundancies was imposed.

Simultaneously, changes in retail distribution and developments in computers were occurring that considerably helped to improve efficiency. There was a surge in the growth of supermarkets and a decline in the number of corner shops, which reduced the number of small deliveries (and the opportunities they presented for 'stock leakage'), and this allowed more intensive use of trucks and drivers. Computers also permitted the development of a specialized and compartmentalized pattern of distribution and the introduction of a real-time stock-control system that removed much staff frustration. These allowed better use of space, a reduction in the shed labour force, and a more efficient recording of damage – which reduced pilferers' exploitation of ambiguity. Fortuitous external changes, the appointment of a new local manager and the introduction of new equipment, together proved enough to prevent closure and ensure viability.

Criminogenic Community Cultures

A 'Criminogenic Community Culture' is the term applied here to define a culture liable to high levels of occupational deviance. As indicated, it appears there are at least two archetypal subcategories dependent on whether fiddled gains derive primarily from goods (as archetypically is the case in docks) or in service occupations (as is typical of holiday resorts and pilgrimage centres).

Because goods have a visible presence, they are rarely left unattended and are subject to security measures – controls over their movement, physical checks, and audits. To regularly bypass these, therefore, needs a degree of organization that invariably involves the coordination and support of several people – a team. But effective deviance cannot be achieved instantly: team members need training

---

18   I am grateful to the late Mr Gerry Leech for details of company developments that happened after I left the site.

and the development of trust – which involves investment over time – and shared risk. The institutionalized theft of goods, as in docks and warehouses, therefore involves participants with access to goods who regularly interact over time.

Given that the throughput of goods in warehouses and in docks tends to be regular – indeed, routine – then a parallel organization is necessary for their subsequent and routine distribution. As in the case of East End Warehouse and in the port of St Johns (Chapter 5 of this volume)., this was well served by the symbiotic constancy of a settled community – one bonded by ties of kinship and residential propinquity. These contribute to a unified, identifiable cultural identity that is able to offer support to its participants at all levels. This makes this kind of deviance extremely difficult to counter and explains why it invariably is accommodated, rather than eradicated. These factors are important in determining the criminogenesis of port communities, perhaps the archetypal context from which goods are pilfered.

The situation in holiday resorts and wherever pilgrims and tourists congregate is very different. Here, distinction lies in the provision of services offered by individuals acting in isolation, not of teams in regular interaction. Also, the focus of exploitation is the irregular victim, not the pilfered item, with each victim being one of an irregular sequence of victims, not part of a regular throughput (as discussed in Chapter 3 under the description, 'passing trade'). Service predators are therefore found acting in isolation or are allocated victims according to some preset criteria. But in neither case are teams usually required and there is therefore no available countervailing worker power. Nor are there parallel distributive networks, nor accepted degrees of accommodation to agreed limits. Punishments for infractions therefore tend to be harsh.

In the absence of teams, the isolation of service fiddlers means an absence of the social controls and mutual support that were well evident in the longshore work gangs discussed in Chapter 5. Such teams effectively self-police their members and invariably place limits on the amounts and categories of goods taken. The absence of such controls among service fiddlers explains why excesses in services, when they do occur, are sometimes spectacularly reported as media scandals – 'Shop Assistant's Home was an Aladdin's Cave, Magistrates Told'.

Whereas entry to a team demands the careful vetting of recruits and a process of socialization, these features are largely absent among service fiddlers. Entry to such jobs is more easily achieved and vacancies more readily filled by part-time, transient and casual workers who may be employed just for the busy seasons. Further, since many such jobs are annually 'renewed' each season, this precludes a lack of continuity, training, and the steady accretion of trust necessarily found in places like docks. There is thus a lack of effective memory (and the safeguards this brings to such trades), which contrasts sharply with the long-term memories, well-rehearsed procedures and often rich folklore associated with fiddling possessed by workers in places such as docks and warehouses. As a result, the criminogenesis of the one is consolidated and becomes embedded within its community culture, while that of the other has to be spasmodically regenerated every season.

There are also occupations and organizations, as against communities, that can be considered 'occupationally criminogenic' because their very structure strongly facilitates deviance – therefore, these operate irrespective of their community settings. Examples of their structural underpinnings are discussed in Chapter 3. They are a particular feature of hotels, garage servicing and driver–deliverers – especially of foodstuffs (Ditton 1977). Worldwide reports – and considerable travel by the author – show the near universality of occupational deviance.

References

Baldamus, W. (1961), *Efficiency and Effort: An Analysis of Industrial Administration*, London: Tavistock.

Colquhoun, P. (1800), *A Treatise on Commerce and Police Forces of the River Thames*, London: J. Mawman.

Colquhoun, P.A. (1806), *Treatise on the Police of the Metropolis*, 7th edition, London: J. Mawman.

Ditton, J. (1977), *Part-time Crime*, London: Macmillan.

Fox, A. (1974), *Beyond Contract: Work, Power and Trust Relations*, London: Faber and Faber.

Henry, S. and Mars, G. (1978), 'Crime at Work: The Social Construction of Amateur Property Theft', *Sociology*, 12, 245–63.

Hobbs, D. (1988), *Doing the Business: Entrepreneurship, Detectives and The Working Class in the East End of London*, Oxford: Clarendon Press.

Institute for Fiscal Studies (1994), Family Expenditure Survey 1971–1993/94.

Larrowe, C.P. (1956), *Shape Up and Hiring Hall*, Berkeley, CA: University of California Press.

Likert, J. (2003). *The Toyota Way: 14 Management Principles from the World's Greatest Manufacturer*, New York: McGraw Hill.

Mars, G. (1974), 'Dock Pilferage', in P. Rock and M. McIntosh (eds), *Deviance and Social Control*, London: Tavistock, 209–28.

Mars, G. (1982/1994), *Cheats at Work: An Anthropology of Workplace Crime*, London: Allen and Unwin; Aldershot: Dartmouth.

Mars, G. (ed.) (2001), *Workplace Crime*, Aldershot: Dartmouth.

Mars, G. (2009), 'East-End Warehouse: A Case Study of 'Organizational Capture' and Cultural Conflicts', *Culture and Organization*, 15, 237–56.

Martin, J. (2002), *Organizational Culture: Mapping the Terrain*, London: Sage.

Whyte, W.F. and Gardner, B.B. (1945), 'The Man In The Middle: Facing The Foreman's Problems', *Applied Anthropology*, Spring, 1–28.

Willmott, P. and Young, M. (1957), *Family and Kinship in East London*, London: Routledge & Kegan Paul.

A Note on Chapters 7 and 8: Organizational Perversion

The following two chapters – 7 and 8 – discuss three case studies that reveal how the aims, resources and structures of organizations may be manipulated and 'captured' by individualist managers for their own short-term opportunist concerns. Chapter 7's two case studies reveal how such 'organizational capture' led to 'organizational tyranny' and the perversion of the organization's objectives – where power is exercised in the absence of inherent checks and balances that have been systematically removed. Chapter 8's account of a factory in Soviet Georgia is concerned with an individualist management's abstraction of power from distant controllers, an example of 'organizational capture' with implications for local autonomy in its opposition to globalized management.

Chapter 7

Individualism and Egalitarianism: 'Organizational Capture' and 'Organizational Tyranny'

Introduction

This chapter introduces the ideas of 'Organizational Capture' and of 'Organizational Tyranny'[1]. Its two cases are based on long-term participant observation, to reveal the processes by which tyrannous organizations emerge and become established. The first concerns the evolution of a group of recruitment consultants; the second, the introduction of change in a business school. Both record the emergence of similar political processes, strategies and techniques to demonstrate their elites' increasing control over information, recruitment, resources and discipline. In both studies, a redundant rhetoric is employed, based on previously held but abandoned values.

The two cases here (and the following one from Soviet Georgia, Chapter 8) well illustrate the advantages of participant observation (PO) as a research method: richly detailed information is obtainable at first hand by direct involvement in social processes. One disadvantage of PO, however, is that it can involve partiality in interpretation and this can distort perceptions of what is happening. In the first case study, since the author describes scapegoat selection and the scapegoat was the author, impartiality might be thought difficult to sustain. The reader, as they say, must be the judge.

Case 1: The Recruitment Consultants

For eighteen years I had the opportunity – somewhat like a cuckoo in the nest – to observe the dynamics and evolution of a small close-knit group of recruitment consultants who serviced the executive selection needs of a large multinational company. The group had a stable membership of approximately ten members who, myself excepted, were all psychoanalytically oriented clinical psychologists. I was involved at all stages as the group moved from being a loose aggregate of segmented individuals, through group-based idealistic egalitarianism – the Enclave – to different stages of bureaucratic control – Hierarchy – and finally to

---

1 'Tyranny' as applicable to organizations was first suggested by Mary Douglas (1992a, p. 144), who focused on the control of information by elites and noted its dysfunctions.

its emergence as a Tyrannous Organization where power was consolidated in the authority of two dominant members.

Though forming an enclave, the consultants were not an extreme enclave like the terrorist groups described in Chapter 4. Their group strength was modified since members had other jobs and were all part-time consultants, but its Enclavism was strengthened by its homogeneous professional membership recruited from an extremely narrow base. As an Enclave group, therefore, they were relatively closed, emphasized Egalitarianism – everyone had to have a fair share of the available work – and regarded each other as professional equals, eschewing rankings and differences in status. They were thus reluctant to legitimize authority, strictly controlled entry, and often ejected 'the internally impure'. They cohered in effect by opposing 'the outside', which they regarded with suspicion.

An opposition has been identified (Hatch and Schultz 1993) between clinical – that is, psychoanalytic – and ethnographic approaches to understanding organizations. Each approach tends to preclude understanding of the other and this proved important in the group's relationship to me as ethnographer. As this group was predominantly clinical, a 'blind spot' allowed structures to arise that traduced those very egalitarian principles in which it saw itself grounded.[2] Conversely, as the only ethnographic member, professionally aware of such cultural changes, I came to be perceived as an unaccountable critical voice – disruptive and an intrusion from outside. Such dynamics have been less readily applied to organizations in the developed world but have been extensively recorded in the ethnographic literature of other cultures. There they have been noted as concerned to establish boundaries against the outside and to reject what has been termed 'insidious harm' within.[3]

In analyzing this case, I examine the political manoeuvrings by which organizational capture was effected to show how this organization changed its form – first by shifting from its enclavic, egalitarian bias to a more stratified and rule-based hierarchic one. The analysis then demonstrates how such deepening of political process led to a further shift – to tyranny.

In the Beginning: The Patriarch and Primeval History

The changes described here took place over a two- to four-year period during the late 1980s and early 1990s. The group, however, had been created in 1947 by Arnold,[4] an entrepreneurial charismatic. Arnold had a distinguished record in World War II, being demobilized in his mid-thirties with the rank of Lt. Colonel. During his war service, he'd played a major role in designing and establishing the famed WASBs, the War Office Selection Boards that chose officers on objective

---

    2   Storr (1997) has noted the propensity to rivalry and boundary maintenance among psychoanalysts.

    3   See, for example, Gluckman 1955 and Douglas 1992b.

    4   Names have been changed.

psychologically based criteria designed to overcome the errors of biased selection that had proved so unsatisfactory in World War I.

On demobilization, Arnold was convinced that principles underpinning the WASBs should be adopted in industry[5] to select trainee executives and he convinced a major multinational company to recruit management trainees according to its principles. Arnold set up a group of part-time consultant advisers to service the multinational's selection needs. The procedures he established are still considered highly successful and have remained largely unchanged for over fifty years.

Applicants, in groups of eight, assembled for a long day of psychological tests, interviews, and the performing of group tasks in which they discussed 'Management Cases' written by Arnold. These tasks were carried out under the watchful eyes of four senior executives, who made the decisions, and two consultant advisers, who administered the tests, interviewed the candidates, advised the executives, and interpreted the process. A junior 'Board Manager' was on hand to organize the board's logistics throughout the day and a senior personnel executive, the 'Board President', oversaw the process.

This company's boards were unique. The selectors were all top senior executives, from the main board chairman down. Arnold had been particularly keen to introduce this feature, which was warmly supported by senior managers, who rarely missed attendance. Their presence served three valued functions: to provide a link between the senior and most junior managers in the company; to form a managerial 'college' in helping managers overcome the insularity of single-company involvement within a large multinational; and finally, to ensure higher management's continuous involvement in selection, which they, together with Arnold, considered a crucial aspect of personnel relations.

Arnold's sharp intelligence, his extensive and comparative experience, and his wide network of contacts developed over long association with this and other companies made him invaluable as an all-purpose 'on tap' advisor and led to frequent invitations to join the board (all of which he rejected). As a result, there emerged an implicit contract between him and the company: in return for Arnold's continuous involvement in its affairs, the company delegated all aspects of selection to him. Arnold was given, in effect, an unencumbered monopoly to run the process: control of selection throughout the company was regarded as his 'property'.

Arnold, active and lively in his eighties, still sat on occasional boards throughout the period described here, indented the company for the consultants' fees, and deducted a levy to pay for secretarial support before dividing the balance. Consultants were paid a fee for each board and averaged service on twenty boards per year. In conformity with their enclavic bias, the consultants' group was much concerned that boards be shared equally.

---

5   Variations on the structure of these selection boards were quickly adopted – and still operate – as integral to UK Civil Service and Foreign Office recruitment. The basic model has now become widespread throughout much of British industry. It is still used within all four UK armed services.

All members of the group, except the author, had backgrounds as career advisers and therapists. However, I, with an industrial and applied anthropology background, had been imposed on the group by Arnold. He was a great believer in multidisciplinary work and a fan of anthropology.

Arnold's imposition of someone not psychoanalytically trained, however, was understandably resented, as was made frequently clear throughout the period I was a member. At one meeting, I was rebuked, to general agreement, for passingly describing someone's behaviour as 'paranoid'. I was not a psychoanalyst and, therefore, not qualified to use the term.

Under the regime Arnold instituted, a group could hardly be said to have existed and at first the co-opted consultants operated more as a loose conglomerate of individuals who met together in pairs at each board; egalitarian enclavism only entered later….

From Enclave to Hierarchy I: An Evolving Structure

The first sign of a shift in the group's structure – and the values associated with it – were initiated by two of its longest-serving members, Herbert and his partner Elaine. Herbert had calculated that the levy deducted for secretarial support by Arnold from the aggregate earnings of the group, was disproportionately large; that, indeed, there should have been a considerable surplus over and above the amount Arnold retained and that his secretary's services were extensively available for purposes unconnected to the work of the group. Arnold, they argued, was exploiting us.

Herbert pointed out to members of the group at different times that, if they were to cooperatively run the group themselves, they could arrange their own secretarial requirements at minimal cost, redistribute the full amount released, and avoid paying the levy. As a result, he said, earnings could rise by approximately 20 per cent. But his big 'selling point' was the opportunity for group's members to 'run their own affairs'.

When Herbert and Elaine were sure of majority support, Herbert approached Arnold, told him that group members now wanted to be autonomous, and that therefore it was time for a change. Though the group would continue working with him as a consultant, Arnold would from then on be merely one among several. They would continue to share the work equally according to availability but now could run their own affairs according to their own criteria. One concern was to gain control over recruitment; another was to deal direct with the company rather than have Arnold act as a monopolist controller of information derived from his dealings with it that affected their interests. Arnold had little choice but to accept what amounted to a *coup d'état*.[6]

---

6   In a sense, Arnold had been hoisted by his own petard. As a psychoanalyst, he had always argued and had taught his followers that a prime aim of consultants should be to encourage clients in self-sufficiency – to 'grow up' without dependence on them. Herbert

Herbert called a meeting of consultants (but without Arnold) to discuss how to liaise with the company and coordinate the group's affairs in the absence of Arnold. Much concern was expressed about the dangers of again having too much power accruing to any one individual and of the control over information this involved. As is usual in enclaves, however, nobody appeared willing to take on either of Arnold's roles. It was finally agreed to have 'Rolling Coordinators' who would each hold office for a month at a time. In a further push to Egalitarianism, and because several women members said they perceived an anti-feminist bias in dealings with the company, it was decided to alternate the coordinator's role: it would be rotated between male and female members month on month. No roster was agreed, but Herbert was chosen as the group's first monthly coordinator and he put the new arrangement to his opposite number, the company's head of recruitment. He, however, firmly rejected the new arrangement, arguing that he couldn't liaise with serially rotated coordinators. To him, consistency was essential: he insisted upon an ongoing relationship with a single individual.

When Herbert announced the head's rejection, there was considerable consternation. The company was seen as undermining the group's Egalitarianism. But again, no one was willing to take on a position of responsibility. After much discussion and to general relief, Herbert reluctantly accepted being co-coordinator for a limited (but unspecified) period during which he 'would see how it goes'. He would only do so, however, if he could delegate some of the tasks to a deputy. Elaine was then prevailed upon to act as deputy, which she, with similar reluctance, eventually accepted on the same terms. This arrangement, however, was to crystallize, with only periodic alternations of the two roles between the two of them.[7]

From Enclave to Hierarchy II: Instituting Rules, Tightening Controls

This new structure facilitated the emergence and consolidation of a powerful executive comprising Herbert and Elaine. This duo had esoteric access to information not generally available, since it was mainly the coordinator and deputy who had access to senior company staff. It was from these contacts that 'spin-off' and lucrative consultancy work often derived. Information was thus able to be differentially allocated, at the duo's discretion, to selected individuals – with some leading to well-paid projects within the company. There were no agreed or specified criteria governing the allocation of such information – and more importantly the projects they led to – which lay entirely at the discretion of the duo. The accounts give no indication of earnings from this source.

However, if an executive is not to be impotent, it needs a consistent source of, and control over, resources to reward those it wishes to favour or, by retention, to

---

was, in effect, arguing that the group had now 'outgrown' Arnold and that it was time for it to be self-sufficient.

7   A very similar arrangement, rotating roles to effect egalitarianism but that similarly crystallized over time, is discussed as occurring in Israeli Kibbutzim. See Mars 1988.

penalize those it does not. Thus by favouring selected members of the group, it can buttress its power – ensuring the compliance of the favoured and the optimism of the disenfranchised. So if it could obtain resources, the duo would hold the power to orchestrate support in favour of itself when needed. Equally, control over resources would give it leverage to increase its own rewards. But how to obtain such resources? The only way was to re-impose the levy, which it could then administer at its own discretion.

To avoid drawing too obvious a parallel with Arnold's individualist practices, however, this reintroduction of the levy had to be cloaked in the rhetoric of egalitarian professionalism. It was suggested, therefore, that, as before, the levy be deducted from earnings but this time would be used to increase the group's professional expertise: it would be spent on 'research' and would thus contribute to the group's overall professionalism. Everyone would therefore benefit.

Research, it transpired, was not defined but emerged as 'inner directed' – that is, as concerned with collecting and processing statistics about the workings of the company's boards and assessing and reassessing their procedures and the processing of candidates through them. This 'research' would be paid for out of the levy at consultancy-level rates to those members of the group selected by the duo. Research in the sense of accessing wider academic expertise of possible professional use to the group, was never considered. Nor was concern to explore the hiring practices of other companies and the nature of their psychological advice. Two members of the group had doctorates and both business and academic research experience – but according to the group's limited definition of research, there was no call for, or need of, their services.

Herbert then suggested establishing a number of administrative procedures. First, regular meetings would be held every month to keep abreast of members' activities at the selection boards. Second, the group, through the coordinator, should be informed of any member's other contacts with the company and its staff. Finally, he suggested a written 'report-back' procedure by which members would complete detailed reports about the events that had occurred at each board. 'It would be a useful source of data,' said Herbert, 'and would underpin the research necessary to enhance the group's professionalism.' These proposals were accepted with little group discussion and considerable enthusiasm, though in total they involved considerable time, extra work and, in their later processing as 'research', considerable expense.

Part of the levy was then used to make sizeable payments to the coordinator and deputy coordinator. A statement of payments for one half year[8] reveals considerable differentials. It shows the average sum paid to all consultants including 'payments for research' was £5,389, while the coordinator and deputy coordinator received £7,976 and £7,076 respectively. The convener received an additional £3,056 as a specific coordinator's fee that took her total receipts to £11,032, while expenditure

---

8   Unfortunately this was the only set of figures available. There is no reason, however, to think that they are atypical.

paid to Herbert as the then deputy coordinator for 'Statistics' and 'Finance/Accts' amounted to a further £1,150. In addition, if we include a payment of £783 for secretarial work by Herbert's wife (who was not a member of the group), this brought his total to £9,009.

Another way of interpreting these accounts is to identify *total* receipts accruing to the four levels to include payments for putative 'research' and other not fully specified payments.

Table 7.1   A comparison of all receipts allocated to the three levels

Level	Notes	Total (£)
Executive Duo		
Coordinator		11,032
Deputy Coordinator		9,009
	(includes secretarial work by the coordinator's wife)	783
Second Level	The Middle Core (average)	6,334
Third Level	The Base of Four (average)	3,832

What emerged within this group of ten, therefore, was a three-level hierarchy, each getting markedly differing receipts. The executive duo, in controlling resources and information, benefited disproportionately from so doing – though their extra earnings from the company are not recorded; the second tier (the core) gained some of the 'research' fees and access to some extra earnings from the company, but this too was not recorded; while the third level (the base) was excluded from such benefits. Some of the base, however, could 'live in hope' and therefore be 'kept on board' as supporters of the elite.

At this point, with three levels of stratification, its institution of rules and procedures, its wide range of pay differentials, the re-imposition of a levy, its restrictive control of information, and its allocation of differential rewards, the group emerges as having negated all the egalitarian principles[9] used to justify its autonomy. The process of organizational capture had effectively passed from Enclavism to Hierarchy. It had, however, further to go.

---

9   Steve Rayner usefully distinguishes two kinds of egalitarianism: 'strict equality egalitarianism', which insists on equity of access and accumulation, and 'equal opportunity egalitarianism', which offers differential access to goods or influence as people choose. This group originally espoused the former, but, after instituting its elite, it quickly moved towards, yet never achieved, equal opportunities. See ch. 2 in Flanagan and Rayner 1988.

From Hierarchy to Tyranny: The Organization 'Digs its Trap'

With the group effectively captured, the elite duo then operated a variety of features that brought the organization to tyranny, with concomitant destabilization, and eventually to its disastrous dysfunction (Douglas 1992a, p. 144). Key to this process is the elite's controls over upward flows of communication and the absence of checks and balances limiting its power. To these I add the introduction of coercive structures through which an elite's power might be applied and the use of these against scapegoats. These features operated in unison.

The control of information: Censorship   Limits on the upward flow of information reveal the essence of tyrannous organization:

> Hierarchy needs information to flow from bottom up as well as top down. The channels of information being organized vertically and authority being centralized, it is a truism of organization theory that sending commands down is easier than receiving news from below as a truly collegial hierarchy would require. The subversion of a Hierarchy into a Tyranny is easy. This kind of society works well in situations needing strong centralized command. To work efficiently it needs good intelligence. But because the system depends on the consent of the majority who benefit only as a collectivity, reasons must be given for explaining why some (only a few) are in the command positions.[10] The value of the reasons depends on the value of the system as a whole to those it privileges least. They need to perceive a spill over[11] from the powerful individual's transactions to themselves as a collective.
>
> Inevitably the command fears its chain of reasoning is not strong enough to be convincing and is tempted to exclude the voices of the followers. When the normative–moral debate becomes an affair of the elite, there is a tendency to reinforce good reasons with censorship. Censorship spells the end of the flow of information on which hierarchy depends and digs its trap. (Douglas 1992a, p. 144)

The trap, as we shall see, involves mounting destabilization because of the inability of tyrannies to adapt to change as they become progressively more insulated from their environments. We earlier saw how this group, in effect, controlled information by its narrow definitions of research and restrictions on which members could carry it out. It is useful, however, to extend the idea of such controls – here termed 'censorship' – to include *all* restrictions and controls on information. This widened definition, therefore, would include the group's insistence on being made aware of 'contacts with the company' that was an early edict of the duo. Crucial too was the group's control over recruitment.

---

10   Not difficult, as here, when there is an enclavic reluctance to accept authority.
11   That is, a trickle down of resources or at least the possibility of this,

Controls over recruitment as a form of censorship Control over boundaries is a feature of all strongly defined groups. One form of boundary control is invariably effected by imposing restrictions on who is recruited. It operated here as a form of censorship, since excluding recruits necessarily also excludes access to their knowledge of, information about, and contacts with the outside.

Restrictions involved all applicants for entry to the group having to possess a clinical background before they could even be considered. This achieved, the processes they were put through – prior consideration by the elite, interviews with the duo, and 'trial boards' – weeded out most applicants. In this case, limiting the entry of new consultants might be seen as an attempt to retain a greater share of total receipts. But the almost continuous rejection of any new recruits more strongly suggests an anxiety to ensure homogeneity of values and, to this end, to limit entry to those sharing the backgrounds and experience of group members and to those whose preferences accorded with those of the elite – as they were discussed with the core before being put to the group as a whole.

There was no circulation of applicants' CVs or discussion of their professional qualifications or experience, nor any definitions of what criteria should govern entrance to the group. The minutes give no effective reasons for exclusion, the decisive factor for which was undefined – with any one member having the power of veto. This again is a feature of Enclavism where there is invariably reluctance to reveal internal discord and suspicion of outside 'contamination'. The minutes of one meeting, record the following comments on four potential recruits:

Lillian X:	'John has reservations. Wait for her to contact us....'
James Y:	'Elaine has reservations. Also wait for initiative from him....'
Alice Z:	'Suggested by Mary: No take up by others....'
Henry C:	'Now working more in the NHS than in career work....'

We are now in a position to assess the extent and results of censorship employed by this group and to consider its effects.

Censoring Action I

The group limited its recruitment to those with a clinical psychological specialization, by far the biggest proportion being recruited from the same training 'stable'.

Main effects

1. The group lost the benefits of wider experience and the information this could have supplied. It selected clones of its members who, similarly, lacked not only exposure to disciplines other than psychology/psychoanalysis but also wider experience of industry.

2. By refusing to acknowledge information that lay outside its experience, the group failed to appreciate explanations of candidates' behaviours, attitudes and values not explained by psychological categories. It thus negated cultural and class influences on behaviour.
3. Being unwilling to spend resources on researching the variant cultures of different companies within the multinational, the group negated possibilities of matching work cultures more closely to candidate characteristics that might have offered it a unique selling point.

Censoring Action II

The group limited its 'research' to assessments of the internal selection processes of the company.

Effect Appreciation of developments in the theory and practice of comparative selection was inhibited.

Censoring Action III

The group's 'inward' research that was limited to its own methods of selection was undertaken by its less qualified group members.

Effect More qualified researchers could have offered access to more relevant research methods and findings.

Censoring Action IV

The group neglected to explore the recruitment practices of rival companies.

Effect The group reduced its ability to assess its own market position vis-à-vis the company employing its members and was in no position to expand its client base when this later proved necessary.

It was the total effects of censorship in influencing, indeed controlling, both internal and external information flows that was to prove crucial in determining the group's fate.

Control and Coercion: Scapegoat Selection without Checks or Balances

Control of information – defined here as 'censorship' – is insufficient of itself to ensure a hierarchy's transition to tyranny. Further requirements have to be met that involve an absence of the more usual hierarchic checks and balances against elite power. This means the elite has to create coercive institutional arrangements. 'Coercive' is used here in the sense that they can be instituted without due process at the instigation of the elite on terms that are invariably ambiguously defined – and that they operate without the constraints of defensive procedures. It is, perhaps, worth reminding ourselves that we are considering this group as a cultural phenomenon, irrespective of its efficacy for its intended task: structural modalities entail unforeseen outcomes and it is the job of the ethnographer to disclose these with as much objectivity as he – in this case – can muster.

Scapegoat accusations in my case focused on breaches of the group's boundary. I spent a social evening with the multinational's head of recruitment and was rebuked by the coordinator for not having reported this as 'a contact with the company'. Later, when asked by the head of recruitment to draft a pamphlet about selection, I raised this with the coordinator as 'a contact' and was told this was 'not an individual but a group concern'. To general agreement, he appointed a group nominee to join me in the task for half the fee. The head of recruitment, however, insisted he wouldn't accept a jointly written pamphlet, asserting I'd been chosen (by his superior, it emerged) because I had writing and publishing experience. Further, there was need to complete the task quickly, which was considered unlikely with group involvement. Since he, as client, 'called the tune', I went ahead and independently submitted a draft. This led to proposals at a group meeting that, as I had ignored group interests, I should still give up half my fee to the group. Discussions were then raised to devise procedures and sanctions for actions seen as 'against the interests of the group'.

This accusation was later augmented by the claim that 'a number of managers' had questioned my interviewing methods. There was an absence of detail about which aspects of interviewing practice were questionable, which managers were involved, how many of them, and how many incidents had occurred.[12] These accusations couldn't be rebutted because they were unspecified – the classic form of an accusation of 'insidious harm'.

At this stage, perceiving the value of installing disciplinary procedures, the duo suggested a working group be established to ensure 'the maintenance of professional standards'. These were undefined. It was then proposed that the working group agree on appropriate sanctions though no grading of penalties was suggested, the only sanction envisaged being dismissal from the group. No appeal processes or independent arbitrational procedures were envisaged. From their reception, it was apparent that these proposals had been discussed within the core of privileged members prior to their presentation to the group as a whole.[13] Before these procedures could be established, I voluntarily left the group.

---

12   A considerable time later, I found that two events six months apart were cited as evidence of an unsympathetic approach to two candidates who had asked for feedback after particularly poor showings at the board.

13   In the event these suggestions were not followed through, possibly because a legal source had suggested they contravened common law and could not be sustained.

The perception of 'insidious harm', the basis of scapegoating and witchcraft accusations, means that accusations cannot be defended: the less explicable the perceived offence is held to be, the greater can emphasis be laid on its unnaturalness or perversity, on, the 'hidden-ness' of its alleged source and power. This characteristic has been observed in various cultures, not least that of the European witch-hunts of the seventeenth century A further characteristic is that it is particularly prevalent in small isolated groups (Douglas 1992b, p. 90).

The 'strategies of exclusion and rejection' on the grounds of 'insidious harm' support tyrannies in several ways. They 'encourage the others'; add to the elite's esteem by having 'unmasked' a threat; confirm the elite's legitimacy; and enhance the elite's hold on power. They increase the group's cohesion, 'by inculpating some, it exculpates others' (Douglas 1992b, p. 94), in the face of a perceived threat. Finally, they institute a new set of circumstances, allowing the jettisoning of the old in favour of the new.

Two years after leaving the group, I met one of its members. 'How is the group getting along?' I enquired. It seemed she too had left it, having also found the atmosphere increasingly not to her liking. Then she said: 'There was one interesting development. Whenever the group found it had a problem, someone would always say, "What would Gerry have said?"' Just as the group had a structural need for a scapegoat, so it seemed it had a similar need for a sustaining legend: their memory of the group's scapegoat had morphed into a benign ancestral myth.

In the End...

It will be remembered that the group's origins lay in its recruitment by Arnold, a figure with charismatic appeal based on the civilian development of his war-time experience and wide and extensive business sagacity that were much appreciated by the multinational's hierarchy. Under Arnold, the group had had nearly fifty years' continual existence, spanning immense change. Socially, economically and in organizational terms, Arnold had managed the group's disposition towards the outside, controlled its internal relationships, and handled its immediate relations with the company. The duo's much more limited experience in all of these spheres – reinforced by their isolation and hubris – were to provide the backdrop to the group's eventual demise.

Decline began with the introduction of new case studies to replace those drafted by Arnold and which were presented to the candidates for discussion. Herbert's view was that Arnold's cases were out of date – and he wrote new ones. These were introduced but found to lack reality by a number of significant senior managers. When it emerged that they had been produced not by Arnold but by Herbert, this highlighted Herbert's lack of comparative experience. Senior managers came to be increasingly absent from the boards and their lack of involvement severed the close link they had with the selection process.

The next step in the group's decline came when the company managers administering the selection boards, came under pressure to cut costs. Without senior management's buttressing of the 'implicit contract' that had granted Arnold – and later the group – its monopoly in selection matters, they proposed that much of the process – including the psychological testing of candidates – should now be carried out at the candidate's own universities by the company's relatively junior managers rather than being done in London by more expensive consultants. They offered to pay the group to train their junior managers in how to administer psychological tests. The duo resisted the proposal 'on professional grounds', insisting that only fully qualified psychologists could effectively test candidates,[14] and they refused to train company executives or collaborate with the amended process, not appreciating the tenuous nature of their now changed relationship with the company. The company's response, not surprisingly, was to seek psychological support from outside the group and an external psychologist was appointed to train the company's junior managers. This proved highly successful and economically viable.

The company's management then considered dissolving 'the implicit contract' by putting the selection process out to tender. In response, the duo sought to solicit selection work with other companies but, lacking both wider external experience and contacts, was unsuccessful. In the event, the company's final decision was narrowly made to retain the group – 'on the basis of the Devil you know' – but in a much attenuated form.[15] It had been confirmed that much of the process could be carried out at the candidate's own universities without any participation of the group. More significantly, only one consultant was to service each London board, rather than two as previously. At a stroke, this more than halved demand for the group's services, which were further reduced by an increase in the recruitment of 'mid-career' applicants, at the expense of graduate recruitment, who were not subject to selection boards.

I have no first-hand information on later developments.[16] The duo, however, ceased work on company selection, while present consultants are not only fewer and earn considerably less than previously but the totality of consultants now apparently retains more of the characteristics of a loose conglomerate than of a group. After nearly fifty years' association with the company, the group had lost its position as putative 'owner' of the selection process, with a resultant loss of earnings.

---

14   In this they followed the official policy of the British Psychological Society that has long held this untenable claim to professionalism – and its buttressing of the earning of its members.

15   As recounted to me later by an involved senior manager.

16   In an attempt to remedy this lack, I offered an earlier, but not too different, draft of this paper to two members of the group with a request for comments and any suggested corrections. They submitted it to the rest of the group, then wrote saying they found 'considerable inaccuracies' but would not specify what these were, and that they would not 'comment in detail'. When I pressed for guidance as to what inaccuracies they referred to, they said the group 'had difficulty engaging with the paper'. To ensure accuracy about events after I had left the group, I then contacted a senior executive of the company who had had close dealings with the group. Some of my account of the group's decline derives from this source.

Did the group's members perceive the looming threat to its existence? It seems not. It is characteristic of enclaves, whose rhetoric they continued to espouse, that much of its energies remained directed at maintaining the group's integrity against a perceived, if inchoate, threat or intrusion. As real threats mounted and in the isolation it had created for itself through censorship, the group directed its attention against 'insidious harm' being perpetrated from within and which led to my own resignation from the group.

The group's demise began when the premises for those intentions departed further and further from the alternative reality of the surrounding context. Finally, as the group diverged from its own egalitarian principles and in order to preserve those self-same principles, the strategies it had orchestrated for its preservation – control, censorship and social exclusion – were the very means that brought about its downfall. Nonetheless, it still maintained an egalitarian rhetoric to justify its non-egalitarian practices – its reintroduction and mal-distribution of the levy, its centralized decision making, differential payments, monopolistic control, and its partiality in allocating information.

Despite its 'founding charter' aimed to remedy the alleged excesses of Arnold by increasing professionalism and preserving egalitarianism, these aims were subsequently negated by the individualist duo: professionalism did not increase and some members became demonstrably much 'more equal' than others.

Case 2: The University Business School – More Business than School?

This second case of organizational capture that led to a tyrannous organization is also based on participant observation. Since it displays the same structural processes and managerial strategies as did the consultancy group, they are not elaborated here to the same degree.

In the late 1980s, I took a job at a university school of policy studies to design and run a Masters degree in Crime Risk Management. Early in my appointment, however, the Policy School – together with me and my course – were absorbed into the university's Business School. At that time, it was well into initiating changes to its administrative structure under the direction of a new director.

Such changes served to devalue the significance of normatively moral values in favour of economic 'rationality', a trend that has now spread to other sectors of higher education[17] – and beyond. This trend however, has proved stronger in university business schools than elsewhere, partly because universities from the 1990s on have been suffering budget controls imposed by government and partly because at that time business schools were enjoying enthusiastic support while they were expanding. Therefore, they were, and to an extent still are, seen as

---

17   In discussing this case, I have been offered details of similar processes that have been introduced in a wide range of normative–moral organizations. These include museums, art galleries and hospitals.

milch cows by their university controllers, who charge levies of up to 60 per cent on their extra-curricular earnings. These derive mainly from consultancies and short courses. It thus shouldn't surprise if university administrators select their directors primarily on the likelihood of their increasing earnings rather than on their academic backgrounds.

This school's director had been recruited from the marketing directorship[18] of a major multinational. He was of minimal academic standing but had nonetheless been appointed ahead of a notable scholar who subsequently went on to revitalize a business school elsewhere.

On appointment, the school's director quickly promoted as his deputy director, a lecturer who, though not shining at research, was nonetheless a whizz at selling short courses and drumming up lucrative consultancy. The director was free to make such a unilateral choice because his new policy allowed him to sit on all selection boards and take key decisions on all cases of promotion. Entering the Business School in the way I did, meant I had bypassed his selection process.

My insights into the workings of the Business School began early. In my first week, I was invited to lunch with the director, A kindly colleague took me aside beforehand. 'Look,' he warned, 'when you meet him – be careful. Don't mention "ologies": they get him very bothered.'

Though he had warned me off 'ologies', he unfortunately hadn't also warned me off 'theories'.

The director was short and brisk, with a self-assured confidence. He appeared concerned to project the image of a practical man with little time for theory and he asked me to explain what the course was about and who it was targeted at.

But it wasn't easy to explain what the course was about without recourse to 'ologies' or 'theories', and it became obvious as the meal staggered on that he was indeed bothered by references to them. He was soon expressing exasperation and it became apparent we had little common ground. Theories in particular seemed to irritate him. This wasn't because of intellectual weakness, but because he apparently wanted his staff to project a hands-on 'practical management' image of the school, its staff and its courses. This, he believed, was what managers wanted – and would, as he saw it, maximize the school's income. I soon surmised he thought me deficient in that role.

As lunch continued, and as I falteringly kept on trying to describe a Masters degree with minimal recourse to either theories or 'ologies', he began to assert more and listen less. He then made his management style clear and announced that after his arrival he had followed a policy of 'prunings', which he explained meant 'sackings and early retirements':

---

18   The same marketing provenance was revealed as applying to many CEOs of banks, including Bob Diamond, appointed in the period immediately prior to the '2008/9 credit crunch' to head the Royal Bank of Scotland, the biggest defaulter of all UK banks. This rise to prominence of individualists is explored more fully in Chapter 9.

I run a tight ship. The first thing I had to do here was abolish tenure. They hated me for that.

My position as an invalidated new arrival was then made clear:

If you don't like the way we play tennis here and prefer to do ballet – then I'd advise you to go where they do ballet....

He was pleased to tell me that the school provided a significant proportion of the parent university's overheads – which is why, I later surmised, the university was so lax in overseeing the quality of what was sold as their Business School's 'products', and why there were surprising variations from the quality standards that (then) were routinely found in other universities.

After his appointment, the pressure to extend economic 'rationality' proceeded apace. It was determined not just by the fee level of its flagship MBA course but by fees charged for tailored short courses – close to £3,000 per head for a weekend's residential course. For consultancies, staff members were charged out at £1,500 per day for a raw lecturer to £2,500+ per day for more senior staff. With income at this level, there were strong vested interests to maintain the school's approach to its market. The university – keen to cherish their milch cow – gave its director a free hand, soon titled him 'Professor', and rapidly promoted him to be the university's deputy vice-chancellor.

One obvious way to understand how an organization works is to comparatively examine its formal procedures – especially its rules. Rules here were manipulated to reduce standards and increase student numbers to raise revenue. Thus, rule bending was extended to the recruitment of students whose fees were a prime consideration in their selection. One applicant for the Masters degree, for example, was given a place despite my revelation that his application was blatantly fraudulent: 'We're too low on numbers to bother about that.'

The easing of standards also applied to research theses. Universities have rules about their length. PhD theses typically range from maxima of 70,000 to 100,000 words; the Business School, however, specified a maximum of only 50,000 words, little more than is normally required for a research Masters degree.

But understanding formal rules must be complemented by assessing *informal* procedures, particularly concerning deviance and rule bending – aspects of organization that didn't feature in the school's teachings on Organization.

Due to the low priority afforded research and the pressure on staff to do consultancy, the research rating of the school, at Grade 3, was lower than that of many non-research-oriented ex-polytechnics.[19] The divergence was only partly overcome by recourse to incessant PR and the school's revamped and much-

---

19   Of six levels of research ratings, the Business School was in the fourth level from the top. In a randomly selected monthly newsletter (Sept. 1992), a column headed 'Papers and Publications' listed thirteen papers, only one of which had been published in a peer-

quoted 'mission statement'. In its reiterated 'false rhetoric', this paralleled the founding assertions of the recruitment consultancy.

The school's system of incentives, encouragement of individualist entrepreneurialism, and subservience to its market meant that staff members were encouraged to informally bend procedures. Some paid more accomplished scholars to write journal articles for them. These were then submitted for onward submission to the RAE (the Research Assessment Exercise that governed the level of government funding). Being sensitive to market valuations, they settled on a fee of £500 per paper.

One difference between 'customers' and 'students' is that commercial undertakings primarily aim to satisfy the perceived demands of their customers, while the prime aim of academic institutions should be to guide their students into areas of education of which they are ignorant. There was an inversion of these aims in the school, which was evident in the reception of proposed short courses.

I was asked to prepare short courses and given a budget for outside speakers. I chose a distinguished anthropologist to talk on development and its problems. This was vetoed: 'She's over seventy. Students won't take her seriously if she's over seventy.' When I proposed a course on Long Wave Economic Cycles – that might help forecast imminent downturns if linked to mounting levels of credit – (the subject of this volume's Chapter 9), it too was vetoed: 'We don't want to spread despondency with our courses.' It may well have been that these assessments of its market did indeed correspond to the views of a majority of managers – though this appears unlikely. But one would have expected the role of the Business School not to foster such bias. However, in catering to its perception of what its 'customers' wanted, rather than what they needed, the school abnegated taking a lead in management *education*: it sold its market short.

The Control and Manipulation of Resources

As was shown, promotions were controlled exclusively by the director, as were other rewards, rather than their being mediated through peer academics as had been previously the case and which is normal university practice. Under his new regime, the director introduced the unilateral granting of 'allowances' – additional increments to selected staff members. These were not made public but given to those he judged as achieving high consultancy earnings or making extensive PR impacts.

The imposition of these differentials, however, divided and polarized staff and precluded the development of collegial collectivity. Good scholars who researched and produced publications yet generated less funding than their consultancy-rich colleagues, were sidelined and many left the school. In an academic variation of 'Gresham's Law, 'bad academics drove out good'.

---

reviewed journal – the rest had been presented at gatherings and conferences. There were no books.

The Control of Information

Hierarchical controls exist in all organizations. But, as we saw in the case of the recruitment consultants, if an organization is to be effective, its elite's power must be modified and alternative interests given their place within a system of checks and balances. Otherwise, an elite's unmodified power will not only dominate and distort the allocation of resources but attempt to monopolize the control of both internal information and of information from 'outside'. This will cause it to lose contact with its lowerarchy. Since lowerarchies are more in contact with an organization's environment than its elite, the elite will progressively lack information about its environment, which will eventually reduce its effectiveness.

The director controlled information both up and down the organization. Missives, commands, injunctions and interpretive views from the top were frequent and indeed almost constant, while collegiate forums able to consolidate or present counter-policies were eroded or eradicated. When individuals expressed dissatisfaction, they were typically ignored or, it was suggested, they moved to 'do their ballet elsewhere.'

This account is not to be taken as applicable to *all* business schools. Indeed, when I gratefully left to take a similar post in another university business school, it was to find an emphasis on high academic standards and an administration where both 'ologies' and theories were appreciated. The big difference was that there, the director was a scholar with an experience of business – rather than a businessman with little scholarship or feeling for education.[20]

If one expects a business school to be primarily concerned with scholarship as applied to business, here we had its negation. But if a business school is to be judged as a business, more instrumental criteria have to be applied.

Conclusion: Organizational Capture and Organizational Tyranny

The transition to tyranny in both case studies reveals a shift from previously held assertions of normative–moral values. This was effected through the adoption of six managerial strategies by which elites are able to capture their organization:

1. The removal of countervailing powers opposing the elite so that a single unopposed source of authority emerged. This was accomplished by:
2. Censorship: the elite's control of information.
3. The elite's control of recruitment.
4. The elite's control and manipulation of resources.

---

20   Two thousand years ago, Plato noted, 'A ship's crew which does not understand that the art of navigation demands a knowledge of the stars, will stigmatize a properly qualified pilot as a stargazing idiot, and will prevent him from navigating.' Quoted in Goodall 2009.

5. The introduction of procedures to eject dissidents without provision of defensive procedures.
6. The use of a redundant rhetoric to justify present policies.

Where the capture of an organization allows these features to be systematically developed – as in both the Business School and the Consultant's Group – then here, it is suggested, we will find a 'Tyrannous Organization' – one manifest in the negation of previously held normative–moral values and justified by the intrusion of rationally economic values. In the Business School this was evident in a reduction of academic standards, while with the recruitment consultants it involved the negation of egalitarian ones. This is not to suggest that the assertion of normative–moral values (often a feature of an earlier stage of an organization's evolution) is ignored. Indeed, such values are often piously and repetitively expressed, often as mission statements. But in tyrannous organizations, normative–moral values are systematically undermined.

Despite what appears to be an increasing incidence of organizational capture and the emergence of tyrannous organizations, their significance within organization theory has been little explored.

References

Douglas, M. (1992a), *Risk and Blame*, London: Routledge.

Douglas, M. (1992b), 'Witchcraft and Leprosy', in *Risk and Blame*, London: Routledge, 83–101.

Flanagan, J.G. and Rayner, S. (eds) (1988), *Rules, Decisions and Inequality in Egalitarian Societies*, Aldershot: Avebury.

Gluckman, M. (1955), *Custom and Conflict in Africa*, Oxford: Basil Blackwell.

Goodall, A.H. (2009), *Socrates in the Boardroom: Why Research Universities should be Led by Top Scholars*, Princeton, NJ: Princeton University Press.

Hatch, M.J. and Schultz, M. (1993), 'Functionalism and Symbolism in Cultural Studies: From Theoretical Prisons to Methodological Interplay', Papers in Organisation no. 13, Copenhagen Business School.

Henry, S. (1988), 'Rules, Rulers and Ruled in Egalitarian Collectives', in J.G. Flanagan and S. Rayner (eds), *Rules, Decisions and Inequality in Egalitarian Societies*, Aldershot: Avebury, 70–97.

Mars, G. (1988), 'Hidden Hierarchies in Israeli Kibbutzim', in J.G. Flanagan and S. Rayner (eds), *Rules, Decisions and Inequality in Egalitarian Societies*, Aldershot: Avebury, 98–112.

Storr, A. (1997), *Feet of Clay*, London: HarperCollins.

Weber, M. (1960), in R. Bendix, *Max Weber: An Intellectual Portrait*, London: Heinemann.

Chapter 8

Individualism and Hierarchy: Management in Soviet Georgia – An Extreme Example of a Local Response to Distant Controls[1]

Co-authored with Yochanan Altman

Introduction

This chapter is based on a specific situation in the USSR under Soviet central planning. It describes the organization of a biscuit factory in Soviet Georgia and in doing so offers a unique and extreme example of the way that controls and targets set from a distance were able to be perverted – that is, circumvented and evaded by its local management.

Though the cultural context of Georgia is highly specific and though the fieldwork on which it is based took place in the 1980s, nonetheless this case offers universal lessons about local managements in a globalized world – one where ownership and controls are increasingly shifting from the local to the distant and where the practice and art of management can be used to adapt and trade-off ongoing patterns of negotiation between different agencies, levels, interest groups, constraints and opportunities. Here, the local managers went well beyond the more common deviance of simply running 'a business within a business':[2] the factory had, in effect, been 'captured' by its local managers, who worked it for their own ends.

This chapter has two aims. First, by providing detail and insight into the role of managers in Soviet Georgia, it seeks to illumine the extreme constraints they faced and to demonstrate how they responded to operate the ingenious institutions they developed to carry out their managerial functions. Second, it attempts to show how these institutions and the management style they evolved were embedded in traditional Georgian culture and how they worked alongside the formal Soviet

---

1   This chapter is an amended version of an article by G. Mars and Y. Altman (2008), 'Managing in Soviet Georgia: An Extreme Example in Comparative Management', *European Journal of International Management*, 2(1), 56–70.

2   In *Cheats at Work* (Mars 1982/1994, pp. 10 and 14), I show how some situations allow workers to bypass their organization's control to the extent that they use the firm's resources to run 'a business within a business'.

economy. An incidental aim is to demonstrate by the use of concepts and methods from social anthropology, the singular contribution of this discipline to the comparative study of management.

Management is by its nature set in widely varying economic environments and social–political–historical contexts that determine its form. Despite these differences, many of management's essential functions are universal: it is how they are achieved that varies according to their context. Variations in performance, however, are difficult to discern from within, which is why comparative studies are valuable. They offer insights – through negation and contradiction – that demonstrate variability in practice, while revealing essential consistencies in function that comprise the daily lot of managers everywhere.

A Note on Method

Much of the data in this chapter was collected by Yochanan Altman under a programme devised and supervised by Gerald Mars during one and a quarter year's in-depth ethnographic fieldwork in 1982/83[3] among a community of some 5,000 expatriate Georgian Jews. Informants had been active in Georgia's hidden economy in the early 1970s and had migrated to Israel in the mid-1970s and resettled en masse. As such, the case represents a version of participant observation at one remove. Since informants came predominantly from one small provincial town and adjacent villages, it was possible for accounts of different informants from various levels in the factory (and of other contexts) both to be obtained in considerable detail and to be effectively cross-checked. Similar details were obtained covering transportation and distribution, and from a range of service occupations that impinged on the factory. This data was supplemented by four short visits to Georgia by both authors before and after the Republic's independence in 1991, by continuous searches of the Georgian and Soviet press, and by access to specialists on Georgia including native Georgians in the UK.

It is necessary in discussing management in Soviet Georgia to describe and analyze the cultural context in which it was set and to do the same for the Soviet command economy system as it existed with some variations, from the time of Georgia's absorption into the USSR in 1923 until its independence in 1991. We then discuss the organization of the biscuit factory and its participation in Georgia's hidden economy.[4]

The Economic and Cultural Underpinnings to Georgia's Hidden Economy

Georgia's hidden economy was regarded as the epitome of hidden economies within the Soviet Union (Grossman 1977), having an estimated 30 per cent that

---

3   Generously funded by the Nuffield Foundation.

4   Variously termed also as its 'informal', 'concealed', 'subterranean', 'black', 'second' and 'parallel' economy.

was 'black' (Wiles 1980). The extent of this formally illicit activity characterized the way of life of its citizens and to a considerable extent that of citizens in other Soviet republics. Whereas the Soviet's formal command economy operated a complex, many-layered bureaucracy that issued decrees, regulations and output demands, it nevertheless couldn't meet the daily needs of its citizenry – particularly failing to supply consumer goods, a fundamental feature of Soviet-type command economies (Castells 1999; Kornai 1992). Georgia's hidden economy worked to remedy this and did so through its exploitation of personal support networks. These monitored and paralleled organizations in the formal economy. Though both economies were in opposition at many points of contact and the hidden economy worked to subvert the formal, while the formal aimed to control the hidden, they were symbiotic – each was necessary to the existence of the other.

Managers, who, as elsewhere, were in post to make the economy work, had in fact to serve two 'masters', with two very different sets of expectations, rewards and sanctions available to them: one, the formal economy, was represented by the State Board for Planning (*Gosplan*) and the State Board for Materials and Equipment Supply (*Gossnab*) in charge of output targets and the provision of related inputs; the other master was the market, with its own modes of regulation and its own ways of reconciling supply and demand.[5]

However, this underground market, the dynamo of the hidden economy, was far removed from the 'ideal' model of a perfect market where perfect competition is based on perfect knowledge. It was, in fact, a series of highly imperfect markets operating within and based upon a form of social organization and culture that controlled information about the availability of goods and their prices. This information was not impartially available but jealously guarded and selectively processed along personal networks. These network-based activities inevitably brought their practitioners and their activities into conflict with the custodians of the formal Soviet economy. It was, however, not the conflict between these two systems (that may also be conceived of as conflict between two aspects of a single system) but the accommodations between them that produced the symbiosis that allowed both to operate. Underpinning the hidden economy was the singular nature of Georgian culture, with its emphasis on honour.

Georgia: An 'Honour and Shame' Culture

Honour, and its corollary, shame, are constant preoccupations in Georgia and determine many normative–moral[6] behaviours and the form of the country's

---

5   These modes correspond to the two archetypal forms of organizing – hierarchies and markets (Williamson 1975).

6   The term 'normatively moral' used here adapts Amitai Etzioni's (1975) usage. He divides organizations into four types, normative organizations being those whose 'rank and file' accept and share the moral norms of its elites as against those with a calculative or coercive involvement as found in commercial or penal organizations.

institutions – especially their type of family organization and the personal networks deriving from them. As such, Georgia shares cultural features with other societies that are found or which derive from around the Mediterranean rim (Peristiany 1966; Davis 1977) and the Caucasus (Tuite 2005).

To be well accepted in Georgian society involves descent and membership in families where both sides are noted for respectability. Though descent is traced bilaterally, there is stress on the male and on the culture and mutual obligations of brothers. Women are important as the articulation points between groups of men and as ensurers of male descent. Whereas the honour of men is achieved by assertion and dominance, the honour of women is passive, largely deriving from sexual modesty. The honour of both genders reflects on their families and to an extent on friends and associates – as does shame, the negation of honour.

Within family groups, spheres of action and mutual expectations are well defined, do not overlap, and are therefore non-competitive – everyone knows their place within the totality of both the nuclear family and its extensions. Family relationships thus provide strong support, security and mutuality.

Beyond the family, however, we find the reverse: an individual's acts are assessed and continually reassessed in the context of his own and his family's honour. Thus, beyond the family, constancy of expectations and reputation do not apply: insecurity and instability in the perpetual ranking and re-ranking of personal relationships is the norm. As a result, males have continuously to prove themselves as men: they are constantly 'on show' and need perpetually to demonstrate worthiness to public opinion and especially to peers. One important way to do this is through conspicuous consumption and the use of goods in display (Altman 1983).

In this kind of 'honour and shame culture' where peer approval is so important, (official) hierarchical relations are resented, resisted, and the sources of perpetual conflict. Since in Georgia, honour accrues to families and families are linked by a common honour, there is little role for the state or any centrally organized hierarchy. Where hierarchy exists, as in most forms of economic organization, relationships need to be personalized – abstraction has little place.

Personal support networks – particularly their 'cores' based on the family – are the backbone of the hidden economy. In Georgia, a man's major social resource is his network – the body of people he can personally relate to, and through whom he can extend reciprocity and incur obligations in exchange relationships with others who were, or might latently prove significant. The extent and 'weight' of a person's network are the primary determinants of the type of occupation he can follow and a man's occupation can facilitate (or hinder) the gaining of honour and in its turn the further extension of his network. Thus, networks are crucial to obtaining and distributing goods and resources and are central to understanding the workings of the hidden economy. We have elsewhere focused upon the role of family and kinship as the bases of personal support networks – what we call 'network cores' – and have devised a method of calculating their 'weight' based on a combination of kinship contingency and power of office (Mars and Altman 1983). 'Kinship cores' are necessarily added to and supplemented by peer group membership. This is why the possession, preferably of a multiplicity of brothers is so valued – they are both kin and the source of same-generation peer contacts. Links to the husbands of sisters are similarly exploitable, but the bond is not usually as significant as with brothers.

Competition, trust and demonstrations of macho risk taking are elements in network formation and their consolidation.

Competition involves conspicuous consumption and display and the involvement of peers in relationships of mutual obligation. Feasts and bouts of competitive drinking to consolidate and extend networks are extensive, while sitting rooms – which in Georgia are often male preserves – are the arenas in which display items are exhibited. Wearing smart dress is important, as is eating out. These activities all affect a man's standing and influence the formation of his network[7] so that they are crucial in influencing the ranges of choice he has in extending his areas of discretion: they are utilized too in choosing spouses and the partners of children – the selection of which can significantly enrich and extend a network. As a result, Georgian males were pressured to obtain resources that the formal economy could rarely supply. It was this dynamic that drove the hidden economy.

Trust is the basis of honour and the cement of networks. A man who is not trusted has no honour: without honour a man cannot be trusted. Trust is crucial to operations in the hidden economy. Since, of course, illegal deals cannot be backed by contract or enforced at law, a man's word has to be his bond. Sanctions for a breach of trust can be serious. An illegal financier who gave loans solely on a man's word of honour told us how someone who reneged would be socially excommunicated. Such discredit contaminates the family not only of the miscreant but also of his in-laws and of others in his network. The resultant shame can extend its stigma through several generations.

Risk taking, which, of course, is essential to business ventures, is a valued macho attribute and one directly linked to the effectiveness of one's network. A large and weighty network, while permitting the taking of extensive risks, reduces the incidence of their negative consequences – and in doing so, permits the projection of machismo. Powerful networks were often crucial in deflecting or avoiding the efforts of officialdom in its continuous attempts to assert control – for instance, in being warned about and being able to take precautions against the numerous 'unscheduled' 'spot' checks that were such a regular aspect of Soviet production (Mars and Altman 1987). The absence of a weighty and effective network may imply that a person is normally limited to less risky jobs or has a greater than usual liability to exposure and arrest (Mars and Altman 1983). If a network fails to prevent an arrest, but is powerful and extensive enough, it can be brought to bear on subverting the subsequent legal process at each of its stages – from influencing the arresting officer through to modifying the final sentence of the judge.

---

7   On recent changes in gender aspects of social positioning in Georgia, see Mühlfried 2006.

In summary, we can see that these features of Georgian culture emphasize the role of the individual and his links within personal support networks at the core of which are kinship and affinal relationships. It is the network that is mobilized to manipulate power; that influences the allocation of scarce resources; that offers personal identity and support; and that is the fundamental building block of Georgian society. We now show how it operated in one Georgian factory.

The Biscuit Factory

This case examines the workings of a medium-sized enterprise, employing some 500 people, that operated in Soviet Georgia throughout the 1970s, the period under Brezhnev, characterized as the epoch of 'economic stagnation'. A more detailed account is provided in Mars and Altman 1987.

The enterprise manufactured biscuits and in addition to its formal output, produced extra biscuits distributed in the informal economy at an average ratio of 4:10 – that is, four 'informal' biscuits were manufactured for every ten 'formal' ones.

The formal enterprise was run by its four top managers, who were also the controlling partners in its illicit activities. Their first objective was always to achieve 'slack' (Kornai 1980) – that is, to obtain surplus capacity, for use in diverting resources to the illicit enterprise. The usual way to achieve this was to obtain lenient – below capacity – targets from the planning authorities when they set the production levels for each periodic 'plan'. It was done by bribing the responsible officials – not by giving 'one-off' payments but by incorporating them 'on the payroll', so they received regular tribute. They, in their turn, passed tribute up to those responsible for appointing them who were also responsible for setting and monitoring their performance and who when necessary protected them from exposure.

Slack was best effected at the time of the plan's formulation, since changes were difficult to accommodate once a plan had been established. The surplus capacity released by 'slack' – mainly production time and use of machinery and tools – then permitted the plant to produce copies of its legitimate product for the private market. However, it could do this only if it obtained extra raw materials for the excess production. As such illicit output was indistinguishable from legitimate output, it was able to pass undetected at all points of its passage from production to consumers.

Ingredients necessary to produce biscuits were in particularly high demand (and short supply): flour, butter, eggs and sugar were often rationed throughout the Soviet period (Kornai 1992). Our entrepreneurs, however, bought these items from the very shops in which they sold their produce, thus creating a 'closed loop' whereby both producer and retailer became locked into a repetitive and balanced exchange. The regularity of this exchange helped prevent the necessity to stock unusually high quantities of raw materials or to stockpile large amounts of finished products, the presence of which could always be detectable on a spot check by the authorities. It was, in effect, a version of 'just in time' production.[8] In the context of Soviet Georgia, however, this was not an aid to efficiency but an expensive managerial gambit – one that involved the weighing of relative risks.

Risk Assessments and Risk Avoidance

By taking more frequent deliveries of ingredients and making more deliveries of final products, the factory's managers reduced stock levels but increased risks of apprehension by the Republic's frequent road patrols. Every road between towns in the Soviet Union was routinely policed by patrols who often checked vehicles to ensure they were on approved journeys and had appropriate documentation to cover what they were carrying. In practice, this meant extra costs in bribes payable to the patrols or/and to their seniors. It also involved extra time and effort spent creating extensive paperwork for these journeys. Obtaining necessary petrol, chronically in short supply, similarly involved more effort and costs directed through more contacts that created further risks. Yet extra petrol beyond that specified by the plan was essential to collect raw materials and deliver final products.

Balancing risks was a perpetual preoccupation of the biscuit factory's managers and one dominating managerial strategies. Since the incidence of risks varied continuously, strategies were continuously amended to accommodate these changes. This can be illustrated by their need to assess and reconcile liabilities to exposure by road patrols when weighed against less frequent liability to exposure through spot checks of the factory's premises. Calculations were based on assessments of comparative incidence and cost of likely sanctions if detected. Road patrols, for instance, were a routine risk activated by low-level operatives and therefore easily avoided at relatively little cost. The incidence of spot checks, however, was instigated by higher and sometimes non-local-level officials and though less frequent, could not often be anticipated. Penalties from exposure by such sources were potentially massive and networks to deactivate prosecutions needed to be extensive and the costs could be increasingly punitive the higher the levels involved.

Risk assessments in Georgia, therefore, had to take account of the level and significance of enforcers, the incidence of their checks, the likelihood of being able to diffuse them, the effectiveness of one's network as a source of warnings or – in the last resort, if it had to be employed – to divert arrest and prosecution. Assessments then weighed the likelihood and costs of alternative strategies. Changes in assessments followed from receipt of warnings from network members about an increase or a reduction in controls or if significant addition or reduction occurred in the strength of a network if weakened by, say, a change of post holder.

---

8   JIT, 'just in time', production involves the close coordination of the arrival of different raw materials or/and components to a plant so that there is a minimum build-up of stock. The process, pioneered in Japanese production factories, requires close coordination of arrivals with the rate at which they are used.

In the example given, of a trade-off between holding stock or making deliveries, this could result in increased deliveries and the holding of less stock or reduced deliveries and holding more stock.

However, the managers' jobs – and the risk assessments they made – were more complex than this relatively simple illustration of a trade-off between two risks might suggest. There were other risks. Obtaining other needed items, such as labels for the illicit biscuit packets, for example, presented especial problems. Printing was strongly controlled in the Soviet Union where even typewriters were licensed, so that penalties for infringing laws governing printing were severe. Managers of printing workshops suffered even stronger controls and stricter rationing of their raw materials – in their case, of papers and inks – than did the management of the biscuit factory. They were, of course, subject to the same vagaries of spot checks on their premises and of their goods in transit. This created difficulties for the factory in obtaining regular supplies of labels. Hold-ups in supply caused bottlenecks in production and added to costs by preventing the smooth, regular, more economically rational throughput that is taken for granted in more liberal economies.

But the labelling of illicit biscuits presented even further problems to the biscuit factory's management. Soviet labels, besides merely illustrating the name of the product, also contained a full history of its production, date of manufacture, batch number, ingredients and price. All and any of these inputs had to marry with the same details on the legitimate products the factory produced, as any lack of alignment could reveal a paper trail leading to exposure.

To expand or not to expand is the ultimate risk question facing enterprises in liberal market economies. This crucial decision in Georgia, however, was based not on assessments of the market (almost always assumed as unsatisfiable throughout the Soviet Union), nor with whether capital or labour was available, but on the effectiveness of networks that could be marshalled by the managers involved (Mars and Altman 1983). There was no point in contemplating expansion to areas where protection from law enforcement agencies could not be guaranteed, or, assuming raw materials and access to plant were available, producing goods for which the paperwork could not be provided, or in a quantity undeliverable by transport and supported fuel, or at a pace unabsorbable by the receiving outlets.

Whether to expand or not in Georgia depended primarily on whether managers could mobilize adequate human and material resources to facilitate illicit provisions, services, access and protection. These were all constrained by the limits imposed by the nature of personal support networks. By definition, these were personal and therefore local. Accordingly, the biscuit factory hardly expanded – its managers serviced its locality and were content at that.

An Inversion of Power

A further source of risks derived from the labour force reveals an inversion of organizational power when compared with the situation in liberal market economies. Soviet organizations, like Western ones, were predicated on the premise that managers have power over subordinates. Indeed, this premise is at the core of the employment contract (Williamson 1975; Jaffee 2001). Not so in the case in the hidden economy.

Due to its organic nature, production in the hidden economy involved a variety of people in a range of specialisms. The factory's management knew that employees were aware of their illicit operations, though without necessarily knowing the details, so it was paramount to secure their cooperation – especially since they were required on occasion to work overtime to achieve the illicit extra produce. Working overtime was not by itself unusual in the Soviet Union and speeding up productivity towards the end of regulatory periods in order to catch up with legitimate production targets – the so-called *storming* phenomenon – was well accepted. Nevertheless, management's vulnerability to the goodwill of their labour force meant they had to be particularly good at man management.

One ex-manager told us, '[As a manager,] you can never be sure, you can never feel safe. Possibly someone will want to take revenge because of something you did to him, or even something you were not aware of doing to him. Or maybe someone envies you and therefore, will try to harm you' (Mars and Altman 1986, pp. 199–200).

Being thus potentially liable to exposure meant the traditional power relationship between management and employees could not be presumed. Subordinates had leverage over their superiors since at any time they might become informers.[9] So employees had to be placated. The easiest way to implicate and integrate them in the informal economy was by providing benefits they would not otherwise be entitled to, and by facilitating scarce privileges. That was the way the biscuit factory management operated.

Keeping the generality of their employees satisfied and cooperative was achieved not through extra remuneration (too open for detection; and besides, money did not necessarily buy goods in a command economy) but through occasional gifts of sought-after items such as sugar, butter, eggs and flour. And workers also expected to take home biscuits for private consumption and for onward redistribution to their own networks. Managers had records of their birthdays and each employee was annually given a birthday cake. Managers would place their own networks at their employees' disposal in cases of sickness to help them obtain scarce medication and be seen by the best doctors. Theatre seats could be obtained through the factory, or seats on aeroplanes when requested. Employees had to be made to feel valued and good man management also meant providing a not-too-demanding working environment.

---

9   Unless, of course, the entire power structure were also enmeshed in the informal economy, which it increasingly became during the 1970s, especially in the Southern Republics of the USSR. When corruption reaches the topmost levels (as eventually it reached Brezhnev's close circle), whistleblowers do not have recourse to a higher authority. Carrère d'Encausse (1991) labelled this a 'Mafiocracy'.

However, some workers and some managers who played more significant roles in illicit production – who did know the detail and who, by the nature of their job, could not avoid being aware of their place in the overall process – had to be differentially rewarded. As examples, both the persons in the office who prepared forged vouchers to cover illicit deliveries and the drivers who carried them received benefits above the general level.

By these means the generality of employees were incorporated into the 'biscuit factory family' and became enmeshed in and collusive to its illicit system of rewards. Illicit production, then, was not only managed through the provision of slack, courtesy of the planning bureau, through supplies of raw materials by courtesy of the shops, through labels via the corruption of printers, and through petrol via deals with the bosses of tanker drivers (as well as the drivers themselves), but it was also subject to the goodwill and cooperation of the factory's labour force.

It is evident that there were two sets of values that operated in the biscuit factory and that they operated in opposition (Mars and Altman 1983; Lawrence 1990). These were, on the one hand, 'the strongly formalised legal/rational values appropriate to a highly bureaucratised command economy' (Weber 1922), technical impartiality, legitimacy of office, adherence to planning command; and on the other, the personal values of partiality, adaptive pragmatism, charisma and rule bending associated with networks (Table 8.1).

These two sets of values were not only operational in the same organizations but focused on the same role holders. The management challenge was how to reconcile these different, indeed opposing, sets of values within the same role and in doing so to give precedence to the informal economy, without overtly antagonizing and openly challenging the ruling powers – the different enforcement agencies, the planning authorities, and the Party.

Management in the Service of Two Masters: Elements in the Role of the Tolkach

Rigidities in a formal system characterized by institutional inflexibility (Soos 1984), meant it could work only by recourse to informal ways. The continuous problems facing the biscuit factory's managers, in achieving both their legitimate and their illegitimate outputs, demanded specialists at bending rules. Normally and throughout the Soviet Union, the people who carried out this function were known as *Tolkachi* (singular *Tolkach*), 'fixers', people with contacts and 'pull', who could 'oil the wheels', the go-between wheeler-dealers without whom the hidden economy could not exist – and neither could much of the formal economy. *Tolkachi* needed extensive and powerful networks, and the economy could be construed as operating a linked system of *Tolkachi*, a network of networks. But this was not the case in Georgia.

Academic references to *Tolkachi*, for example by Nove (1977) and Berliner (1957, 1983), have focused on their role as having been a product of the formal economy, a means to achieve required output targets in the context of inefficiencies such as delayed supplies, unfixed broken machinery, and poor-quality raw

Table 8.1   Formal (bureaucratic) Soviet command economy values vs. Georgian hidden economy values

Soviet command economy values	Georgian hidden economy values
Separation and insulation of private life from work life	Fusion of work life and private life
Since private and work lives are conceptually separate, they are not rated vis-à-vis each other nor seen as competing for personal resources	Since private and work lives are fused within one conceptual system, the resources of one can be used in the service of the other
Sourcing (including human resources) is a derivative of official plans	Sourcing (including human resources) is subject to market needs and network demands
Recruitment and promotion are based on impartial universalistic merit	Nepotism is a moral duty
Hierarchical organization: directives go down; information flows up	Patron–client directives come from where the real power is vested: information flows along network lines
Officials are accountable to the official above them	Officials are trustees of an enterprise conditioned by and confined to a network's capacity
Officials are in charge of subordinates	Officials are dependent on the action (and inaction) of subordinates
A long-term view of targets	Pragmatic adaptation to short-term pressures

materials. They saw the role as upheld by single individuals located within organizations and dedicated to the furtherance of legitimate ends by flexible and sometimes illegitimate means. This, however, is a misreading of the role that leads to misinterpretation of its nature and functions. First, it was in the service of the hidden economy that the role found its natural niche and where it appears to have been most developed. Yet in Georgia the word was not used and indeed was hardly known: there were no individuals who, as specialists, carried out its functions. This was because *all* managerial roles in Georgia contained elements of *Tolkachi* functions: the total 'role set' fed off each of its parts.

Since *Tolkachi* functions were so crucial, they had to be institutionalized and managerial roles requiring a substantial 'tolkachic' element that could only be filled by incumbents who not only had to be formally qualified but had to possess useful networks – available when needed and powerful enough to be effective. Each of the four partners in the biscuit factory was, in this dual sense, a *Tolkach*.

They all spotted opportunities, negotiated deals, established alliances, and paid off officials. Their dual areas of specialism – technical expertise plus network effectiveness – necessarily overlapped with both the factory's formal and hidden economy needs. Balancing the demands of the two was crucial to the smooth running of both.

The engineering manager, for example, was expected to solve bottlenecks involving machinery breakdowns, but he needed to balance formal and hidden outputs to optimize both sets of requirements. All machinery was scheduled by the plan to last for specific periods with normal use, so that breakdowns from over-use were not covered. If extra spare parts above the normal were required and could not be obtained legally, this could cause bottlenecks – not just to illegitimate- but to legitimate production also. Failures in maintaining production would not only negate agreements in the hidden economy but invoke massive penalties from the formal economy and – worse – could engender enquiries that might uncover hidden economy activity.

The production manager had similarly to ensure adequate (and motivated) labour to meet orders from both sets of consignees. Near the end of a planned production period, he could – if short of legitimate biscuits – make up the shortfall with illegitimate ones. In the same way, the accountancy manager would keep two sets of books and had to be adept at shifting assets between different headings and over different timescales if he were both to satisfy legitimate needs and effectively to order illegitimate ones. Balancing the needs of both frameworks was vital. Similar balancing was necessary to ensure order in the regular throughputs of payments for favours to factory employees as well as to cooperating officials of impinging outside bodies. Regularity had to be maintained even if receipts were irregular: the two sides of the Georgian managers' role were symbiotic.

While offering obvious benefits to a hidden economy manager's persona, this symbiosis also benefited their formal managerial function: having to balance the demands of two areas of operation gave extra flexibility in operating both.

To return to the biscuit factory: while the need for basic ingredients was relatively constant (though they were never easy to obtain), it meant that the means of obtaining them, once established, would not need too frequent changes. It was problems affecting security – crises that could not be readily scheduled, especially those that could involve exposure and prosecution – that could be crucial and critical and which demanded the most powerful networks. The specialist networks of the four partners when combined in the face of such threats were more powerful, other things being equal, than the network of a single *Tolkach*. But, of course, in Georgia each network itself was fostered and developed. It is no accident that Georgia should have led the Soviet Union in the percentage of GNP attributed to its hidden economy.

The Inherent Weaknesses of Soviet Formal Managements

We have seen that in the hidden economy there was an inversion of powers vis-à-vis workers and their managers. There was a similar but stronger inversion in the formal economy. In an economy that could not satisfy the demand for consumer goods, where 'the producer [rather than the consumer] is King' (Nove 1977), salaries were unable to buy the goods people needed and wanted. Accordingly rewards and incentives, such as promotions that merely offered higher salaries, were hardly effective as an incentive. In the liberal economies, assessing and allocating rewards brings a degree of order into work organizations that justify the evaluation of performance. The core difficulty for people management in the Soviet Union's command economy was a structurally imposed imbalance in the nature of its employment relationships. It stripped managers of the power of making discretionary allocations and therefore gave no purpose to evaluations of performance.

If the formal manager could not allocate carrots, neither did he have access to sticks. Absenteeism was a common problem throughout the Soviet Union – as was drunkenness at work – but a manager's ability to discipline workers was strongly compromised. Sacking a worker was not an option, since 'the right to work' was a fundamental building block of the socialist economy, and attempting to sack someone would have involved a variety of agencies. Nor could there be any guarantee that a new hire could be put in place because the organization would not normally have authority to hire directly – manpower was allocated, as were all other resources, by centralized planners. Nor did managers have the power to assign work so that a worker might be given a less salubrious job. The detailed 'standardization' of jobs by the planning authorities clearly defined them by content, context and time. And since salaries were fixed and external to the system, the opportunity to use them as a management tool further limited a manager's autonomy.

The Soviet Union in effect recognized these inadequacies by acknowledging that workplace managements might resort to more direct and less elegant forms of reward. Rewards could be allocated at the discretion of management, that to some degree allowed workers to 'jump the queue' for items such as cars or even housing – where average waiting times in the 1980s were twelve and eight years respectively (Kornai 1992). An unanticipated consequence of such discretionary preferment, of course, was that it made extra resources available to fuel the hidden economy. And offering employees lunches in the workplace was standardized throughout the Soviet Union, with quality and quantity standards specified so that, in addition to their welfare element, they were a means of controlling or at least encouraging attendance at work. But they could not be offered or withdrawn at the discretion of a manager.

The Soviet's formal system, therefore, presented to its managers little opportunity to offer incentives and few means of applying discipline. The hidden economy, while making its managers vulnerable to exposure, at least offered them considerable power over incentives. The formal economy gave managers neither carrots nor sticks (and gave birth to the well-known cynical idiom, 'They pretend to pay us – and we pretend to work'). The hidden economy had an ample supply of carrots, a whole range of incentives and rewards. It also had a variety of sticks at its disposal – first and foremost, the withdrawal of participation in the hidden economy that could amount to potential exclusion from social networks, an equivalent to a material and social 'death'.

Concluding Notes on the Bypassing of Targets

Though overall it was parasitic on the formal authority, the hidden economy as derivative of the Soviet-type command economy emerges as by far the most dynamic, adaptive and innovative element in the entire economy of the Soviet Union. Its managers paradoxically emerge as a standard for entrepreneurship, innovation and exemplary human resource management. The region's seemingly unprecedented, 'unique' transformation into a capitalist market economy (Kornai 2006) is nothing less than naive if one fails to acknowledge that long before the collapse of Communism the socialist command economies were in the grip of a feudalized market economy, albeit hidden to those who did not wish to stare it in the eye. Equally naive would be to believe that the practices characteristic of the hidden economy have not survived into the new era, under new names and disguises (Lacko 2000).

This episode in twentieth-century social history exemplifies the vagaries of an overly rigid system, aspects of which are also to be found everywhere in the liberal economies, since laws, regulations and plans are not the prerogative of command economies alone. It is not unheard of that managers need to resort to 'informal' means in order to achieve their targets; and, with apparent transparency now a common feature of all domains of an economy, private, public and voluntary sectors included, the achievement of specified objectives has become the gold standard of executive success. To exceed targets – the surest way to promotion and an annual bonus – managers need the support of their subordinates, an understanding and sympathetic superior, and resort to extra means and resources – not unlike their forerunners in Soviet Georgia. Today's managers are equally dependent on the goodwill of their subordinates, not only since the latter can vote with their feet but also because they have a variety of means to make their voices heard: periodic job satisfaction surveys, 360-degree feedback, the annual performance review, and last, the now standard exit interview.

The deeds of managers in Soviet Georgia's hidden economy throw into sharp relief what contemporary managers in liberal market economies and under 'normal' circumstances have to endure in order for them to succeed and thrive. And with the advent of globalization and greater international competition, target setting by distant power centres, with fewer and fewer secure jobs and a rapidly changing technology, even the *angst* that characterized managing in the hidden economy, seems to be hanging in the air around us too.

In this case, we have a clear example of conflicting moralities and systems of ethics in the same milieu – one derived from the rigidly hierarchic bureaucracy of

Soviet central planning, the other from the counter-dominance of networking and of individualist family organization inherent to Georgian culture. The forms of deviance that emerge in organizations vary, therefore, not just with how work is organized but with aspects of the indigenous culture in which they are set. Together, but with different emphases in each case, the way that work is organized, distorted, amended to effect deviant aims, is a theme further developed in the following chapter, which deals with the excesses characteristic of economic upturns as evidenced in the current downturn.

References

Altman, Y. (1983), *A Reconstruction, Using Anthropological Methods, of the Second Economy of Soviet Georgia*, Ph.D. dissertation, Middlesex Polytechnic.

Berliner, J.S. (1957), *Factory and Manager in the USSR*, Cambridge, MA: Harvard University Press.

Berliner, J.S. (1983), 'Managing the USSR Economy: Alternative Models', *Problems of Communism*, January–February, 40–56.

Carrère d'Encausse, H. (1991), *La Fin de l'Empire Sovietique*, Paris: Fayard.

Castells, M. (1999), 'The Crisis of Industrial Statism and the Collapse of the Soviet Union', in *End of the Millennium Vol. III: The Information Age*, Oxford: Blackwell Publishers.

Davis, J. (1977), *People of the Mediterranean*, London: Routledge and Kegan Paul.

Etzioni, A. (1975), *A Comparative Analysis of Complex Organizations*, Glencoe, IL: Free Press of Glencoe.

Grossman, G. (1977), 'The Second Economy of the USSR', *Problems of Communism*, 26, 25–40.

Jaffee, D. (2001), *Organisation Theory: Tension and Change*, New York: McGraw-Hill.

Kornai, J. (1980), *Economies of Shortage*, Amsterdam: North Holland Press.

Kornai, J. (1992), *The Socialist System*, Oxford: Clarendon Press.

Lacko, M. (2000), 'Hidden Economy – An Unknown Quantity? Comparative Analysis of Hidden Economies in Transition Countries, 1989–95', *Economics of Transition*, 8(1), 117–49.

Lawrence, P.R. (1990), 'US and Soviet Contemporary Decision-making Theory', in P.R. Lawrence and C.A. Vlachoutsicos (eds), *Behind the Factory Walls: Decision Making in Soviet and US Enterprises*, Cambridge, MA: Harvard University Press.

Mars, G. (1982/1994), *Cheats at Work: An Anthropology of Workplace Crime*, London: Allen and Unwin; Aldershot: Dartmouth.

Mars, G. and Altman, Y. (1983), 'The Cultural Bases of Soviet Georgia's Second Economy', *Soviet Studies*, 35(4), 546–60.

Mars, G. and Altman, Y. (1986), 'The Cultural Bases of Soviet Central Asia's Second Economy', *Central Asian Survey*, 5(3–4), 195–204.

Mars, G. and Altman, Y. (1987), 'Cases of Second Economy Production and Transportation in Soviet Georgia', in B. Dallago and S. Allessandrini (eds), *The Unofficial Economy*, London: Gower Press, 219–46.

Mühlfried, F. (2006), *Postsowjetische Feiern*, Stuttgart: Ibidem-Verlag.

Nove, A. (1977), *The Soviet Economic System*, London: G. Allen & Unwin.

Peristiany, J.G. (ed.) (1966), *Honor and Shame*, London: Weidenfeld and Nicholson.

Soos, K.A. (1984), 'A Propos the Explanation of Shortage Phenomenon', *Acta Oeconomica*, 33(3–4), 305–20.

Tuite, K. (2005), 'The Autocrat of the Banquet Table: The Political and Social Significance of the Georgian Supra', Conference on Language, History and Cultural Identities in the Caucasus, School of International Migration and Ethnic Relations of Malmö University, Sweden, 18 June.

Weber, M. (1922/1968), *Economy and Society: An Outline of Interpretive Sociology*, New York: Bedminster Press.

Williamson, O.E. (1975), *Markets and Hierarchies*, New York: Free Press.

Wiles, P. (1980), 'Anti-Systemares Verhalten in der Sovjetwirtschaft', Bundesinstitut fuer Ostwissenschaftliche und Internationale Studien, Bonn.

Chapter 9

Individualism versus Hierarchy: Kondriateff and his Crime Waves; the Behavioural Underpinnings of Booms and Slumps

Co-authored with Michael Thompson

History does not repeat itself; at best it rhymes.

Attributed to Mark Twain

Introduction

Chapter 1 demonstrated that Cultural Theory (CT) is essentially a dynamic theory by showing how its different constituent cultures interact and by examining the effects of intrusions on particular locations as illustrated in Chapters 3, 6 and 7 (this volume). There is, however, another aspect of intrusion: economic change that has powerful and often rapid implications for the culture of organizations and the perception of behaviours appropriate to them. Not the least of these perceptions results in the labelling of actions as deviant or otherwise. These topics are the subject of this chapter.

CT's dynamism will now be demonstrated by examining the alternating dominance of two of its archetypal cultures – Individualism and Hierarchy[1] – over the extended periods of economic cycles. We shall see how pressures to innovate in periods of expansion – the upturns – favour individualists who, valuing autonomy and the freedom to transact, act as society's risk takers. Relatively unencumbered by group constraints, their aim is 'to make things happen' and in doing so to be primarily concerned with the short term implications of their

---

1   We have restricted the analysis to the interactions of just two of the theory's four archetypal cultures purely for simplicity of presentation. However, in reducing the overall variety from four to two, we come perilously close to the conventional markets-and-hierarchies framing (Williamson 1975), the sort of framing that gives us a pendulum-like oscillation between 'light-touch' and 'heavy-touch' regulation. If we include Egalitarianism (the enclaves) and Fatalism, thereby restoring the 'requisite variety', we get a much less deterministic (and more realistic) kind of cycle (see Thompson 2008).

actions. The alternating downturns favour hierarchists, who are characterized by caution, risk aversion, the long term implications of policies and actions and a concern with regulation.[2] As their mutual dominance alternates, so it appears that society's prevailing definitions of deviance change also.

Though these considerations make comparisons between periods difficult, they do not make them unsustainable. And though deviance and criminality (problems of definition apart) appear more common during upturns than downturns, comparisons over time are difficult to assert. Records of earlier cycles are scarce and unmatched variables intrude. In addition, definitions of fraud – let alone of deviance – overlap with those of embezzlement, corruption and other offences, while many cases are often not prosecuted or even recorded (Levi 2008). Further, examples often do not emerge until long after they have been committed. Statistics of variations over time are therefore, as Levi asserts, problematic.

If it can be established that economic cycles follow a consistent 'shape' comprising two roughly equal periods – upturns and downturns – (booms and slumps) – then we can perhaps, determine whether the incidence and types of deviance also coincide with these variations. But since perceptions of deviance appear to shift, so we need to assess why the perceptions of acts considered morally neutral (or even laudatory) at one time should be reassessed as deviant – or indeed criminal – at another. Consider for instance, current proposals to criminalize the manipulation by banks of Libor interest rates: to reduce the bonuses of business executives and to eradicate previously tolerated tax avoidance schemes – all of which were tolerantly accepted during the prior upturn. To further these concerns therefore, it will first be necessary to determine whether the cycles are indeed cyclical – or random.

Regular Waves – or Random Fluctuations?

Long-wave economic cycles were first promulgated by N.D. Kondratieff (1921) and later elaborated by others. It is now necessary to examine their bases and to consider the criticisms to which his work has been exposed. Four cycles will be discussed and comparatively assessed to examine the nature of behaviours that characterize the two halves of the cycles.

The validity of Kondratieff's cycles has been subject to considerable criticism – not least that their occurrence should be regarded as random rather

---

2   Downturns also favour egalitarian (enclavic) actors, these being the most cautious and risk averse of the solidarities. Hierarchical actors, as is evident from their concern with regulation, are focused on control, 'risk steering', as it is called in the financial sector (see Ingram and Thompson 2011).

than cyclical.[3] So these criticisms will have to be addressed if the cycle's links to deviance and crime and to regulation and control are to be sustained.[4]

The Details of Kondratieff's Cycles

Kondratieff's hypothesis, in brief, is that under capitalism both upturns and downturns are regular features of economic life and that after each downturn comes economic resurgence – an upturn. Unsurprisingly Kondratieff was denounced by the Soviet authorities, since he contradicted the Marxist doctrine of the unsolvable contradictions of capitalism and the unstoppable process of mounting crises leading to its final collapse. The idea of capitalism's periodic resurgence was too much for the Soviets to take and in 1928 Kondratieff was removed as director of the Conjuncture Institute in Moscow. Arrested in 1930, he later died in Siberia.

Kondratieff's evidence was based on just two and a half cycles beginning in the 1780s and calculated on commodity prices – the cost of industry's raw materials – and on wages and interest rates in England, France and the United States as well as levels of foreign trade. He found these were linked and ran from trough to peak to trough in cycles of approximately fifty to sixty years, with each demonstrating two very different phases: an upturn lasting roughly half the cycle (twenty-five to thirty years) and a downturn for a similar period. Kondratieff made no attempt to account for variations in the length of his cycles or to ascribe any behavioural bases to them or to link them to rule bending and deviance during the upturns. These are the concerns of CT and will be explored in this chapter.

Kondratieff argued that, despite problems of statistical comparison, this long-wave pattern was roughly the same in all the countries he investigated. Since then, we have had roughly one and a quarter more cycles, very much of the same shape as he described for his two and a half cycles – an accumulation of data that considerably weakens the 'random fluctuations' argument (Figure 9.1). He describes 'the shape' of these long waves as follows:

> The upturn of the first long wave embraced the period from 1789 to 1814, i.e. 25 years; its decline began in 1814 and ended in 1849, a period of 35 years. That cycle was therefore completed in 60 years. The upturn of the second wave began in 1849 and ended in 1873 thus lasting 24 years. The downturn of this second wave began in 1873 and ended in 1896, a period of 23 years. The overall length

---

3   Such criticisms have been levelled at all economic waves and cycles, not just the Kondratieff. Even the well-documented trade cycle has its deniers. For careful treatments of these criticisms – treatments that come down in favour of regular waves – see Freeman (1983) for the Kondratieff, and Matthews (1959) for the trade (and other associated cycles).

4   Again, something of a simplification. Since there are few 'points of inflexion' in the curve for one cycle (one at the trough, one at the peak, one halfway through the upturn, and one halfway through the downturn), we should really speak of four quarters, not two halves (see Ingram and Thompson 2011).

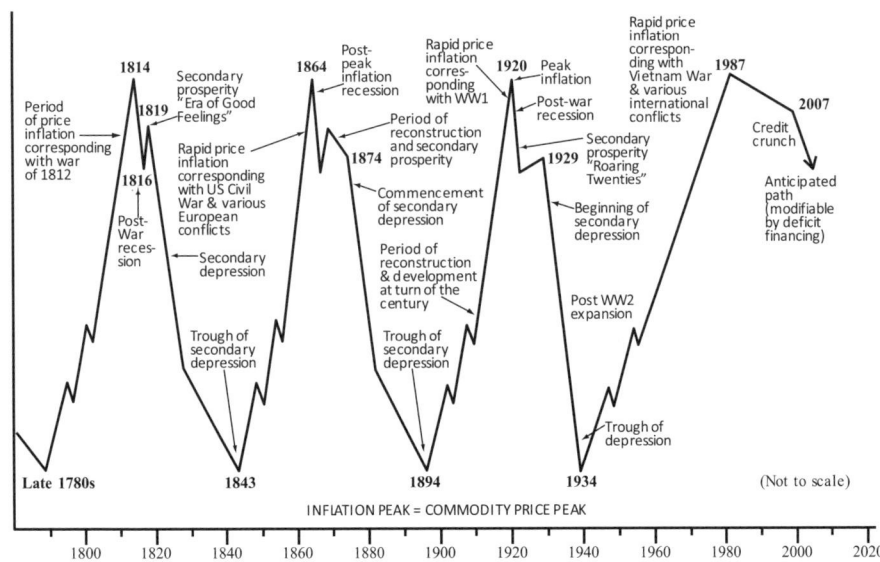

Figures within the chart:

Period of price inflation corresponding with war of 1812

1814

1819

1816
Post-War recession

Secondary prosperity "Era of Good Feelings"

Rapid price inflation corresponding with US Civil War & various European conflicts

Secondary depression

Trough of secondary depression

1864

Post-peak inflation recession

1874

Period of reconstruction and secondary prosperity

Commencement of secondary depression

Period of reconstruction & development at turn of the century

Trough of secondary depression

Rapid price inflation corresponding with WW1

1920 Peak inflation

Post-war recession

1929 Secondary prosperity "Roaring Twenties"

Beginning of secondary depression

Post WW2 expansion

Trough of depression

Rapid price inflation corresponding with Vietnam War & various international conflicts

1987

Credit crunch

2007

Anticipated path (modifiable by deficit financing)

Late 1780s   1843   1894   1934   (Not to scale)

INFLATION PEAK = COMMODITY PRICE PEAK

1800   1820   1840   1860   1880   1900   1920   1940   1960   1980   2000   2020

Figure 9.1   Four long wave cycles, late 1780s–2010+ (adapted from Beckman 1983)

of the second wave was 47 years. The upturn of the third wave began in 1896 and ended in 1920. (Kondratieff 1921 and 1926)[5]

The second and third waves had similar patterns to the first, though the first was shorter. When Kondratieff forecasted the crash of the third wave as due in the late 1920s, and that it would lead to a depression, he was proved spectacularly right.

Each wave begins its upturn after a long trough of depression (the late 1780s, early 1840s, mid-1890s, mid-1930s). Economic activity then gradually increases, along with inflation and overall prosperity. Big profits are made, but risks are incurred because of uncertainty as to whether a general upturn is occurring or merely a blip, since minor recessions recur in each upturn. Then rapid increases in investment, credit and prices follow as the upturns escalate and confidence rises. This phase appears relatively risk free – and that is its danger, because entrepreneurs shift from strategic investment to speculation. Then comes a crash and recession followed by a deceptive 'double dip' so that, based on their previous limited experience, most people at first don't appreciate how bad are the imminent bad times to come.

---

5   Kondratieff might have calculated his first long waves from the peak of the wildly speculative 'Tulipmania' in Holland in 1636 or the classic collapse of the South Sea Bubble in 1720. That he did not do so was perhaps because of the paucity of commodity price statistics in these periods.

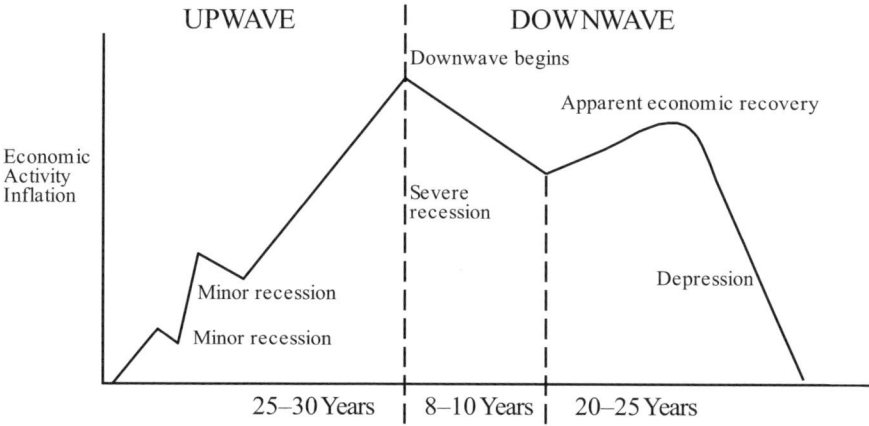

Figure 9.2   Idealized model of an economic long wave (after Beckman 1983)

The regular incidence of 'double dips' at the beginning of downturns (1814–19, 1864–74, 1920–29 and 2007/8 on) is noteworthy – though admittedly not directly relevant to linking Kondratieff waves to deviance. They are discussed here for the purpose of topicality – to show how optimism about an imminent resurgence is recurrently fuelled by the hopes, false assertions, assumptions and conscious lies pronounced by pundits, business leaders, politicians and other vested interests. These peddlers of rose-coloured spectacles share an aim – to bolster business and 'talk up' public confidence. They do so by suggesting that the double dip is no more than one of the recurrent 'hiccups' or 'blips' common to upturns that run counter to an overall upward trend. In this they argue from restricted experience – invariably so, having had limited personal exposure to a downturn, though they may well have had experience of lesser recessions. But despite protestations to the contrary, hopes of recovery fade as overall demand continues resolutely to fall and a crash proceeds, followed by an unmistakeably steep decline into depression: widespread bankruptcies, liquidations, deteriorations in output, prices and employment. Then comes stagnation, characteristically continuing for a decade or more, after which the cycle slowly returns to the starting point of a new upturn – when the process begins anew.[6]

---

6   The alleged inevitability of this sequence was countered by Keynes (1936), who argued that increasing consumer demand through deficit financing and public works was the way to kick-start a new upturn. But European governments and American Republicans, at the time of writing, appear unwilling to accept Keynesian arguments (despite the example of Roosevelt's 'New Deal' of the 1930s). The principle intellectual opposition to Keynes was mounted by F.A. Hayek in 1944 – see *The Road to Serfdom*, in which he advocates free markets involving the withdrawal of all government intrusions into financial affairs.

Though this alternation of upturns and downturns has long been recognized, its contribution to a theory of regular economic variation has faced criticism because of its apparent unpredictability: a criticism that we shall now show would be valid only if the cycle, like the disciplined sine curve associated with the oscillations of a pendulum, was deterministically generated.

The Irregularity of Long Waves: Does It Matter?

Kondratieff's critics insist that, since the lengths of cycles have fluctuated between fifty and seventy years (with the most recent taking close to eighty years), it is their very erraticism that suggests their incidence is random. This is the basic criticism that needs to be refuted if we are to use long wave cycles to locate and contextualize certain kinds of deviance in time – that is, as especially appropriate to the upturns – and to identify controls as appropriate to the downturns.

Long waves certainly do not operate with the regularity of train timetables. Kondratieff himself argued that they have no strict regularity. Though crests and troughs continuously recur, they do not do so at rigid intervals – 'blips' are numerous, while the economies of particular industries, sectors and different countries, frequently anticipate or lag behind overall movements.

Long-wave variances, therefore, certainly go deeper than 'blips', 'lags' and 'double dips'. But critics argue that too many variables intrude, making the cycles' lengths too widely different. This, it is claimed, means that 'a regular time scale cannot be taken for granted' (Mandel 2005) and the cycles therefore would better be described as 'waves'. Gordon (quoted in Weber 1981) puts it like this:

> Although business cycles represent alternations of prosperity and depression, virtually all authorities agree that there is nothing periodic about these movements.

Others (for example, Shurig 1984) have sought to relate the irregularity of the cycles/waves to the various clusters of technological innovations that they see as their initiators. The Industrial Age (1787–1842), they argue, was triggered by steam power, iron, cotton and textiles; the Railway Age (1843–97) by railways, coal and steel; the Mercantile Age (1898–1953) by electricity and the internal combustion engine; and the Information Age (1952–) by the computer, microelectronics and telecommunications. And since these sorts of 'system-transforming' technologies tend to come somewhat erratically, it is hardly surprising that the long waves are not perfectly regular.

These objections – 'they're not cycles; at best they're waves' – have mounted as the long-delayed crash of Kondratieff's fourth upturn – 'due' in the late 1970s – failed to materialize (though lesser recessions occurred in 1975 and again in 1987). And it has to be admitted that the last upwave has indeed taken an exceptionally long time to crash – some seventy-eight years (from 1929 to 2007/8).[7] Indeed, its continued deferral appeared to support the then British Chancellor Gordon Brown's confident assertion in March 2000 to have 'eradicated boom and bust'. Nonetheless the inevitable bust arrived, albeit well out of sync, in 2007/8. How, then, can these irregularities be explained?

Four Explanations for the Unpredictability of Long Waves

We shall now set out four explanations for the irregular lengths of the cycles that together, we believe, not only restore the integrity of long wave cycles but help explain the extended length of the most recent upturn.

First, Schumpeter's (1939) refinement of Kondratieff's cycles maintains an overall cyclical element while accounting for some of their varying lengths.[8] Schumpeter recognized four shorter cycles as operating within the longer Kondratieff waves. These are the Kuznets cycle of eighteen years and the Juglar cycle (Juglar 1862) lasting eight to ten years, both of which, like Kondratieff's cycles, are based on commodity price variations, and the shorter Kitchin cycle (Kitchin 1923) of approximately forty months based on bank clearings, commodity prices and interest rates. It is the simultaneous movements of the four cycles, Schumpeter argued, that define Kondratieff's turning points. So that 'of greatest interest are those periods when all three[9] cycles have moved in tandem' (Beckman 1983, p. 86), with the result that their individual troughs coincide.

This synchronicity occurred at times when commodity prices peaked, as they did preceding the crashes and the subsequent great depressions of 1873–78 and 1929–32. They appeared to do so again in 1974/5. That year saw a stock market collapse and a recession and, in the UK, the failure of secondary banks. But though there was then a secondary recovery, it was not followed by an expected crash. The last crash, when it did occur, did not do so until 2007/8. So why the delay? Synchronicity goes only some way to facilitating the turning points of cycles.

Alongside synchronicity there appear two further reasons for the extended deferral of the fourth wave's crash. One, we suggest, is to be found in the globalized extension of world markets created initially by the emergent Chinese and Indian economies, later by the subsequent Asian 'Tigers', and then by the rise of the South American economies. By 2008 China and India were together

---

7 It took eighty-eight years, if we count the 1929 crash as originating in 1920 – at the start of that wave's double dip.

8 Schumpeter saw sequences of capitalist economic activity – with upturns manifesting excessive innovation, too fast a level of growth, followed by downturns that eradicated the excess through a process of 'creative destruction'.

9 Some commentators ignore Kuznets cycles, arguing that they are no more than two Juglar cycles end to end.

contributing approximately 11 per cent to the world's GNP,[10] with the rest of the Tiger Economies and those of South America almost equalling this. Their contributions, in extending economic activity to its current global extent, helped defer an otherwise imminent crash. The other additional reason for the deferral of the fourth wave's crash focuses on the innovative cohort of individualist decision makers who manipulate economic affairs during each upturn. As CT demonstrates, under modern conditions the increase in Individualism allows innovating actors to extend the cycle: they are placed in positions where, increasingly, they can manipulate the usual economic indicators as agents of change, not subjects. This moves explanation from the economic to the behavioural aspect of downturns.

Several authors have noted a link between cohort values and beliefs. Galbraith (1955) observed, 'The suicidal tendencies of the economic system have occurred with some persistence every fifty or sixty years for as long as reliable records have been in existence.' This interval, he suggests, 'was perhaps roughly related to the time it takes for men to forget what happened before' (1955).

Beckman (1990, p. 363) is more specific. What he called 'the oblivion interval' seems to be about two generations. 'So the grandparents, who could not forget [the turmoil of the previous slump], constantly reminded their children, who could not remember.' Kaldor (1982) also uses an 'oblivion interval' to focus similarly on the contrasting behaviour of alternate generations. He suggests too that this is why Kondratieff's work tends to be ignored during upturns – which perhaps explains why we have heard relatively little of his relevance this time around, and especially since this upturn has been so protracted and the downturn so long delayed.

The intergenerational 'oblivion interval', however, has been extended. Between 1931 and 1981 average life expectancy for males in the UK and other economically developed countries has increased by approximately a third – from about 60 to almost 80[11] (a figure mirrored in the US and which is even higher in Japan). The financial decision makers' cohort, with its collective memory and its shared values and attitudes matching those of CT's individualist culture, may therefore be considered to have contributed to the extension of this latest cycle by approximately twenty years.

We can gain further insight into the decision spans of innovative cohorts by examining cycles that occurred when life spans were shorter than at present. It is intriguing to note that waves of only forty years' duration have been identified as occurring in Roman Britain – where life expectancy averaged less than fifty years (Parkin 1992, p. 144). The Roman waves were identified through archaeological evidence of pottery production that rose and fell in a series of cyclical phases and 'in a pattern that matches ... increases and decreases in the speed [velocity] of silver coinage [which] circulated in the first to early third centuries AD' (Going 1992).

---

10   Data derived from the IMF via http://en.wikipedia.org/wiki/International_ Monetary_Fund (accessed 30 June 2012) .

11   *Trends in UK Statistics since 1900*, House of Commons Research Paper 99/111, 21 December 1999.

So it would be a mistake to see entrepreneurial behaviour as *determined* by the structure of Kondratieff waves. Entrepreneurs are independent agents. The possibilities open to them are shaped by their interpretations of the opportunities that structures present. As Lukes (2005) explains, where structure ends and agency begins is arbitrary. So when an upturn ends it will present an opportunity to an astute agent to get out of the market at the right time, while those who are less astute stay in.

So far we have had three contributory explanations for the irregular patterning of long wave cycles that *together* help explain why the last upturn should have persisted for so long. First, there is Schumpeter's inclusion of Kuznets, Juglar and Kitchin cycles, which necessitates the synchronization of four waves that increase vulnerability to a crash. Second, we have the global extension of world markets created by China, India, the Asian Tigers and the South American economies that have sustained economic opportunities to the rest of the world. And finally, there is the cohort (or memory) explanation that has extended the manipulative and innovative controlling cohort's span of control following increases in the lifecycle.

Our fourth explanation is of a different order and, if correct, totally invalidates the criticisms that the first three have sought to counter. Those criticisms, and the arguments advanced to counter them, all assume that the socio-economic system we are dealing with is a *simple* system (deterministic, equilibrating, insensitive to initial conditions, and so on). The fourth explanation argues that the system is *complex* (indeterminist, far from equilibrium, sensitive to initial conditions – i.e. 'path dependent' – and so on).

For ease of explanation, we have framed our treatment of Kondratieff waves in terms of just Individualism and Hierarchy, and if that was *all* that was driving the cycle then it would indeed be simple, in which case the waves should certainly be regular, that regularity being inherent in the equation we can write for these pendulum-like systems. But, once we go beyond two solidarities – by bringing in Egalitarianism and Fatalism – our system, like a forced pendulum, becomes complex; there is no longer any equation we can write to predict its behaviour. All we can do, when faced by three - or fourfold systems like this, is build a computer simulation (an agent-based model, as it is called), set it going, and then see what happens.

What happens (with all four solidarities, but not with three or just two) is that, while the system never settles down (there is never 'no more boom and bust'), we do see the emergence of cycles – fairly regular alternations that are consistent with Kondratieff waves. But those cycles are erratic in both their amplitude and their timings, as is only to be expected if the system from which that behaviour is emerging is complex (see Thompson 2008; Ingram and Thompson 2011; Ingram, Taylor and Thompson 2011). So Kondratieff is not just being let off the critics' hook; there *is* no hook. Indeed, it is the critics who have been hooked, by their erroneous assumption that all cycles are simple cycles!

Though the varying lengths of the cycles since the 1780s and the delayed crash of the fourth wave do not lessen the validity of Kondratieff's theory, they do mean that his cycles have to accommodate wider inputs to the economic sphere (the complex dynamics of technological evolution, for instance, that deliver the 'system-transforming' innovations) while also admitting to only a low level of accuracy in forecasting.[12] This latter, however, is not a weakness of the socio-economic system: being complex is of its very nature unpredictable. That we cannot predict the cycles' exact dates and turning points comports with Mark Twain's assertion that history does not repeat itself. That we can be aware of the wider pattern, and some of what it is that fuels its periodic transformation, confirms that history, at best, rhymes. And that is Kondratieff's great achievement: he picks up the rhymes in economic affairs while resisting the temptation of claiming that those affairs repeat themselves.

Those patterns – the rhymes – are evident in the successive upturns and downturns exhibiting the same basic forms, each upturn being marked by innovative manipulation that eventually leads to speculative mania, followed by a crisis (a crash), a secondary ('double-dip') recovery, and then a downturn that is always marked by reactive caution, regulation and control.[13] But, though we have now gone a considerable way towards authenticating long wave economic cycles and towards understanding their shape, we have yet to consider the vital part that ideas play in determining that shape.

Two Cycles in Unison: Economic Long Waves and CT – The Behavioural Underpinnings of Economic Behaviour

We have suggested that economic cycles reveal the alternating dominance of the opposed values of Individualism and Hierarchy. In brief, and in repetition, upturns emphasize innovative and manipulative Individualism, which exhibits short-term optimism and entrepreneurialism. It supports bold risk taking, the legitimating of highly differential rewards, the sanctity of free markets, competition, freedom from controls, and, on occasion, a readiness to bend rules. It is the exuberance of upturns that facilitates organizational deviance, but it also enables innovation, which inevitably involves taking risks that can have good or bad effects.

---

12   But when, one might ask, has there ever been an economic forecast that was accurate?

13   In their excellent *Manias, Panics and Crashes*, Kindleberger and Aliber choose a model of general financial crises that 'centres on "the episodic nature of the mania and subsequent events" … [and that] differs from those that focus on the variations and the periodicity of economic expansions and contractions' – thus, they do not mention the work of Kondratieff. We concentrate on Kondratieff's long wave cycles because they offer more distinctive parallels and contrasts than would the inclusion of the lesser periods discussed by Kindleberger and Aliber that cover lesser recessions as well as the major downturns. By using Kondratieff's cycles, we are more readily able to point up the parallel behaviours that derive from CT.

Downturns, as stated, exhibit the reactive opposite: the emergence of Hierarchy emphasizing caution, control, risk aversion and regulation.

Individualism is associated with a general widening of previously restrictive boundaries, a process that accelerates as upturns proceed. As one might expect, upturns manifest not only a growing liberal relaxation of economic controls but an overall society-wide relaxation of constraints. These are manifest in increased sexual permissiveness and radical innovations in literature, drama and throughout the arts; women's fashions become more revealing; music, religion and technology more drastically inventive; conspicuous consumption more lauded (Beckman 1983, pp. 42–7). Attention is forward looking, while the past tends to be discounted. In CT terms, we see an overall reduction in Grid.[14]

As an upturn proceeds, speculation – based on weakened regulation and the growth of extended credit – intensifies. This is supported by a shift of accountancy practice from 'rule observer' to 'rule manipulator'. Since in upturns attention focuses on the future, the past can offer only limited lessons (and warnings). Creative accountancy is thereby able to calculate collateral valuations within widened parameters, as we shall see when discussing Enron and the widespread application of the Black–Scholes formula.

Since a key individualist value is optimism, the conventional wisdom is that prosperity and rising prices will continue indefinitely – with successful entrepreneurs supportively lauded as folk heroes. Some may well believe the upturn will continue forever, but those who don't will have to act as if it will – innovators cannot stop innovating. And regulators are also concerned that the upturn should not stop. They too have a vested interest in acting like innovators. But upturns always end in the same way – with a crash.

With a crash, the values of Individualism become discredited. Calls are increasingly heard that 'this must never happen again'. It is then that the values of Hierarchy emerge. There is a tightening of regulations to curb speculative excess; lessons are sought from the past; and there is widespread denigration of those heroes of the previous upturn – the entrepreneurs.

Hierarchic values also extend to wider societal concerns: boundaries tighten and pressures mount to roll back the perceived excesses and tolerances of the prior upturn. There are calls for increased controls over immigration. Sexual constraints are promoted; female fashions become more modest with longer hemlines and covered shoulders.[15] Conspicuous consumption is frowned upon. In CT terms, there is an overall increase in Grid. But economic affairs post the crash, are at the core of this wider ideological shift. These cyclical swings from tolerance to control are repeated in each cycle. In upturns, as will be shown, controls on credit are progressively relaxed until the crash, when we have a liquidation of credit followed by a re-imposition of controls.

---

14 Paradoxically, this does not appear to apply to punitive penal sanctions, which have increased in severity during the past upturn in both the US and the UK.

15 For a fuller and more extensive account see Beckman 1983, pp. 333–47.

The economic cycle is, therefore, seen as running in parallel with a cultural cycle – one half of which in the upturn, dominated by the values of Individualism, licenses regulatory freedoms, supports risk taking, and permits the expansion of credit, first for investment and then for speculation. The cycles' second halves, the downturns dominated by Hierarchy, put a regulatory brake on these activities.

Upturns, Bubbles, Crashes – and Deviance

The structure of bubbles/crashes has been noted as similar in each case (Whalen 2008). The market expands as new and inexperienced investors, funded by economic surpluses from earlier in the upturn, are enticed into the market. At first their investments earn a reasonable income and their appreciation is considered adequate. As an upturn proceeds, borrowings on credit increasingly finance speculation (defined as buying assets intended for resale at a profit, irrespective of their derived income). More investors enter the market, resulting in a sharp upswing in the price of assets. A positive-feedback cycle then develops that inflates prices still further and a 'bubble' progresses powered by euphoric bidding, increasingly available credit, and a generalized belief that prices will rise in perpetuity. These bubble conditions are then exploited by a network of market manipulators.

Entering the market in the expectation that repayments will accrue from gains to be financed by later waves of borrowers, is the mechanism of Ponzi schemes.[16] These are inherently unsustainable because they require a continuous inflow of new buyers that is inevitably limited, and because any sudden rush of withdrawals can be fatal. When the market slows and anticipated income is threatened, and especially when it becomes insufficient to meet the interest on indebtedness, it can then precipitate criminality and deviance.

The 'tipping point' that heralds a crash and the beginning of the downturn has been termed 'The Minsky Moment'.[17] There is no economic formula that can indicate a Minsky Moment. The percentage of private debt as a ratio of GDP increases *vulnerability* to panic, but the activating triggers are not economic; they are social and psychological – the suggestion of an imminent bank failure, a massive financial scandal, a rumour or maladroit government action, anything that makes enough overcommitted risk takers simultaneously attempt to sell their assets. It commonly occurs when shrewd – invariably insider – investors secretly decide to sell and knowledge of their selling becomes public. Then a massive sell

---

16   This was the practice defined as 'a pattern of financial transactions when a firm's interest payments are larger than its cash flows from operations' (Minsky 1975/2008). It developed and was made notorious by Charles Ponzi in the mid-1920s, the most dramatic example being that of Bernie Madoff, whose Ponzi scheme crashed in 2008.

17   This is the economic phenomenon that occurs when over-indebted investors are forced to sell good assets to pay back their loans, causing sharp declines in financial markets and jumps in demand for cash (*The Guardian* 2007; and see Minsky 1992.)

off follows and prices collapse. But it is just at this time that banks limit their credit: new loans are not readily offered and old loans not readily renewed. (The 'credit crunch' is not unique to this downturn!) Even a small disruption to the flow of credit repayments or a slight rise in interest rates can rapidly snowball to entail massively disproportionate effects. Among these is increased deviance as those who are 'crunched' try to avoid or at least delay their liability in the hope that things will improve.

It is towards the end of an upturn when euphoric, credit-based speculation has ousted orthodox investment, that deviance and crime can be expected to mount as panic rises and crises occur. Minsky (1992) has argued that crises are integral to financial markets, being essentially linked to their preceding upturn. As he puts it, 'Stability breeds instability.' The longer an upturn lasts, the more risks borrowers will take and the wider the reverberations when commitments cannot be met.

Four Cases

Four examples of upturns, each culminating in a crash followed by a downturn, are now discussed. These range from brief accounts of Tulipmania and the South Sea Bubble in the seventeenth and eighteenth centuries, to more detailed discussions of the two most recent upturns that culminated in the 1929 crash and the 2007/8 crash and 'credit crunch'. We thus have two historic 'classics' and two more recent cases spanning nearly four hundred years. They have been selected to demonstrate similar structural characteristics, conformity with Kondratieff's cycles, and apparent similarities in deviant practices. And though the methods and instruments used show consistency, they have over time developed in both sophistication and scope.

Tulipmania: Setting the Scene for Understanding 'Boom and Bust'

Tulipmania is the name given to a massive speculation in tulips and their bulbs that occurred in Holland in the seventeenth century. It created the first relatively well recorded major financial bubble, leading to a crash in 1636 that was followed by a downturn.

Tulips had been introduced to northern Europe in the mid-1500s from the Middle East and southern Europe. By the late 1570s, they had become fashionable at courts and among the aristocrats of France, Germany and England. By the end of the century, a taste for them had spread to the richer middle classes of Vienna and Holland, for whom they became a status symbol – a demonstration of wealth and good taste. As prices rose, collections came to include ever more refined and rarefied specimens. These were graded and classified, and the prices of the rarer ones attracted substantial premiums.

The early to mid-seventeenth century was Holland's Golden Age. At the hub of a trading empire with colonies in Asia and America, she had a vast maritime fleet and dominated the lucrative East India trade. She also had a developed banking system that facilitated the creation of credit – though much credit was also supplied by vendors. The trade in tulips, therefore, could readily be fuelled by a prosperous middle class with surplus funds accumulated from a rise in prosperity from 1622 and particularly during the first half of the 1630s.

Holland was thus well set to exploit the rising demand for tulips, and its soil and climate were particularly conducive to producing them. As trade in tulips in the 1620s extended well beyond its borders, methods of harvesting, storing, packing, transporting and securing tulips had to be developed. A new industry and new specialisms emerged: expert tulip assessors appraised new mutations, insurances were arranged, and the banks undertook large investments in especially designed tulip vaults (Beckman 1983, pp. 15–16). The credit they offered became integral to the new industry and to Holland's economy, which became dependent on the trade in tulips.

Speculation mounted in the early 1630s. At Tulipmania's peak, prized bulbs were selling for over 4,500 florins and the average price of a single bulb exceeded the annual income of a skilled worker. 'Four fat oxen could be bought for 480 florins', while the price paid for the rarest bulb of all, one of only two specimens, was

> 4600 florins, a new carriage, two grey horses and a complete set of harness ... Many individuals grew suddenly rich. A golden bait hung temptingly out before the people and one after the other, they rushed to the tulip-marts, like flies round a honey-pot. Everyone imagined that the passion for tulips would last forever and the wealthy from every part of the world would send to Holland and pay whatever prices were asked for them. (Mackay 1993, p. 91)

Beckman (1983, pp. 17–18) records a variety of scams during Tulipmania: 'Tulip Jobbers ... accrued huge profits by buying massive quantities each time there was a fall in price and rapidly selling out on every rise.' They could do this because of the tight networks in which they operated, while simultaneously spreading rumours about the market's inherent stability.

More obvious criminal activities developed:

> manipulators of the tulip market trained animals to dig up and devour bulbs for the purpose of creating a scarcity of selected strains, thus forcing prices higher. Ducks, cats, geese, pigs, chickens and various other household livestock were turned loose on the multifarious tulip patches to create havoc for the tulip breeder, grower and profits for their owners. (Beckman 1990)

In a foretaste of insider trading, 'tulip riggers' emerged who purchased the stocks of a specific grower and then spread rumours of calamitous destruction.

> The price of tulips from that region [would rise] to astronomical heights in anticipation of a permanent shortage of the species destroyed. They would

then sell ... to unsuspecting buyers preparing for further price rises. (Beckman 1990)

What later came to be known as rings were established:

> Tulip riggers would form a pool and choose a particular species of tulip that was out of favour ... By buying and selling among themselves, the riggers would make it appear that the selected species was suddenly in demand. (Beckman 1990, pp. 25–6)

They would do this repetitively, moving from one stock to another. But at the mania's peak some dealers, well aware that perpetual upward prices were beginning to appear unsustainable, sold out. As selling mounted, panic also mounted and tulip prices dramatically collapsed.

After the crash, as with all crashes, there was a public outcry and calls for regulation and control. In November 1636, the Dutch government ineffectually declared 'that all contracts made at the height of the mania or prior to the month of November 1636 should be declared null and void and that after that date purchasers should be freed from their engagements on paying ten percent to their vendors' (Mackay 1993, p. 6).

Tulipmania set the scene for our understanding of subsequent crashes. It demonstrated a dependence on a surplus of funds from earlier in the upturn, a ready supply of available credit, and a generalized belief that prices would rise in perpetuity. It embraced a network of market manipulators who knowingly encouraged this belief and a refined development of criminal and deviant specialties. Together these contributed to euphoric bidding that rose to a peak and was followed by a sudden crash, a downturn (lasting in this case until approximately 1650), public outrage, and resultant moves for government regulation.

The South Sea Bubble of 1720

In the early eighteenth century, England was the trading centre of the world. Its economy was booming with a wave of developments in construction and transport, and its trade was supported by the unrivalled power of its empire. Large profits were simultaneously accruing to its trading companies operating abroad, such as the Hudson's Bay Company and the West and East India companies. As in Holland a century earlier, there was a prosperous and investment-conscious middle class with funds to spare. The situation was thus well set to launch a company that offered trading opportunities in the South Seas and beyond.

The South Sea Company's principal asset was a monopoly granted by the British government in 1711 to exploit the riches of the South Seas (which extended also to South America, the West Coast of North America, and onwards to the Far East). It was granted, together with the right to obtain the revenues of certain taxes, in return for accepting responsibility for the national debt – swollen by liabilities in maintaining unmanageably expensive Army and Navy debentures. These costs were causing mounting government concern because they involved unsustainably high taxes. Since the South Sea Company had explicit government support, the new enterprise seemed to be following the precedent of the lucrative East India Company and it was enthusiastically oversubscribed.

After its launch in 1711, the stock suffered various setbacks but the directors, 'by various arts' (Mackay 1993, p. 65) and then with specific government backing, encouraged

> the most extravagant rumours [about supposedly emergent treaties] between England and Spain ... whereby the latter was to grant a free trade to all her colonies; and the rich produce of the mines of Potosi-la-Paz was to be brought to England until silver should become as plentiful as iron. For cotton and woollen goods, with which we could supply them in abundance, the dwellers of Mexico were to empty their gold mines. The company of merchants trading to the South Seas would be the richest the world ever saw, and every hundred pounds invested in it would produce hundreds per annum to the stockholder. (Mackay 1993, p. 51)

In little over the ten years of its existence, the enthusiasm of investors had at different times faltered then been maintained by the spreading of false rumours, by paying, on occasion, double the expected level of dividend, at others by the issuance of new stock and by the use of 'tame' journalists. One such journalist was Daniel Defoe, who, when the shares were at their peak, wrote a journal article 'puffing' the price further. It is suggested that he owned shares in the companies he promoted, an early example, it is claimed, illustrating the later venality of much of the press that had become well established by the time of the 1920s upturn – many later examples of this are offered by Kindleberger and Aliber (2011, p. 146).

But the exuberance surrounding the South Sea Company had simultaneously encouraged nearly a hundred fraudulent joint stock companies largely funded by credit,

> each more extravagant and deceptive than the other ... promoted by crafty knaves, then pursued by multitudes of covetous fools, and appear[ing] to be, in effect, what their vulgar appellation denoted them to be – bubbles and mere cheats.' (Mackay 1993, p. 54)

Some bubble companies were established merely with the view of raising their shares in the market. 'The projectors took the first opportunity of a rise to sell out, and next morning the scheme was at an end' (Beckman 1990). Some of the schemes were clearly ludicrous. One, for instance, was

> for a wheel for perpetual motion – capital one million pounds ... another for a company for carrying on an undertaking of great advantage, but nobody to know what it is ... it was computed that near one million and a half sterling was won

and lost by these unwarrantable practices, to the [eventual] impoverishment of many a fool, and the enriching of many a rogue. (Mackay 1993, pp. 54–5)

The growth of the more obviously fraudulent companies was soon seen as posing a serious threat to the South Sea Company, since money invested in them was not available to it. When, in 1720, the South Sea Company's share price again wavered, its directors sought support from the government – many members of which were shareholders. In 1720 it passed what came to be called 'The Bubble Act', which outlawed companies without a royal warrant. The move was successful and the price of South Sea shares rose to its peak at £1,000.

The directors owned significant blocks of shares and were able to collateralize them and use the funds raised to invest in real estate. Their central concern was then to boost the value of the stock to effect a capital gain, and the spreading of rumours was integral to this. The company chairman Sir John Blunt 'had six contracts to buy estates … another [insider] had four … on which he owed £100,000'. It was therefore necessary to increase capital and the price of stock simultaneously and at an accelerating rate 'as in a Ponzi scheme' (Kindleberger and Aliber 2011, p. 14).

Despite the company's efforts, the peak price of £1,000 was not sustainable. The chairman, his close associates, various directors and members of the government, well aware the value of their assets was minimal compared to their stated values, sold out. When knowledge of this became public, the stock crashed and soon was worthless.

As with Tulipmania, popular clamour was again raised that 'this must never happen again'. Mobs rose and pressure mounted on the government to regulate market excesses, which in part it did by outlawing the issuing of stock certificates, thereby abolishing limited liability. This law was not repealed until 1825 and thereby helped inhibit the subsequent recovery.

The 1929 Crash (and its Precursor, the Florida Land Boom)

The 1929 Crash followed a similar progression to its predecessors and exhibited similar (though more sophisticated) behaviours. Its sequence began in 1920–22, with a recession in wholesale prices of 42 per cent and a fall in the Dow Jones Index of 33 per cent. Similar or worse falls were recorded in France, the UK and elsewhere, though the markets recovered fairly quickly.

However, there was a further portent of disaster when massive speculation in land based upon exploiting Florida's warm sunshine led to the Florida land boom and the emergence of Charles Ponzi. As many as twenty-three building sites per acre, together with streets laid out on sub-marginal land, were offered that were larcenously described as 'being on the seashore when they were up to 15 miles inland' or, in Ponzi's sales pitch, described as 'being "near Jacksonville" when they were up to 65 miles distant from the city' (Galbraith 1994, pp. 62–3). But in their scramble to invest, buyers were not bothered by such detail – they were in the market to speculate, not to reside in Florida. The end, in 1926, was swift:

the supply of new buyers ran out and land prices crashed. 'Some land having passed through the hands of half a dozen speculators, each reaping the rewards of leverage, was returned, in successive defaults to the original owner ... In 1925, bank clearings in Miami were $1,066,528,000. By 1928 they were down to a mere $143,364,000' (Galbraith 1994, p. 64, quoting Allen 1931, p. 282).

Nevertheless, the 'Roaring Twenties' roared on and a record number of new and inexperienced investors with surplus funds from the prior boom began to gamble on the stock exchange. They focused particularly on the newly emergent industries and technologies dominated by automobiles and radio. As in Holland three hundred years earlier and in England a century after that, financial affairs in this period were similarly 'noted for manipulation and swindling. Interest brokers, blockers, traders and owners banded together to manipulate stock prices by trading them between each other for slightly more each time. An ignorant public noticed the trend and invested through credit whilst the manipulators sold at a healthy profit' (Beattie 2012). Meanwhile, the market soared.

One important reason it soared was that shares could be bought from brokers 'on margin' in anticipation of their imminent rise for as little as a 10 per cent down payment of the purchase price (though some purchasers were required to offer up to 50 per cent). The balance was borrowed from the broker, who in turn borrowed from the banks.

Galbraith suggests a second, more sophisticated example of leverage effected through 'closed ended investment trusts' that could effect multiple levels of leverage – and which, when they crashed, involved multiple scales of de-leverage. These trusts were pioneered by Goldman Sachs in 1928 when it created a company, Goldman Sachs Trading Corporation, whose sole function was to own other companies' stock. It issued securities amounting to $100 million (a billion dollars at 1994 prices), 90 per cent of which was sold to the public, with 10 per cent being retained by Goldman Sachs. The Trading Corporation issued common stock, bonds and preferred stock. The latter two had fixed returns that did not rise with the price of the stock, so that all gains accrued to the price of the common stock. Goldman Sachs then sponsored a further company (whose initial issue was said to have been oversubscribed sevenfold) and that company sponsored yet another. All the intervening companies in their turn issued the three types of security. The large gains in the stock of the final company soared as its holdings boomed and these went 'in powerful concentrations' to add to the stock of the intervening companies until it was fed into Goldman Sachs. The Goldman Sachs initial issue sold at a hundred and four and after the crash was worth one and three quarters (Galbraith 1994, pp. 70–74).

Galbraith notes that there followed many other examples of closed-end trusts, some even more spacious in scale and imagination. As a result of this explosion of highly leveraged credit, equity prices rose to a peak of thirty times earnings (Beattie 2012). Then, between September 1929 and the end of that October, and without apparent warning, the Dow Jones fell by 40 per cent. There followed a further, albeit slower but nonetheless precipitous, collapse, so that by July 1932 the Index had fallen 90 per cent from its 1929 peak.

Speculation had thus again been facilitated by an explosion of unregulated credit. Its level had risen from 45 per cent of US GNP in 1945/46 to over 150 per cent in 1929 (Elliot 2011). When prices fell, speculators were then required to fund a higher percentage of their margins. But the banks would not extend further credit and debts were liquidated in a self-feeding chain reaction that rapidly extended throughout the global economy. Once again, there was public clamour.

Much of this clamour was directed against the banks. During the upturn, many US banks had established security affiliates to float bonds and underwrite corporate stock issues. In this they had benefitted from banking's two classic profit-making strategies: the ability to 'create credit' by increasing the margin of lending as a proportion of assets and the ability to use such resources to engage in risky ventures. The banks made massive profits until the crash of 1929. In 1932, after nearly five thousand banks had failed, an appalled Congress, responding to vigorous public pressure, passed the emergency Glass–Steagall Act as part of Roosevelt's New Deal. The Act imposed controls on bank lending and reintroduced the boundaries that traditionally had governed their activities – notably by separating their commercial and investment functions, thereby reducing their ability to take risks.

The Glass–Steagall Act's provisions were made 'permanent' in 1945. But the next upturn's lobbying, spearheaded by the financial services sector, again mounted for a loosening of financial controls. Reagan and later Clinton's congresses responded favourably and the Glass–Steagall Act was emasculated by the Gramm–Leach–Bliley Act of 1999. This imposition of controls during a downturn and their later removal through the lobbying of financial interests in the subsequent upturn, as might be expected, follows the alternating domination of hierarchic and individualist ideologies.

The Housing Bubble and Credit Crunch of 2007/8

The housing bubble and credit crunch of 2007/8 was distinctive in two ways. First, it was a product of an upturn that had lasted longer than any other; second, and integrally linked to its length, it was fuelled by greater excess credit.[18] This was sourced from the earning surpluses of developing countries – mainly China – and the recycling of surplus commodity earnings, especially from Australia and Canada. This massively available credit coincided with the Federal Reserve's determination, post the dot-com bust of 2000, to keep US interest rates low, which pressed down global interest rates. As a result, surplus available credit at low prices meant that global returns from investments such as government bonds declined to record low levels. Low returns then encouraged investors to assume more risk by seeking higher returns wherever they could be found. They were found in funding mortgages for the housing market, particularly in the US.

---

18   In the US at the peak of the boom in the last decade, it had reached 300 per cent (a record), while in the UK, as the boom mounted, people had withdrawn £300 billion in equity withdrawals from domestic property (Elliot 2011).

Sub-prime mortgages, sold by 'bonus-fuelled' lenders, led to a US domestic property boom that quickly extended globally, particularly to the UK. It was backed by a general supposition that home prices could never decline and it was further boosted by the increasingly frenetic activity of an orchestrated financial services sector that was extensively backed by cheap credit.

The US financial services sector was – and still is – dominated by the relatively small number of firms that emerged after a series of amalgamations in the 1990s. In 2006 it comprised five investment banks – Morgan Stanley, Lehman Brothers, Goldman Sachs, Merrill Lynch, Bear Stearns – and two conglomerate firms – Citigroup and JP Morgan Chase (which straddled several functions). They were supported by AIG, the world's largest insurance company, and three assessment agencies – Moody, Standard & Poor's, and Fitch. Acting in unison, these companies were integral in exploiting the domestic housing market and ultimately in creating the 2007/8 crash.

The investment banks bought up large numbers of mortgages, which they combined ('bundled') into units called 'collateral debt obligations' (CDOs), a new form of financial 'instrument' known as 'derivatives'. Investors bought CDOs based on the AAA ratings they were awarded by the main rating agencies that, assessed them as investments. The assessors do not face financial liability if their ratings prove erroneous, though, they argue, they stand to lose credibility.

Each segment of the US financial sector had close links to government and to validating consultancy advice, in that senior office holders in different companies rotated positions between themselves, government regulatory posts and university business school professorships (Ferguson 2011). The companies therefore comprised individualist networkers rather than insulated company-oriented hierarchists.

However, a new, sophisticated and highly influential development made its appearance during the past upturn. A mathematical formula was devised by which elements of risk could be calculated and factored into transactions. Loans could be made and profits gained by lending to people not considered safe by orthodox measurements and then insuring against the odds of their failure to comply (Black and Scholes 1973). The formula was massively applied to value derivatives, enabling them to be traded as commodities prior to maturity.

The financial services industry avidly embraced the Black–Scholes formula, and

> by 2007 was trading derivatives valued at one quadrillion dollars per year …
> 10 times the total worth, adjusted for inflation, of all products made by the world's manufacturing industries over the last century. The downside was the invention of ever-more complex financial instruments whose value and risk were increasingly opaque. (Stewart 2012)

In buttressing speculation on a massive scale, the Black–Scholes formula facilitated speculating on speculation. It eventually failed because its mathematics didn't take account of imponderables that would eventually, and inevitably did, intrude – as they had when Lehman Brothers collapsed in 2007. This provides a further reason for the extended length of the last upturn, as to why the current long-delayed downturn is likely to prove particularly disruptive.

CDOs, however, were known as being far from safe investments (Rajan 2005) because they included some 30 per cent of sub-prime mortgages – mortgages granted to those with little hope of sustaining them. They also comprised risky car financing and student loans. But, because the assessors had rated them AAA, they were eligible to be purchased by retirement funds and other agencies and by individuals wanting safe investments.

There is considerable evidence (for example, Ferguson 2011; Lewis 2010; Beattie 2012) that the five major US investment banks were well aware of the insecure nature of the housing market and of the CDOs they were selling – for which they took out insurance against the likelihood of a drop in the housing market. When the CDOs proved toxic, their purchasers, including retirement funds,[19] took massive losses, as did the retirees dependent on them and AIG – also rated AAA – who was the insurer of last resort. But, as with the banks, AIG was deemed 'too big to fail' and it required more than $150 billion in taxpayers' emergency aid. The same rating agencies had similarly awarded a triple-A rating to Lehman Brothers – until it too crashed in 2007. As Beattie (2012) records,

> In 2006 and 2007, the Goldman Sachs Group, aware of the imminence of a tipping point, [had] peddled more than $40 billion in securities backed by at least 200,000 risky home mortgages, but [had] never told the buyers it was secretly betting [through insurance] that a sharp drop in US housing prices would send the value of those securities plummeting.

Another commentator (McClatchy 2009) noted,

> Goldman's sales and its clandestine wagers, completed at the brink of the housing market meltdown, enabled the nation's premier investment bank to pass most of its potential losses to others before a flood of mortgage defaults staggered the US and global economies. Only later did investors discover that what Goldman Sachs had promoted as AAA rated investments were closer to junk.

Indeed, after the crash they turned to junk.

> Now, pension funds, insurance companies, labour unions and foreign financial institutions that bought those dicey mortgage securities[20] faced large losses.

---

19   Retirement funds were prevented by their legally backed constitutions from investing in anything other than AAA securities.

20   Most of whose constitutions forbade them investing in anything other than AAA investments.

Parallel deception was evident in the UK when Fred Goodwin, head of the Royal Bank of Scotland, the UK's largest bank (at one time the world's largest), was publicly denying his bank held sub-prime securities when in fact it was so heavily involved with them that they eventually brought down the bank.

In the UK, Margaret Thatcher's pro-individualist government, in power during the 1980s upturn, as in the US, was dedicated to the deregulation of industry and commerce. It too was also subject to lobbying by the financial services sector, which resulted in the large-scale scrapping of financial regulations – known as 'the big bang'. Its various building society acts permissively allowed building societies to demutualize and become banks. Their buying of sub-prime mortgages then mirrored the US banking experience. Again, large profits were made – and large salaries and bonuses paid to their executives based on short-term profits. This continued until – and indeed after – most of these banks had crashed in 2007/8.

As the 1990s advanced, the upwave moved towards its peak and the scale of imaginative innovation grew. But by no means all classic examples of deviance were restricted to the financial services sector.

In the US, the Enron debacle was massive. Originally trading in electricity, natural gas, water and broadband, and then widely extending its interests, its stock had risen by 1,700 per cent. Described by *Fortune Magazine* for seven consecutive years as 'the most innovative corporation in the US', in its final year its share price fell from an opening price of $61 to a closing price of 20 cents (Cruver 2003). 'At its peak its market capitalization had been $250 billion, the market value of its stock ... over $200 billion and its publicly owned bonds $40 billion' (Kindleberger and Aliber 2011, p. 129). It rapidly reached this pinnacle in part by refining versions of the South Sea Company's share-boosting techniques. Enron's senior managers were incentivized by the award of stock options as bonuses so that the bigger and more consistent its profits, the more their options were worth.

Enron ensured that reported profits were consistently high by over-valuing futures contracts and including their revised valuations in current profits as well as engaging in complex sale and leaseback arrangements. Both methods increased their stated current assets at the expense of future profits. Further, they borrowed in ways that avoided balance sheet notations through legalized accountancy finagling and then used the funds to support their own stock price (Kindleberger and Aliber 2011; Cruver 2003). By these means, the company was able to boost earnings while concealing its debts. But it could do so only as long as its share price remained buoyant.

To this end, and like the South Sea Company, Enron used the press. As well as buoyancy, the consistency of its share price was important to Enron since the financial press made quarterly assessments of company incomes. A fall in a single month's assessment could lead to a 20 per cent drop in the share price. Enron therefore ensured that earnings were 'smoothed' with larger than necessary increases in profits being deferred by delaying receipts or prepaying expenses. When profits were less than deemed necessary, they practised the reverse. Their efforts were eased by payments to some financial journalists – who were paid on retainers of $25,000, for attending one meeting per year.

In upturns, there is a general loosening of auditing standards that reflect the overall climate of deregulation, and it was this that facilitated Enron's strategies. After the upturn post the 1890s crash, there had developed a progressive reduction in the expected distance between auditors and those they audited until their interests were thought to merge and the profession lost public credibility. In 1913 a new firm, Arthur Andersen, was established. It proclaimed a fresh moral approach and its success in emphasizing conformity to downturn hierarchic values was marked. It quickly rose to become one of the US's top four accountancy firms. It is ironic, therefore, that in the period of deregulation during the last upturn Arthur Andersen should have become auditors to Enron.

As Enron's auditors, Arthur Andersen merged the incompatible functions of both auditor and highly paid consultant. For these services, Enron paid it $2 million and $25 million per year respectively. These dual roles facilitated a whole set of ingenious, accountancy-based scams until the market crashed in 2000 and both firms collapsed together. This was despite consistently positive assessments by Standard & Poor's who assessed it as a suitable vehicle for investment. This it did, awarding it continuous AAA ratings and – with other rating assessors – maintaining this until Enron could no longer juggle its liabilities and crashed. The assessing agencies argue that their assessments were largely dependent on the distortions issued by Arthur Andersen.

Enron was perhaps the upturn's most dramatic corporate failure. But this failure, as Nelken (2007) has noted, represented 'the flip side' of the company's previous success. Enron had been a genuinely innovative company. Following opportunities offered by the Black–Scholes formula, it had successfully been making money out of risk and thus conforming to the essence of modern capitalism: it was, in effect, selling insurance (Nelken 2007). Enron's rise and fall nicely illustrates the shadowy line between parasitism and making a profit and between illegality and being within the law.

The ebullient 1990s and 2000s also included Bernie Madoff's individualist Ponzi scam, the greatest in history. When the stock exchange crashed in 2008 and his clients attempted to withdraw $11 billion from his fund, they found it wasn't available and the scale of the fraud was then revealed. Estimates of loss range from $20 billion to over $60 billion. Madoff, however, was distinctive only in the scale of his fraud. He was at the forefront of a wide range of lesser Ponzi schemes that flourished through the upturn.

Many forms of upturn deviance involve the manipulation or theft of information, which not only includes the spreading of false rumours and the commissioning of journalists 'puffing' articles, as in the four cases, but theft of information that facilitates insider dealings. It is widespread and can offer lucrative benefits.

On 13 April 2011 Raj Rajaratnam, founder of the Galleon Hedge Fund, was convicted in New York of insider dealings. The judge estimated his takings were 'well over $50 million', derived from corporate acquisitions and by benefiting from inside knowledge of large changes to corporate earnings. Rajaratnam was later jailed for eleven years and fined $10 million (*New York Times* 2011). He worked through a network of executive informants in major companies and was arraigned with twenty-six others, accused of passing or applying confidential information.

As the current downturn proceeds, another aspect of managerial behaviour is increasingly seen as deviant (though not criminal), which was not considered so during the upturn. Senior UK managers (mirroring similar changes in the US) increased their pay from a multiple of 14.5 of average worker's pay in 1979, to a multiple of 75 in 2009–11. This discrepancy is widest at the very top. In 2011, the average CEO of a FTSE 100 company was taking home 145 times the basic pay of an average worker, *plus* bonuses, pension payments and share options – averaging, in all, £4,365,636 against average worker earnings of £25,900 (High Pay Commission 2011).

These differences are accelerating. Top managers in 2009–10 increased their takings by a further 30 per cent and in 2010–11 by 49 per cent compared to their workers' average increases of 2–3 per cent and 2.5 per cent. These later increases were awarded after the current downturn was well established and when some businesses – and especially banks – were not even covering the cost of their capital in terms of the risks taken.

How is it that managers have been so successful in increasing their share of company profits, in many cases irrespective of company performance? It has been suggested this is due to a progressive uncoupling of the balancing elements in corporate governance. In the conventional wisdom, the power of managers, 'independent' directors and shareholders (the owners) is expected to balance to ensure businesses are run for the long-term benefit of owners and to control inherent managerial excess. This has signally failed as shareholders have progressively abnegated their powers to managers and withdrawn oversight as long as they produced favourable, albeit short-term, results.[21]

Managers have also benefitted because of the tendency to pay them bonuses, thus again encouraging short-term tactics at the expense of dividends and longer-term strategic investments. With reduced shareholder restraints, we have also seen widespread 'organizational capture' by individualist managers.

Similarities in Variation

The four selected cases show that, though history may not repeat itself, it most certainly rhymes. In each period, there are evident variations in institutional structures, dominant technologies, and in the sophistication of deviant and fraudulent practices.

---

21   Lord Myners (Financial Services Secretary, October 2008 – May 2010), quoted in a radio programme 'In Business – Corporate Governance', presented by Peter Day, BBC Radio 4, 14 August 2011. This accelerating process was described by Warren Buffet (2001) as operated by 'Ratchet, Ratchet, Ratchet and Partners'.

But the structures of each upturn remain similar: they reveal the same patterns of bubbles followed by the same patterns of crashes. While methods of manipulative innovation become progressively more complex, they too remain essentially the same. And each sequence 'fits' the amended regularities of Kondratieff's economic cycles: history's 'rhymes' apply not just to the structure of bubbles and crashes but also to the structure and styles of their deviance and criminality.

We find that, as markets rise, deviant insiders have attempted to boost their company's prospects by lying in public pronouncements, planting false rumours, and by secretly selling out at what they believe is the top of the market while continuing to encourage sales to the wider public. These were the practices during Tulipmania in 1636; of the South Sea Company directors in 1720; they emerged again prior to the 1929 crash; and yet again in the housing crash and credit crunch of 2007/8.

In the more obvious examples of deviance, we therefore see variations of practice yet consistency in the principles employed. The extensive operations of 'riggers' in Tulipmania are paralleled by the escalation of contemporary 'boiler shops' whose principals trade with each other to increase the price of stocks they hold, the resulting rise in price encouraging repetitive 'cold-caller' sales to gullible investors. Other consistent variations involve borrowing on overstated assets to buy lavish lifestyles – as the directors of the South Sea Company did in 1720 and the directors of Parmalat did before it crashed in 2010.[22] And after each crash, public perceptions of what is and isn't deviance shift, and pressures[23] mount to demand government regulation against entrepreneurial excess.

Overall

The longer the upturn, the greater the excess. This is to be expected as more transactions become dependent on increasing credit and because the longer manipulative practices flourish, the more accomplished and confident their practitioners become. The more sophisticated the practices, the bigger they are likely to grow and the more concerned will practitioners be to ensure their continuance.

The pattern and extent of corporate activity during upturns exhibits a consistent prioritizing of short-term interests over longer-term concerns. Indeed, short-termism is both a cause and a consequence of upturns. In upturns, money is made by being short termist, whereas money in downturns is made or at least retained, by being long termist. Short termism in an upturn appears the most logical response to prevailing conditions. Entrepreneurs, having no experience of downturns, base their practices on the limited experience of their own pasts. And they are buoyed by the prevailing wisdom of every upturn – that it will last forever. In emphasizing

---

22   The dairy foods manufacturer, the eighth largest firm in Italy, failed to meet interest liabilities of 18 billion euros.

23   It is intriguing, at the time of writing, to note a possibly marginal shift by advertisers from using images of 'Executives' to those of 'Professionals'.

this process, we are not negating the consequences that follow many of their actions but attempting to explain how they come about.

Where Now?

At the time of writing,[24] the reassertion of hierarchic values associated with downturns, is slowly becoming evident in public attitudes to the excesses of the last upturn. Shareholders are starting to campaign against the 'bonus culture', that epitome of individualist short termism, and to point to its effects on dividends and the neglect of long-term investment. There have been few results to date, and the gaps between top and bottom pay levels are still widening. But they can be expected to narrow as the austerities of the downturn kick in, leading to further denunciation of entrepreneurs and a redefinition of many of their behaviours as deviant or indeed as criminal. There is a danger, however, that the resurgence of hierarchic values may swing regulation and controls so far that it inhibits the enterprise necessary to power the next upturn

So far there have been insubstantial attempts, on both sides of the Atlantic, to make the Assessment Agencies accountable for their assessments, to control pay differentials, or to institute a Financial Services (or 'Tobin') Tax. Attempts in the US to limit banking excesses on the lines of the Glass–Steagall provisions have so far been unsuccessful and in the UK have been sidelined to 2017. Transition from the institutions and practices of Individualism to those of Hierarchy, therefore, currently appear limited, possibly because the financial service industries – and much of manufacturing and commerce – are now unquestionably global in their influence while their opponents are limited to mobilizing only as competing national entities. But, as the pressures of austerity mount, the pressures to institute hierarchic controls can also be expected to mount.

References

Beattie, A. (2012), Items 6 and 10, 'Market Crashes: The Grand Depression (1929)' and 'Market Crashes: Housing Bubble and Credit Crisis (2007–2009)', via www.investopedia.com (accessed 30 June 2012).

Beckman, R. (1983), *The Downwave*, London: Pan Books.

Beckman, R. (1990), *Crashes*, London: Grafton Books.

Black, F. and Scholes, M.S. (1973), 'The Pricing of Options and Corporate Liabilities', *Journal of Political Economy*, 81(3), 637–54.

Buffett, W. (2001), Berkshire Hathaway 2001 Chairman's Letter, at www.berkshirehathaway.com/2001ar/2001letter.html (accessed 30 June 2012).

Cruver, B. (2003), *Enron: Anatomy of Greed*, London: Arrow Books.

---

24   Mid-2012.

Ferguson, C. (2011), *Inside Job: The Financiers Who Pulled Off the Heist of the Century*, Oxford: Oneworld Publishers.

Freeman, C. (ed.) (1983), *Long Waves in the World Economy*, London: Butterworth.

Galbraith, J.K. (1955), *The Great Crash, 1929*, London: Hamish Hamilton.

Galbraith, J.K. (1994), *The World Economy since the Wars*, London: Sinclair-Stevenson.

Going, C.J. (1992), 'Economic "Long Waves" in the Roman Period? A Reconnaissance of the Romano-British Ceramic Evidence', *Oxford Journal of Archaeology*, 11(1), 93–117.

Guardian (2007), 'In Praise of Hyman Minsky', 22 August, 00.

Hayek, F.A. (1944), *The Road to Serfdom*, Chicago, IL: Chicago University Press.

High Pay Commission (2011), *Final Report, the High Pay Commission*, London: Compass.

Ingram, D. and Thompson, M. (2011), 'Changing Seasons of Risk Attitudes', *The Actuary* (US), Feb./Mar., 20–24.

Ingram, D., Taylor, P. and Thompson, M. (2011), 'Surprise, Surprise: From Neoclassical Economics to E-life', *ASTIN Bulletin: The Journal of the International Actuarial Association*.

Juglar, C. (1862), *Des crises commerciales et de leur retour périodique en France, en Angleterre, et aux Etats-Unis*, Paris: Guillaumin.

Kaldor, N. (1982), 'Economic Prospects of the 1980s', in *Experiences and Problems of the International Monetary System: Economic Notes*, Siena: Monte dei Paschi di Siena.

Keynes, J.M. (1936), *The General Theory of Employment, Interest and Money*, Cambridge: Cambridge University Press.

Kindleberger, C.P. and Aliber, R.Z. (2011), *Manias, Panics and Crashes*, 6th edn, Basingstoke: Palgrave Macmillan.

Kitchin, J. (1923), 'Cycles and Trends in Economic Factors', *Review of Economics and Statistics*, 5(1), 10–16.

Kondratieff, N.D. (1978), 'The Long Waves in Economic Life', *Lloyds Bank Review*, 129, 41–60 (originally published in German, 1921).

Levi, M. (2008), *The Phantom Capitalists: The Organisation and Control of Long-firm Fraud*, Farnham: Ashgate Publishers.

Lewis, M. (2010), *The Big Short*, London and New York: Allen Lane/Penguin Books.

Lukes, S. (2005), *Power: A Radical View*, 2nd edn, London: Palgrave Macmillan.

Mackay, C. (1993), *Extraordinary Popular Delusions and the Madness of Crowds*, New York: Barnes and Noble.

Mandel, E. (2005), 'Long Waves', in T. Bottomore et al. (eds), *A Dictionary of Marxist Thought*, 2nd edn, Oxford: Blackwell Publishing, 324–5.

Matthews, R.C.O. (1959), *The Trade Cycle*, Welwyn: James Nisbet & Co.; Cambridge: Cambridge University Press.

McClatchy (2009), 'How Goldman Secretly Bet on the U.S. Housing Crash', at http://www.mcclatchydc.com/2009/11/01/77791/how-goldman-secretly-bet-on-the.html (accessed 1 November 2009).

Minsky, H. (1975/2008), *John Maynard Keynes*, New York: McGraw-Hill Professional.

Minsky, H. (1992), 'The Financial Instability Hypothesis', The Jerome Levy Economics Institute Working Paper Series, reprinted in G. Argyrous and F. Stilwell (eds) (2003), *Economics as a Social Science: Readings in Political Economy*, North Melbourne: Pluto Press, 201–3.

New York Times (2011), 'Galleon Chief Sentenced to 11-Year Term in Insider Case', Business Section, 13 October.

Nelken, D. (2007), 'White Collar and Corporate Crime', in M. Maguire, R. Morgan and R. Reiner (eds), *The Oxford Handbook of Criminology*, 4th edn, Oxford: Oxford University Press.

Parkin, T.G. (1992), *Demography and Roman Society*, Baltimore, MD: Johns Hopkins University Press.

Rajan, R.G. (2005), *Has Financial Development Made the World Riskier?* International Monetary Fund.

Schumpeter, J. (1939), *Business Cycles*, 2 vols, New York: McGraw Hill.

Shurig, R. (1984), 'Morphology: A Tool for Exploring New Technology', *Long Range Planning*, 17(3), 129–40.

Stewart, I. (2012), *The Observer*, 12 February.

Thompson, M. (2008), 'Beyond Boom and Bust', *Journal of the Royal Society of Arts*, Winter, 34–9.

Weber, R. (1981), 'Society and Economy in the Western World System', *Social Forces*, 59(4), 1130–48.

Whalen, C.J. (2008), 'Association of Evolutionary Economists', *Journal of Economic Issues*, 42(1), 248.

Williamson, O.E. (1975), *Markets and Hierarchies*, New York: Free Press.

Appendix
A Practical Guide to Doing Organizational Ethnography: LISTOR/SPARCK

LISTOR/SPARCK is a dual acronym devised to guide the ordering and systemizing of ethnographic fieldwork in a CT frame. It was developed in an earlier study of the culture of households and refined during studies of building workers. It is applicable with a minimum of adaptation to a variety of contexts. As applied here, it is appropriate to groups and occupations within organizations. It is not designed as a qualitatively sophisticated tool but within its limitations has proved effective in achieving what engineers call 'quick and dirty' assessments.

To carry out ethnographic assessments of an organization using CT first requires awareness of the main characteristics of the four cultures (solidarities) that are spelled out in Chapter 1. Armed with this background, the next step requires identification of the organization's workgroups and jobs. It is suggested that grid/group scores can then be assessed by observation – ideally by participant observation, rather than by issuing questionnaires. This involves collecting and comparing data (while noting that the comparisons are essentially relative) under the following headings. The analysis involves assessing six grid components and six components of group incorporation.

The six grid constituents comprising **LISTOR** are assessed by raising the following questions:

- Labour divisions: extensive or absent? Are specific tasks considered appropriate only to specific roles and ranks (indicating strong grid) or are tasks performed as adaptability, availability, urgency and skills determine (weak grid)?
- Information: restricted or open? Is it restricted on a 'need-to-know' basis and validated only if derived from 'approved' sources via accredited conduits (indicating strong grid)? Or is it free flowing and multi-sourced (weak grid)?
- Space. Is space primarily used to buttress rank, restricted and allocated to office (indicating strong grid) or is its use adaptive to functional needs (weak grid)?
- Time. Is time used as a social organizer and a source of control (indicating strong grid) or as a fluid resource that allows personal autonomy (weak grid)?
- Objects. Are these primarily allocated to rank irrespective of function

(indicating strong grid) or as determined by functional needs (weak grid)?

- **Resources.** Are resources controlled from the centre and distributed according to traditionally validated principles (indicating strong grid) or allocated to specific functions as required (weak grid)?

Group incorporation can be assessed by applying the second acronym, **SPARCK**, also by using six constituents:

- **Selection and promotion.** Are selection and promotion influenced by ascribed characteristics (indicating strong group) rather than on achievement criteria (weak group)?
- **Propinquity of residence.** Do subjects live in the same neighbourhood (indicating strong group) or are they residentially dispersed (weak group)?
- **Association at work.** Do people work on collective tasks and make collective decisions (indicative of strong group)? Or are these activities disproportionately focused on individuals (weak group)?
- **Roll-over of work and leisure.** Are co-workers mutually involved in leisure activities (indicating strong group)? Or are there minimal off-site social activities with co-workers (weak group)?
- **Common histories.** Do members of the group have similar shared experiences (indicating strong group)? Or is this absent (weak group)?
- **Kinship.** Are there significant kin relationships within the workplace (indicating strong group)? Or is this absent (weak group)?

Grid and Group ratings for each set of constituents can then be allocated numerical strengths of between 1 and 6 as follows:

- Weakest   1
- Weak   2
- Moderately Weak   3
- Moderately Strong 4
- Strong   5
- Strongest   6

It has been found that both LISTOR and SPARCK constituents tend to occupy similar overall ratings. If one or more constituent scores diverges widely from the others, it points to that area as worthy of further enquiry. It might, for instance, indicate the source of an emerging shift within or between cultures or the intrusion of external forces.

To gain readings for both the Grid and Group dimensions, the figures for their constituents can be added and divided by six. The two resultant totals should then represent the overall rating of Grid and Group. These numbers can next be plotted on a Grid/Group chart with Grid on the vertical axis and Group on the horizontal, to give an overall allocation to cultural category as follows:

Armed with this method of allocation, the values, attitudes and ideal behaviours of each cultural category can then be assigned and 'read off' – as these are listed in Chapter 1.

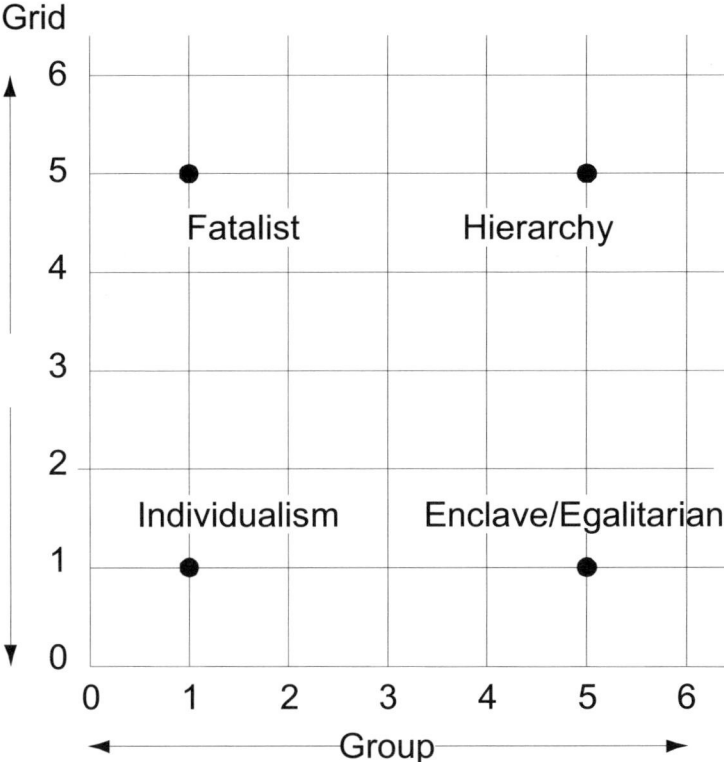

Figure A.1   Plotting Grid and Group

Index

Advances in Criminology

Full series list

Re-Thinking the Political Economy of
Punishment: Perspectives on Post-Fordism
and Penal Politics
Alessandro De Giorgi

Transitional Justice
Images and Memories
*Edited by Chrisje Brants, Antoine Hol and
Dina Siegel*

The Arts of Imprisonment
Control, Resistance and Empowerment
Edited by Leonidas K. Cheliotis

The Hidden Order of Corruption
An Institutional Approach
*Donatella della Porta and
Alberto Vannucci*

Comparative Criminal Justice and
Globalization
Edited by David Nelken

Racial Criminalization of Migrants in the
21st Century
Edited by Salvatore Palidda

Pervasive Prevention
A Feminist Reading of the Rise of
the Security Society
Tamar Pitch

Children's Rights and the Minimum
Age of Criminal Responsibility
A Global Perspective
Don Cipriani

Hate on the Net:
Extremist Sites, Neo-fascism On-line,
Electronic Jihad
Antonio Roversi

Decisions to Imprison:
Court Decision-Making Inside
and Outside the Law
Rasmus H. Wandall

The Policing of Transnational Protest
*Edited by Donatella della Porta,
Abby Peterson and Herbert Reiter*

Migration, Culture Conflict, Crime
and Terrorism
*Edited by Joshua D. Freilich and
Rob T. Guerette*

Re-Thinking the Political Economy
of Punishment:
Perspectives on Post-Fordism
and Penal Politics
Alessandro De Giorgi

Deleuze and Environmental Damage:
Violence of the Text
Mark Halsey

Globalization and Regulatory Character:
Regulatory Reform after the Kader Toy
Factory Fire
Fiona Haines

Family Violence and Police Response:
Learning From Research, Policy and
Practice in European Countries
*Edited by Wilma Smeenk and
Marijke Malsch*

Crime and Culture:
An Historical Perspective
*Edited by Amy Gilman Srebnick and
René Lévy*

Power, Discourse and Resistance:
A Genealogy of the
Strangeways Prison Riot
Eamonn Carrabine